The Limits of Atlanticism

The Limits of Atlanticism

*Perceptions of State, Nation, and Religion
in Europe and the United States*

By

Gret Haller

Translated by

Alan Nothnagle

Berghahn Books
NEW YORK • OXFORD

Published by
Berghahn Books

www.berghahnbooks.com

German edition
© Aufbau-Verlag GmbH, Berlin 2002
Negotiated by Aufbau Media GmbH, Berlin
Originally published as
Gret Haller: *Die Grenzen der Solidarität. Europa und die USA
im Ungang mit Staat, Nation und Religion*

English-language edition
© 2007 Berghahn Books, Ltd.

Library of Congress Cataloging-in-Publication Data

Haller, Gret, 1947–
    [Grenzen der Solidarität. English]
    The limits of Atlanticism : perceptions of state, nation, and religion in
Europe and the United States / by Gret Haller ; translated by Alan Nothnagle.
        p. cm.
    Includes bibliographical references and index.
    ISBN 978-1-84545-318-3 (hardback : alk. paper)
        1. Europe—Foreign relations—United States. 2. United States—Foreign
relations—Europe. 3. Human rights—Europe. 4. Human rights—United
States. 5. Religion and state—Europe. 6. Religion and state—United
States. I. Title.

D1065.U5H2513 2007
327.7304—dc22

                                                                2007020710

British Library Cataloguing in Publication Data

A catalogue record for this book is available from the British Library.

Printed in the United States on acid-free paper

Contents

Preface to the English Edition   vii

Preface to the First Edition   xi

Chapter 1

Bosnia   1
From Strasbourg to Sarajevo, 3
Background, 4
After Tito, 6
Monolithic Ethnic Identity, 7
The Alternative, 11
Astonishing Observations, 13

Chapter 2

Transatlantic Differences   16
State, Nation, and Religion, 17
Freedom and Attachment, 26
Law and Morality, 40
Should We Grow Together or Stay Apart?, 55

Chapter 3

The "Western Europe/East Central Europe/United States" Triangle   67
Bosnia in the Transatlantic Tug-of-War, 68
Community and Statehood, 80
The Future of the Nation in Europe, 91
Freedom through Shared Sovereignty, 106

Chapter 4

    Western Europe   124

        The Role of Statehood, 125

        The Pivotal Role of Law, 132

        The French Revolution Continues, 143

        Intellectual Offerings, Sense of Mission, and National Interest, 151

Afterword   163

Bibliography   167

Index   172

Preface to the English Edition

The original German edition of this book appeared in 2002. The English translation is based on the unabridged text. The book has been neither revised nor updated. There are two reasons for this. The first has to do with the political developments that have occurred during the intervening years. The original German edition appeared almost one year before the start of the second Iraq war, which suddenly thrust the relationship between Europe and the United States back into the headlines and which has also further transformed this relationship. After the citizenry impressively proclaimed their overwhelming opposition to this war on the streets of all European capitals in February 2003, it would have been nearly impossible to rewrite the text in the relatively detached and sober style in which it was originally drafted in 2001–2002. Because of these events, revising the book's content would have meant practically writing an entirely new text, since the emotionality surrounding the conflict over the Iraq war, which plainly revealed the different conceptions over the relationship between law and military force, was simply too great.[1]

These political developments have also brought new insights in another regard. Among other things, this book describes how and why the 1995 Dayton Agreement obstructed the reconstruction and pacification of the country of Bosnia and Herzegovina: the new state was conceived along precisely those fault lines that had led to the war in the first place, and a thorough ethnicization of a kind that had never existed in Bosnian history for centuries occurred all the way down to the state's most minute structures. In the first years of the Agreement's implementation, this faulty design appeared justifiable. A different result could not have been reached in Dayton with the previous war parties, it was said. The reconstruction attempts in Afghanistan and Iraq are remarkably similar. In all these crisis regions, attempts were made to impose a structure of order upon ethnic or religious groups. Both of the latter attempts at "nation building" were—and to some extent still are—strongly, if not exclusively, dominated by the United States. Thus, hidden in the pages of this book on Bosnia from 2002 we can also find insights that can help contribute to an understanding of nation building—and particularly of its possible failure—in the two other crisis regions. However, a revision of the text including the two new crisis regions and their commonalities would have gone far beyond the boundaries of the original book, both in terms of my own experiences in Bosnia and my theoretical reflections on these experiences.

But most of all—and today, this second consideration appears even more critical to me—this book is based on concrete experiences dating to the years between 1996 and 2000. It does not compare Europe and the United States under George W. Bush. Instead, it compares Europe and the United States under the Clinton administration. The American actors, whose points of view differed from those of the European actors, had all been sent to Bosnia by leaders from the Democratic Party. It is no accident that the book concludes with a reference to the public caveats, warnings, censures, and cautions provided by the incumbent secretary of state, Madeleine Albright. Against this background, it is worth mentioning the recent book by the now former secretary of state in which she also criticizes the Bush administration.[2] Several statements in this book are interesting in connection with the present volume and its theoretical reflections.

Albright sets a clearly different tone to the Bush administration in the relationship between power and law: "A policy of supremacy contradicts the self-conception of the United States and is a poor means to protect our interests."[3] However, her tone sounds remarkably similar when it comes to the relationship between law and morality, which amounts to an exacerbation of what is stated in this report on Bosnia. What stands out most of all is that she in no way questions America's claim to leadership in many areas, such as the deployment of international peacekeeping troops and, in general terms, with regard to human rights and humanitarian issues. And the basis of this claim to leadership is a moral one. One of the differences between the Bush administration and Albright's view seems to lie in the fact that the Bush administration bases America's leadership claim on both military superiority and morality, whereas Albright's version is restricted to the moral foundation and relies on military power only with great restraint. Thus, morality is transformed into the central concept of foreign policy legitimacy, a standpoint Albright traces back to the days of the Founding Fathers: "In his first inaugural speech as President of the United States, George Washington mentioned our debt to God when he said that every step America has 'advanced to the character of an independent nation seems to have been distinguished by some token of providential agency.' Americans should repay this debt, Washington said, by ensuring 'that the foundation of our national policy will be laid in the pure and immutable principles of private morality.'"[4]

This addresses the close connection between religion and morality, leading us to a statement by the former secretary of state that is of central significance to this book. In a brief overview of the objectively determinable differences between the United States and Europe, and following a warning against generalizations—because the truth is always more complex—Albright mentions that "Europeans do not equate religion with morality."[5] One reviewer placed her finger on the counter-position of the United States: "Albright seems to believe that religiosity can be distilled into morality."[6] The former secretary of state leaves no doubt about this, and prefaces her statement with the programmatic sentence: "It is also a question of which behavior is right and righteous."[7]

As I write this preface to the English edition in July 2006, the war in Lebanon is claiming victims every day. In Europe, people are increasingly asking whether the struggle against terrorism, as it is being conducted today, is failing because of the methods used. The dogma is that no one who is on a list of terrorist organizations can be negotiated with. The parties are divided into "good" and "evil," after which an appeal is made to the "good" ones to join forces in combating the "evil" ones. The reason for this is obvious: exclusive moral claims, that is, moral claims to leadership, are humiliating to those who cannot participate in the definition of that which is morally "good." This demonstrates an ancient piece of European wisdom: in Europe, "law" is the name for collectively proclaimed valid morality. And collectively proclaimed valid morality is "lawful" only for those who have participated in making this collective proclamation of morality. The procedure of collectively proclaiming valid morality cannot be reconciled with exclusion, nor can it be reconciled with a morally based claim to leadership.

Perhaps one day we will view the failure to talk to the democratically elected Hamas government, which is a direct outcome of this posture, as a critical error. In the period leading up to the Palestinian elections, I was continually reminded of events in Bosnia as described in this book. There is no question that intense international cooperation is essential in the struggle against terrorism. And yet, this fact should in no way prevent the European states from challenging America's role as the world's moral leader, nor from pointing out that this role is based on exclusive claims on the definition of morality that humiliate those who are excluded. European history is rich in examples of humiliations that were later bitterly avenged. It is to be hoped that the European learning process will continue to bear fruit in these matters and will not be ignored. To ensure this, an open debate over the relationship between law and morality, as urged by this book, is of decisive importance.

Many Europeans assume that a change of government in the United States from the Republicans to the Democrats will again normalize the transatlantic relationship and lead us all back onto the familiar pathways of the Cold War era. However, the debate over the transatlantic differences in dealing with law and morality still leads me to doubt that such a normalization will come about any time soon.

July 2006

Gret Haller

Notes

1. See Gret Haller, *Politik der Götter: Europa und der neue Fundamentalismus* (Berlin, 2005). The transformed situation in Europe is also described here in emotional terms.
2. Madeleine Albright, *The Mighty and the Almighty: Reflections on America, God, and World Affairs* (New York, 2006).
3. Ibid., 326 (German translation).
4. Ibid., 36.
5. Ibid., 10.
6. Annette Bingemer, *Neue Zürcher Zeitung*, 24 June 2006.
7. Albright, *The Mighty and the Almighty*, 23.

Preface to the First Edition

On the afternoon of September 11, 2001, when the radio broadcast the news of the terrorist attacks in New York City and Washington, DC, which were later confirmed by the horrific images of the collapsing World Trade Center, I was just penning the last lines of a lecture I was planning to deliver on the topic "Deregulating Human Rights." I had already completed most of the preliminary work for this present volume, and had borrowed a few comments on transatlantic differences regarding divergent understandings of the state and the nation from my book notes with the intention of including them in the lecture. I immediately realized, however, that I could not depict those differences in the current situation, since doing so might be construed as showing a lack of reverence toward the September 11 victims. I then rewrote the lecture text and attempted to put my rational analysis into a form that included this reverence. Before long, I realized why the media commentators were right, at least for the moment, when they spoke of September 11 as a turning point in history: all of a sudden, a whole range of things could no longer be stated as they had been previously. The question of faith took center stage as never before.

On that fateful day, the image of the collapsing towers of the World Trade Center displaced the older image of the ruined tower of the *Oslobodenje* newspaper building in Sarajevo as the symbol of a new age. After a few days, cool heads began explaining publicly that this event did not represent a confrontation between the Islamic and Christian worlds. Had I not spent years discussing the question of whether Islam and modernity are reconcilable—arguing, of course, that they are? Had my inner clock started to turn backwards? When I took another look at my manuscript, it suddenly began to resemble a history book and not, as I had thought, a report on matters that still had a certain topicality. After just a few weeks, the vast public media discussion of the 9/11 horror began raising questions that may not have been identical to the ones I had brought up in my manuscript, but which, as time went on, pointed increasingly to similar thought structures. It became more and more evident that the

United States and Europe would not react to the same things in the same way. And more and more people began posing questions regarding transatlantic differences. These questions also touched on areas that had already been raised in perceptions regarding post-war Bosnia. It would have been desirable if these perceptions, which I will discuss in the following pages, had not come to be framed by the horrors of September 11, 2001. It would have been desirable if this book's topic had not become so dreadfully topical.

May 2002   Gret Haller

Chapter 1

Bosnia

One day in early 1995, my office phone rang. The caller asked if I would like to go to Sarajevo as an ombudswoman for human rights. I was told that while the Dayton Agreement had not yet been signed, it entailed such a function, and that would not change before the signing. I spontaneously told the caller that I did not want to assume this function. At the time, I was an ambassador to the Council of Europe, I was leading an interesting life in Strasbourg, and I could not think of anything that could persuade me to trade all this in for a job in a country that had just barely left the most dreadful war atrocities behind it. When later that evening the fax machine spat out the legal basis for the newly created office, I glanced at it anyway. At first it looked like a dry legal document. But then I realized that this was virgin territory: the European Convention on Human Rights was to be applied directly in Bosnia and Herzegovina without being ratified by this state under international law, since this country was not yet a member of the Council of Europe. Individuals in Bosnia would thus be able to appeal to this convention and file complaints. However, the European Court of Human Rights would not be able to rule on these cases, even though it was normally responsible for all of Europe.

There were opportunities lurking in this arrangement, but also dangers: maybe it would be good to cooperate after all, because I had been familiar with European human rights culture for years. This led to my second spontaneous reaction the next morning, which in the end won out over the first. It was the people of Bosnia and the horrific things they had experienced that finally made me change my mind. Could I have imagined from my perusal of an annex to the Dayton Agreement one evening that I would soon be in Bosnia,

---

Notes for this chapter are located on page 15.

confronted with a vast array of cultural differences between Europe and the United States? Hardly. But looking back, I have come to realize that my second spontaneous reaction unveiled a previously unknown perspective from which I would be forced to make observations over the following years that would first amaze me, then infuriate me, and ultimately move me to write this book.

Shortly before Christmas 1995, the Hungarian president of the Organization for Security and Co-operation in Europe (OSCE) appointed me to my new position, which had been formally created with the signing of the Dayton Agreement in December. Over the following months, alongside my work in developing this institution, I also had to acquaint myself with the situation in the country. To the extent that they were picked up by the media at all, the images of the war atrocities in Bosnia had reached Western Europe. But what was the history behind all this? What conditions had led to these horrors? From what vantage point could one confront the causes? How was the international community reacting? On the one hand, I was part of this international community. On the other, I also stood outside it, since the institution I was now directing was formally regarded as an institution of the state of Bosnia and Herzegovina.[1] It was international only in the sense that the officeholder in the first five years was not permitted to be a citizen of Bosnia or of a neighboring state.

Right from the start, most of the institution's staff were Bosnian assistants who were at first supported by international lawyers with expert knowledge in dealing with complaints in accordance with the European Convention on Human Rights. After all, this had not been part of legal training in Bosnia, or if it had been, the Yugoslavs had always cited it as a negative example of Western imperialism. Toward the end of my five-year term, the Bosnian lawyers were already working pretty much independently, so that the presence of the international experts faded. Thus, from the first day I looked at events from the Bosnian point of view, which does not mean that my Bosnian colleagues all saw things the same way. Nevertheless, it was precisely this Bosnian viewpoint that showed me that there were more transatlantic differences than I had previously imagined. They extended from the understanding of legal, governmental, and political notions all the way to the understanding of the notion of democracy.

There were comprehensive discussions on transatlantic differences in the fields of economics and security policy, and occasionally also in the field of culture, but less in the area of basic values, provided that they did not directly touch on the desirability of a stronger or weaker welfare state. This was no coincidence: in economics, in culture, and in security policy there are direct sources of friction between Europe and the United States. In legal, governmental, and political matters, however, this friction is indirect; normally, one perceives it only when one comes face to face with it in a specific situation. In this respect, the activity of the international community in Bosnia represented an exception. While it was strongly dominated by the United States, the intention nevertheless was to erect a European state in Bosnia despite this dominance, so that from a longer perspective, transatlantic differences in legal, state, and political matters could be perceived on a one-to-one basis. Since I carried out my task over the course of several years, which is fairly unusual on missions in regions like this, and since I supervised a state institution in the legal-political field, I could not fail to notice these differences sooner or later.

From Strasbourg to Sarajevo

We flew to Sarajevo for the first time in mid-January 1996. The flight time from Strasbourg to Sarajevo was exactly 80 minutes, and on that day I finally realized once and for all how incorrect my geographic notions had been since the early 1990s. Bosnia lies practically in the center of Europe, not far away as I had deluded myself during the war years. However, our actual arrival was postponed considerably following this brief flight. It was apparently not so easy to receive landing permission for non-NATO flights, even if they had been requested and approved in advance. This was an experience that would later be repeated many times. We finally landed on the bumpy airstrip of an airport that had been transformed into a military landing field and whose buildings had been largely destroyed. The letters "AERODROM ... EVO" could still be seen. The rest had apparently been shot away. Walking between high walls of sandbags, we reached a makeshift office located in a part of the airport that still had intact foundation walls on the main floor. Here we were greeted by the staff of the local OSCE mission. Already on our approach we had seen the completely destroyed buildings around the airport. As we later learned, some of these buildings had served as the Olympic Village in 1984.

On the drive into town I received my next impression of the destruction from the *Oslobodenje* newspaper headquarters. A modern building of what had once been impressive architecture, it had been transformed into an even more impressive memorial: the central part of the tower still rose into the sky while parts of the floors of the individual stories barely clung to its skeleton. The ruin of the National Library, a richly decorated building erected in Moorish style, was particularly impressive. It was completely burned out, so that the sky shone through the gaping windows. This was another impression that would repeat itself continually over the coming years. The Ring Road around the old city of Sarajevo, upon which the city's venerable streetcar would soon again go clattering and ringing on its rounds, functions as a one-way street going counterclockwise, around the National Library as its easternmost tangent. Whoever enters the town in a car regularly first drives past the southern, then the eastern, and finally the northern side of the National Library—or, more accurately, its ruin—a ritual of probably more lasting significance than many international visitors may have realized in the confusion of the moment.

Already on the second or third trip through town, our driver showed us the street corner on the banks of the Miljacka, the narrow river that flows through Sarajevo from east to west, where the Austrian heir to the throne, Franz Ferdinand, and his wife were shot in 1914. There was no time to pepper the driver with questions because there was too much to be arranged. I would have to ask or read about the historical background later on.

Background

For centuries, the town of Sarajevo had symbolized the peaceful cohabitation of different peoples, cultures, and religions. Here there were Bosnians of Islamic faith (today they call themselves "Bosniacs"); Bosnians of Serb descent and of largely Orthodox Christian faith; Bosnians of Croat descent and of largely Catholic Christian faith; and what had been a sizable Jewish community before World War II. Above all, there had been a tradition of tolerance. This was also known across Europe, and those who did not know it beforehand came to understand it later on during the siege of the town from 1992 to 1995: artistically creative people in Sarajevo, regardless of their ethnic group, not only stubbornly insisted on remaining in the besieged town, but also demanded that their culture continue under unimaginably difficult conditions, such as snipers and artillery fire. Sarajevo preserved its symbolic meaning throughout the war, thanks to the unparalleled dedication of all those who refused to abandon this town and those who could not leave it even if they wanted to and who then tried to make the best out of the situation. One can hardly call the cohabitation that emerged after the war peaceful, since conditions were extremely difficult. But the town's essence survived, and after the war, it began to spread—if only slowly—once more. The historian Eric J. Hobsbawm described the past century as "the short twentieth century," which he said lasted from 1914 to 1991, both beginning and ending in Sarajevo, from the previously mentioned murder of Archduke Franz Ferdinand, which led within a few weeks to the outbreak of World War I, up until the siege of this town at the end of the same century, when it once again became the focus of global interest.[2] Not only did the siege affect the town and its population; it also represented an attack on the symbolism of the peaceful cohabitation of different peoples, cultures, and religions.

I gradually learned just how unperturbed this cohabitation had been in Sarajevo before the war from the accounts of my Bosnian staff members: the Catholic, Orthodox, and Muslim holidays all fell on different dates, and many people visited families or clans of another religion to celebrate the holiday together. The fact that this lovely tradition meant a whole series of school or work-free days was merely viewed as a side effect. In many families, interreligious marriages were perfectly normal. In fact, this interreligiosity was not even an issue in itself, at least not in the towns—including not only Sarajevo but also Tuzla, Banja Luka, Travnik, and others. Cultural blending has always worked better in towns than in the countryside. In the rural environment, one encountered the same interreligious openness to a large degree, although there were also villages with clearly defined ethnic majorities. Here, however, the other groups were tolerated, and marriages took place across religious boundaries. In certain areas, villages with different majorities all blended together, which also eased the interethnic exchange. This blending became painfully clear when one flew over Bosnia after the war: like a patchwork quilt, one could see entirely intact villages and, immediately next door, villages whose houses had been shattered to the foundations, the signs and results of "ethnic cleansing," if I am permitted to utter these abhorrent words. In the towns, by contrast, there were often no ethnically divided quarters or streets. There, the blending succeeded on the smallest scale imaginable. One has to assume that such straightforward interethnic cohabitation was a largely urban phenomenon that in Bosnia had become possible for a large portion of the population only with the rise of urban lifestyles and that had also been influenced by industrialization, which did not begin on a large scale until after 1945.

Ethnically motivated migration movements have always been present in the Balkans. Ethnically motivated, systematic expulsions began only in the twentieth century, starting with the Balkan Wars of 1912–1913. The first Yugoslavian multiethnic state—namely, the Kingdom of Serbs, Croats, and Slovenes—was created after World War I. Within the framework of this state, attempts were made to promote a pan-Yugoslavian identity, at which time a common Serbo-Croatian language was created. This state collapsed during World War II, and it was followed by the next phase of brutal, ethnically motivated cruelty. In Josip Broz Tito's post-war Yugoslavia, new attempts were made to promote "Yugoslavism." In the process, the population's ethnic identities and religion were pushed into the background. This was facilitated on the one hand by the new state's federalist structure, which organized the country in autonomous republics, and on the other hand by the communist ideology, which made ethnic or particularly religious identity largely unattractive, since party membership was always the decisive factor. When census takers asked people about their religious status, atheism had its own box next to those set aside for the Catholic, Orthodox, Muslim, and other religious faiths. For those persons in mixed marriages or for those who for fundamental reasons saw little meaning in an identity based on ethnic background, an "x" in this box provided a simple and frequently chosen solution. These were often the same people who called themselves Yugoslavs when they were asked about their ethnic affiliation, and there were more than a few who did so. Ethnic and religious affiliation vanished as indicators of identity, taking a back seat to citizenship, which had become more or less the norm in Western Europe over the course of the past two centuries, although the reasons were not the same: in Western Europe, genuine civil identities emerged, while for many people in Yugoslavia, this identity offered a way out of an increasingly illusory or consciously rejected ethnic classification. Even so, there is no doubt that an ethnically tolerant atmosphere developed in which Yugoslavia's opening to the West and the resulting migration of guest workers also played a part. These guest workers brought back not only their wages but also Western perspectives. But why did this relatively untroubled cohabitation end so suddenly?

After Tito

When the disintegration of Yugoslavia became a genuine possibility follow-ing Tito's death in 1980, and when it also became clear after the fall of the Berlin Wall in 1989 that communism as an ideology had lost its power base in Eastern Europe, some people who had grown up in the Communist Party of Yugoslavia began looking for a new ideological foundation that would main-tain their power. One did not need much imagination, just a good memory or some knowledge of the history of the past several decades to discover ethnon-ationalism—an ideology in which one's identity is derived entirely from one's descent from a particular population group—as a suitable basis.[3] This ideology is linked to claims to one's own territorial region, which should be placed at the disposal of this population group in the form of a nation-state. In the former Yugoslavia, the conditions for the conversion of the power base from communism to ethnonationalism were ideal from a historical standpoint. In particular, one could draw on the country's experiences during World War II. The population was called upon to reflect on its ethnic background and to do so using a wide variety of methods, ranging from subtle insults of other ethnic groups to pseudo-scientific racist theories to ethnic agitation during mass events. The goal was to incite hatred toward the other ethnic groups and to cultivate violent attitudes. A Bosnian co-worker, who was and always had been a resolute advocate of the peaceful co-existence of peoples, told me more about these hate campaigns. When they started, she had been spending a long vacation on the Adriatic coast, that is, in the former autonomous Yugoslav republic of Croatia. As a Bosnian, she had been surprised by the Croatian hate campaign. Yet the depictions on Croatian television were so drastic, so sophis-ticated, and so convincing that she almost believed the claims being made, even though she, as a Bosnian, was not of Croatian descent.

In this way, the groundwork was systematically laid for what followed. After the autonomous republics of Slovenia and Croatia had made preparations for their separation from Yugoslavia through laws and constitutional amend-ments in the late 1980s and early 1990s, they conducted referendums on state sovereignty. Both declared their independence on 25 June 1991. On 15 January 1992, the European Union recognized the former component states as sovereign states. The autonomous republic of Bosnia-Herzegovina with its three popula-tion groups—in 1991, 40 percent were counted as Bosniacs (Bosnians of Muslim

background), 31 percent as Bosnian Serbs, and 17 percent as Bosnian Croats—was left in a hopeless situation. Already on 15 October 1991, the parliament of Bosnia-Herzegovina in Sarajevo proclaimed sovereignty; however, it
expressly declared that the republic would remain within the existing Yugoslav
federation. This, however, was conceivable only if Slovenia and Croatia also
remained members. The Serb members of the Bosnian parliament had demon-
stratively walked out of the hall following the vote and proclaimed their own
Serb Republic of Bosnia-Herzegovina as early as 24 October 1991. Following
the recognition of Slovenia and Croatia by the European Union, the Bosniacs
and the Bosnian Croats now likewise pushed for the creation of a sovereign
state of Bosnia-Herzegovina, since they feared they would be dominated by
the Serbs if they remained in Yugoslavia. The referendum on independence of
1 March 1992, which was approved by 99.4 percent of the voters (the Bosnian
Serbs had boycotted the vote), was followed on 3 March by the proclamation
of the Republic of Bosnia-Herzegovina. Even before the European Union and
the United States agreed on 7 April 1992 to recognize the new state, units of
the Serb-dominated Yugoslav People's Army implemented the long-planned
siege of Sarajevo. Although the Yugoslav state presidium ordered all soldiers
and officers from Serbia and Montenegro to leave Bosnia-Herzegovina, it was
an open secret that the army had become a Serbian force.

An extremely cruel war began, in the course of which the Yugoslav People's
Army, together with irregular troops, swiftly conquered 70 percent of Bosnia's
territory. The war in Bosnia lasted almost four years. Thousands were killed
and wounded, more than a million persons were displaced, and human rights
were systematically violated. The murder of more than 7,000 Bosniac men in
Srebrenica and the rape of countless Muslim women in specially established
camps demonstrated this horror to a global public. This brief summary would
not be complete without mentioning the advance of the Bosnian Croats and the
Bosniacs in West Bosnia in May 1995, as well as the offensive of the Croatian
army in August 1995, as a result of which the Serbian units were driven back
into Bosnia and Croatia. Finally, the war was formally ended in the peace agreement that was negotiated in Dayton, Ohio, and signed in Paris on 14 December
1995. The peace agreement was preceded by the lifting of the siege of Sarajevo
on 14 September 1995, as well as by a regionally limited armistice after NATO
units, acting under UN orders, launched massive aerial attacks against Serbian
units in the region around Sarajevo and later throughout the country.[4]

Monolithic Ethnic Identity

The war left the people in Bosnia with deep wounds, and nobody was spared.
Those who had not themselves been physically injured mourned the dead and
injured in their families. Older people especially suffered from loneliness after
their friends and relations, particularly the young, fled abroad. Added to this

was the profound injury they felt due to the fact that Europe and the world as a whole had allowed a series of events to occur that no reasonable person had ever imagined was possible and that should have been avoided at all costs. The fear of renewed violence and a general fear of the economic future—which, looking back, proved to be more than justified—continued to gnaw at people.

It is understandable that after the war many Bosnians were capable of thinking only in terms of ethnic categories. Many had experienced for themselves how once-friendly neighbors had become enemies overnight because they belonged to another population group, and how these neighbors had suddenly armed themselves, had threatened them, or had driven them out of their own houses at gunpoint. Others had seen with their own eyes how neighbors, who had suddenly become enemies, did not hesitate to commit cold-blooded murder. Family members were slaughtered in plain view of their parents, siblings, or children. People who suffered such losses, not to mention those who were tortured or raped, were traumatized. Even with the best of will and the application of the highest reason, it is no longer possible for a person who has experienced such things to live in the certainty that ethnic background does not or should not play a role in a person's behavior and basic values. But also those who were spared such horrific experiences scarcely had an opportunity to avoid thinking in ethnic categories. Everybody was aware of these terrible events, and this knowledge disturbed people greatly, whether or not they knew the victims personally. For reasons of pure self-preservation, many had been forced during the war to join groups that, on account of their ethnic background, at least were not threatened, for there were not many places in which multiethnic cohabitation remained possible throughout the entire war. The non-Serbian occupied section of Sarajevo was such a place.

There were also places in which "ethnic cleansings" occurred, but where members of a minority group survived after deciding categorically not to bow to the ethnic pressure, choosing to die rather than move away. For all those who made such a decision, thinking in non-ethnic categories must have been an important concern, for otherwise they would not have done so. If they survived the war, then they scarcely had a chance to return immediately and unobserved to a position where ethnicity could be ignored and/or reduced to its pre-war status. Living with constant, ethnically based threats leaves behind traces that extend deeper the longer the situation lasts. Furthermore, the formal end of the war did not eliminate the dangers. Years later, members of some ethnic minority groups could not return to all villages, even if some progress had been made in the meantime.

Ethnically Understood Law

Edin Šarčević has presented the effects of this sort of "ethnicization" on legal thinking in a brochure concerning the final phase of the Bosnian constitutional process. Human actions are no longer viewed as actions undertaken by a particular person; rather, it is assumed that a person has performed an action exclusively as a member of an ethnic group. Sometimes ordinary petty criminals are no longer called to account because their arrest would be considered an attack on their ethnic group.[5] In such a situation, even the criterion of common crime is subordinated to ethnic status: a member of one's own ethnic group simply cannot be a criminal, just as a member of another ethnic group is a criminal by nature. An ethnically defined person therefore no longer possesses autonomy as a person and is reduced entirely to his ethnic background. He does not even have the autonomy to commit a crime and thus cannot be tried neutrally before a criminal court. This creates the basis for the horrific human rights violations that the Balkans have experienced. An ethnically defined person no longer possesses dignity as a person; dignity is conferred instead through membership in an ethnic group.

There is no doubt that one could strive to overcome thinking in ethnic categories and return to some kind of normalcy. Many have attempted it, and some have achieved it: they have not forgotten, but they have learned to forgive. Others cannot do this, or at least will not be able to do so for a long time to come. No one has the right to reproach them for it. I was not present at an event that occurred in a Bosnian village a year or two after the end of the war. It had been organized by an international or non-state organization and was intended to reopen the dialogue between the population groups. The organizers were profoundly moved by what happened, and most of the international workers in Sarajevo heard about it later on. The dialogue, we learned, began slowly and cautiously, but the balancing act between wounded silence and explosions of hatred was successful at first. Shortly before the end of the event, a man, holding his four- or five-year-old son on his knees, raised his hand. After relating what his family had suffered at the hands of irregular soldiers belonging to another ethnic group during the war, he proclaimed the following: he would never stop telling his son every day that he must never, in any situation, trust a member of the other ethnic group, and as his son grew to adulthood he would make him vow to take revenge on arbitrary members of the ethnic group whenever he could, just as it would remain his, the father's, duty to do the same. Father and son had previously listened to the dialogue in silence, but after the father's declaration, they left the assembly. There is no guarantee that the son will still see things the same way in the future. Sometimes such declarations represent the culmination of a reflection process and can lead to new ways of thinking. But this was also a post-war reality, and it is possible that such statements are still being made today.

That was the situation in which the population of Bosnia found itself immediately after the war. Whether consciously or unconsciously, intended or unintended, people were stamped with a "monolithic identity" based on ethnic criteria.[6] This meant that the first or even the only criterion for judging a person or situation was that person's ethnic affiliation. It is highly presumptuous for an outsider to think that he or she would act differently in a comparable situation. State institutions such as municipal administrations or administrative authorities of any kind, police forces, or the army in the normal sense of the word—in many places, these institutions had long since ceased to exist. All of these functions not only had been turned upside down by the war, but—to the extent that they still existed—were now organized along ethnic lines. This was particularly the case for army units identified with ethnic groups, which had battled with other groups in the cruelest way imaginable. Police units too were organized ethnically. Members of another population group could not hope for police protection; instead, they lived in fear of attacks on their bodies, lives, and property by these ethnic groups. Administrative authorities, if they still functioned at all, basically consisted of members of a single ethnic group and acted correspondingly: on the one hand, to protect their own group and, on the other, to defend themselves from the other groups. In this situation, tribes and family clans achieved positions of power, with mono-ethnic clans having the greatest opportunities. Most economic relations operated within such structures, which were often organized, Mafia-style, along ethnic lines. For many people during and immediately after the war, precise knowledge of these structures was a question of survival. But mere knowledge and use of these structures did not necessarily mean that one supported the ethnic point of view.

The Ethnic Lens

Other identity characteristics besides those of origin had basically been swept away by the force of events. It was as if everyone had been issued a pair of spectacles that made one's entire field of vision appear in blue, red, or yellow light, according to one's ethnic background. It was not just that people on the street, or the houses in which they lived, were suddenly tinted red, blue, or yellow. It went much further than that. The tree in one's neighbor's yard was no longer green but blue, as long as the house and garden were used by members of a certain ethnic group. And if they moved away and a member of another ethnic group moved in, then the tree became red or yellow. The same thing applied to all social events: they too bore the colors of the origins of those persons who participated in them. People who feel uneasy with this point of view constantly search for images whose contours are blurred. They want to get rid of the spectacles as quickly as possible. Others feel threatened when things can no longer be so clearly classified. They cling to the spectacles for a variety of reasons. After the long war years, there were many people who scarcely had the energy to think about such things as the spectacles they wore. The exhaustion was too great, and the ongoing everyday struggle for survival was almost overwhelming.

I use the image of the spectacles here in order to illustrate the monolithic ethnic identity. The colors have no political meaning, and I have not assigned them with any conscious intent. Some Bosnians, mostly those who were convinced that their own group was principally affiliated with the victims and not with the perpetrators, have occasionally blamed me for consistently refusing to apportion guilt among the ethnic groups. Within the framework of the coping process described here, I can understand this position. The question of collective guilt—as opposed to individual guilt, which is a matter for the courts—does, however, play a role in this process. Nevertheless, I have consciously refused to take part in the blame game, for this would have made my work impossible. By contrast, the occasional reproach I received for not taking a stand on the question of collective guilt troubled me less. And one more clarification: if on the one hand it was right to show understanding for Bosnians who for personal reasons were not at first in a position to deal with their traumatic experiences and who therefore clung to their monolithic ethnic identity over a long period of time, then on the other hand an absolutely uncompromising approach was essential toward those people who had stoked the ethnically oriented identity in all groups of the Bosnian population, who had exploited this identity, and who had sought to maintain it because they had used it to construct political power positions, usually in connection with personal economic benefits. In dealing with the latter group, mere understanding was clearly the wrong strategy. So what was the solution? It would have made little sense to explain to the Bosnians that this monolithic identity would never get them anywhere, something that many of them already knew or sensed anyway. A true alternative was urgently needed.

The Alternative

After the war, the alternative to the monolithic ethnic identity was actually plain for all to see. In Bosnia the state order had vanished, and many of the former state functions either had ceased to exist or had been organized along ethnic lines. The precondition for a normalization of the situation was thus the replacement of this identity by a different identity, and this could only be a civic one. At issue were two sectors, an institutional one and a personnel one: on the one hand, the state institutions had to be rebuilt; on the other, persons who came to work for these institutions, that is, for the public, would have to understand or else learn again what such an activity meant. This was new insofar as in the old Yugoslav state system, the administration had stood entirely under the control of the political party. To "learn again" is also a fairly accurate description, for the Yugoslav state was not entirely comparable with other communist states. In any case, there certainly was some basis for overcoming the monolithic ethnic viewpoint, although not for overcoming party dependence.

Various Complaints

The first-named sector, the building of new state functions in an institutional sense, does not require any further description here, although it proved to be enormously difficult for reasons to which I shall return later on. Regarding personnel issues, a few examples will illustrate what I mean by overcoming the monolithic ethnic identity and replacing it with a civic identity. First of all, I need to provide a brief description of the action radius of the institution I was in charge of. The position of ombudswoman was formally created as an institution of the state of Bosnia and Herzegovina with the signing of the Dayton Agreement in December 1995 in Paris. In the first five years, the position was to be staffed by someone who was not a citizen of Bosnia or any other neighboring state, but who nonetheless acted in the name of the Bosnian state. The ombudswoman's task was to evaluate complaints from private persons who could demonstrate that their fundamental rights had been violated by an authority or by a person acting in an official (state) function. These could be authorities from all levels in the complicated structure of the Bosnian state apparatus: municipal authorities; authorities of one of the two component states, the Republika Srpska and the Federation of Bosnia and Herzegovina; or finally authorities of the state as a whole. The catalogue of guaranteed rights was contained within the Bosnian constitution, which is a component of the Dayton Agreement, and a long list of international human rights agreements was appended to the respective annex of the Dayton Agreement. After years of "ethnic cleansing," it came as no surprise that more than 90 percent of the cases that reached us referred to apartments and houses that the petitioners were seeking to have restored to them.

We were continually confronted by cases of inactivity on the part of administrative authorities. In the numerous areas that after the war were solely or largely occupied by members of the same groups, it is understandable that during this period the authorities were exclusively made up of members of the same group. Nevertheless, there were cases in which persons from another ethnic group addressed themselves to these authorities, whether because they could remain in the area in question or because they wished to return to it. In the first months of 1996, such petitions were often left unprocessed. When viewed from a monolithic-ethnic perspective, they were, so to speak, "non-petitions," since they came from "non-fellow citizens." Particularly astonishing was the absolute serenity with which members of these authorities and government representatives declared that an equal treatment of the various ethnic groups was simply impossible. They usually justified their attitude with descriptions of what the other group had done to their own group during the war, and how under these conditions no one could demand equal treatment by the authorities. Whether and how powerfully the notion of vengeance played a role in such cases depended on one's personality and one's war-related traumatization. By no means did all administrators argue in this way. But apparently, in general terms, the state order structure had over time organized itself in such a blatantly ethnic way that the ethnic organization had entirely displaced statehood. This development could not be reversed overnight since it had burrowed into the people's hearts and minds over many years, not in a superficial or merely intellectual fashion, but rather in life-threatening situations—in hunger, cold and fear, suffering and mourning.

Civic Identity

The most challenging aspect of our work thus lay in slowly and cautiously leading the people in this war-ravaged country out of the blind alley of monolithic ethnic identity back to a civic identity, which is based on the notion that every citizen, or every inhabitant of this country, is equally protected by the state and is entitled to participate and share in public affairs. If one were to fulfill this task in a sustainable fashion, one would have to be in a position to point out the difference between an ethnic and a state order structure and to explain to one's dialogue partners in a credible manner why only an order structure based on public authority provides lasting security, both to society as a whole and to one's own group.

Our dialogue partners were at first the authorities against whom complaints had been filed, and speaking with them initially proved to be quite difficult. But the complainants often turned out to be our dialogue partners, and they themselves frequently thought in purely ethnic terms in the first months or even years following the end of the war. We frequently heard them say "my human rights as a Bosnian Croat," "my human rights as a Bosnian Serb," or "my human rights as a Bosniac." We tirelessly explained to the people who filed their complaints with us that a person had human rights only because he or she had been born as a human being, and that they possessed no human rights because of a particular characteristic, whether it was ethnic background, race, sex, family background, religion, or anything else one could come up with.

Civic instruction would have been critical in the first post-war phase, less in terms of actual classes than in the form of public discussions, personal conversations, and, particularly, very clear language on the part of the international community toward the Bosnian authorities on all levels. This would not have brought about a normalization of relations immediately, but even so it would have helped uproot the very problem that had formed the basis for the still ongoing military violence, for the disorganization, chaos, and corruption, and thus, indirectly, also for the protracted collapse of the economy. Such an approach would at least have strongly accelerated the normalization process. The military pacification of Bosnia was considerably more expensive than the entire non-military activity of the international community. This was inevitable, and there is no doubt that the military presence on the scale at which it occurred was utterly essential to the pacification of the country. And this is all the more reason why civic instruction, which is so much cheaper than the other activities, should have been carried out all over the country. Unfortunately, this did not happen.

Astonishing Observations

In tandem with the staff of our institution, numerous international organizations attempted to propagate civic identity as an intellectual alternative to the monolithic ethnic identity. Nevertheless, the alternative was never effective. It did not work for all the people it might have and should have helped, that is, for those who had already taken off their ethnic spectacles or who were about to do so. The international community could all agree, "That is not the way to go!" But the question "What then?" did not meet with a unanimous response when it came to civic identity. The international organizations displayed even less enthusiasm and clear conviction, both of which would have been essential in order to leverage a breakthrough for the intellectual alternative of civic identity. It is true that many internationals worked with admirable dedication and clear concepts, but there were also internationals who—as it seemed to me—had little concept of what they were doing. In the early days, I often asked myself what in the world ever motivated them to take on a mission in such a difficult country when they often did not even know what they had to offer the people in the way of ideas. It was only toward the end of my first year in Sarajevo that I realized that this question—as I had formulated it at first—was incorrectly phrased.

It finally became definitively clear to me that the phenomenon which I at first could not explain was related to the powerful presence of the United States and to the dominant position that it took within the international community. But I also realized that the lack of a clear concept that I had been observing represented a concept in itself. The Americans often had no clear understanding of what a functioning state meant from a European perspective. The United States itself acted as a state with a well-organized foreign policy, as everyone in Bosnia could see on a daily basis. So what was the concept that it wanted to bring to bear as an alternative?

During my activity in Bosnia, I observed a great deal that later helped me to find answers to these questions. At the end of my mission, I was able to assemble the fragments of the mosaic into a clear picture. To be sure, during my years in the Balkans, I had little opportunity to publish anything on the transatlantic differences, since my work in Sarajevo and Banja Luka was not the sort of job one performs in studies or in libraries. I made up for this after my return from Bosnia. Thus, I have developed through personal observation, on the one hand, and subsequent research, on the other, my own conception of the relevant differences between Europe and the United States.

Notes

1. Bosnia and Herzegovina is the name of the state that was created by the Dayton Agreement. Both the autonomous republic of the former state of Yugoslavia and the subsequent independent republic bore the name Bosnia-Herzegovina. The component "and" in the current name thus serves to distinguish it from previous states and/or forms of government.
2. Eric J. Hobsbawm, *The Age of Extremes: A History of the World, 1914–1991* (New York, 1994).
3. In *Das Fanal von Sarajevo: Ethnonationalismus in Europa* (Zurich, 1996), Urs Altermatt discusses the term "ethnonationalism."
4. An account of these events can be found in Wolfgang Petritsch, *Bosnien und Herzegowina fünf Jahre nach Dayton: Hat der Friede eine Chance?* (Klagenfurt, 2001). A shortened version can be read in Michael Thumann, "Der unvollendete Triumph des Nationalstaats—Bosniens Weg zum Abkommen von Dayton," in *Deutsche Aussenpolitik 1995*, ed. Auswärtiges Amt (Bonn, 1998), 15–28.
5. Edin Šarčević, *Die Schlussphase der Verfassungsgebung in Bosnien und Herzegowina* (Leipzig, 1996), 51f.
6. In visual terms, a monolithic ethnic identity is made up of a single piece of rock from the same rock formation.

Chapter 2

Transatlantic Differences

There is no ideal type of European or American. It will always be possible to find countless Americans who are much more "European" than many Europeans. And it will always be possible to find countless Europeans who are much more "American" than many Americans. Free societies—and we are talking about free societies on both sides of the Atlantic—are characterized by the way that the individual chooses his or her identity. What this chapter and the book in general are intended to discuss is the social backing that is offered to individuals as they develop their freely chosen identity, a process within which the transatlantic differences become noticeable. There is no question that this social backing influences our collective self-image, even if individual persons do not actually need this backing or consciously choose to distance themselves from it. It even holds sway when a society functions in a highly individualistic fashion and where it is almost considered good form to distance oneself from it. This is particularly the case in periods of crisis or in other times of collective regression to familiar values, as could be observed in various cultural circles worldwide after September 11, 2001. With this in mind, I will nevertheless speak of "Europeans" and "Americans" in the following pages.

Western values are generally considered to be informed by the two continents of Europe and North America, and Japan is often included in an economic sense. The fact that the terms "West" and "Western culture" are still in common usage is hardly surprising since they are both products of the Cold War, which ended not much more than a decade ago. These terms are appropriate to the extent that Europe (or at least Western Europe) and North America can point to more or less the same standards, achievements, and failures, as in the way they

---

Notes for this chapter begin on page 56.

distinguish themselves from other continents and continue to show evidence of a parallel development. Thus, it was clearly correct for observers to apply the vulnerability that so traumatically thrust itself into human consciousness with the terrorist attacks of September 11 to the West as a whole. But in the coping process following this event, differences kept cropping up. Even the choice of words in Europe was not always the same as that in the United States. Differences between Europe and the United States had always existed, but the constellation of the Cold War did not permit people to make an issue of them, if they were even aware of them in the first place. We will look at some of these differences in the following.

Transatlantic differences have been particularly discussed in economic terms, mainly in connection with debates on the desirability of a stronger or weaker welfare state. In the wake of the attacks of September 11, the topic of worldwide social differences was once again discussed in depth. In this book we are mainly concerned with non-economic areas, which are nevertheless influenced by economic conditions. Conversely, some economic phenomena have their roots in entirely non-economic areas, which is why the discussion of these phenomena in purely economic categories cannot take us very far. Furthermore, I will not directly address the cultural conflicts of interest between Europe and the United States insofar as they apply to actual cultural activity, its distribution, and its promotion. By contrast, culture in the broadest sense of the term will be the central theme of the following comments, particularly with regard to legal and government culture.

Finally, I would like to make one more clarification regarding this chapter's title. "Transatlantic" refers exclusively to the relationship between Europe and the United States. Thus, the term is not used in this book to mean any other states across the Atlantic. Canada in particular is much more European than the United States in many matters, an issue that was often spoken of by the Canadians I dealt with in my work. They frequently criticized the way Americans mean only the United States when they say "America" and never the entire North American continent. With regard to the topic of this book, Canada would have to be considered part of Europe in some cases, part of North America in others, whereas in other respects—particularly regarding multilingualism—it is in a unique situation that cannot be included in one or the other. Addressing these issues would go far beyond the framework of this book.

State, Nation, and Religion

One important component of American identity is distrust of the state. The origin and basis of this peculiarity have been described many times. One American expert can stand in for many here: "In the United States, the state was defined in a very unusual way right from the beginning.… The Founding Fathers placed supreme value on preventing the state from intervening in

social developments. Instead, its task was to guarantee undisturbed development by protecting free discussion and the open exchange of views. Americans
in the early period were convinced that a good and just society would develop
if the government avoided all attempts to influence the direction of social and
economic transformation."[1] This basic attitude has remained formative for the
United States up to the present. The reasons behind it have to do with the relationship between state and religion, which we shall look at first.

State and Religion

The reasons for the divergent development of Europe and the United States are
of historical origin. Following the Middle Ages, Europe's hierarchical social
structure disintegrated, and a process of individualization began. The individual wanted to decide for himself what he considered to be religiously and morally correct. The Reformation summed up this development when it declared
that the individual could stand in a direct relationship with God and no longer needed the intercession of the church, as the Roman Catholic Church
continued to maintain. The wars of religion were one fateful consequence
of this. Previously, the individual had been integrated in a pre-set "divinely
ordained" order. When embarking on a war, he did so in the interest of a goal
that he himself did not have to accept, let alone formulate. Individualization
also characterized the course of the wars of religion, which were largely dominated by military entrepreneurs—today we would call them warlords—and
by private mercenary troops. European thinkers responded to this situation
with various demands. The legal system, they said, should be independent
of religious-cultural premises, and religion should be shifted from the public
sphere to one's own private conscience. War was to be nationalized or, if you
will, "statified," meaning that only states should be permitted to fight wars and
to possess a monopoly on violence.[2] With the 1648 Peace of Westphalia, which
ended the Thirty Years' War, some of these thoughts were implemented. The
European powers agreed not to fight any more confessional wars, leading to
the formula "cuius regio—eius religio" (whose region, his religion), that is, the
confessions would henceforth have a territorial basis. This meant that the king
or prince determined the state religion. At the same time, the right to emigrate
was granted so that persons of different faiths would have an opportunity to
practice their religion, although at a new location. The new territorial order
thus brought about "massive 'religious cleansings.' It provoked migrations,
particularly of Protestant Christians: from Germany to the East, from France
to the North, from Europe to the West, into the New World."[3]

Individualization led not only to the Reformation and the religious wars, but
also to many subgroups and schisms in the form of faith communities. Some
of these differed little from the large religions, while others were sects. Such
groups were not tolerated in the Catholic countries nor, to some extent, in the
Protestant ones, particularly if they were suspected—justly or unjustly—of not

recognizing or of disrupting the public order. The greater this incompatibility, the greater the impetus for their members to emigrate, particularly to the "New World." Thus it came about that America was shaped by free churches from the very beginning. Many emigrants may have embarked on the journey to America out of economic distress or as a quest for adventure—or a combination of both. By no means did all of them have a clear position in matters of religion and the state. But to the extent that they had a conviction in these matters, they distinctly recruited themselves from those portions of the general European population for whom the pursuit of their religious convictions dominated all other values. Emigration represented a sort of Darwinian natural selection in favor of sect-oriented religious thinking. Added to this was the New World's colonial situation in which "alongside sects coming from the Old World, new ones were hatched, and dogmatic conflicts within individual sects caused the number of these groups to increase even more."[4] This had various consequences, and one of them, which is still effective to this day, lies in the United States' more or less pronounced wariness toward the state. The Israeli sociologist Schmuel N. Eisenstadt, who was one of the first scholars to compare European, American, and Japanese modernity from a religious-sociological perspective, points out not only that mistrust toward a strong state has become a firm component of the American political tradition, but also that no genuine "concept of the state" has ever developed beyond it.[5]

Europe chose the opposite path after 1648. The Westphalian order of religion and the state became the basis for the creation of political nations in the eighteenth and nineteenth centuries. Today, particularly since 1989, this order has been shaped by other developments, but it remains effective to the extent that it laid the cornerstone for modern-day international law.[6] And it remains historically relevant, since the year 1648 brought about the intellectual historical crossroads where Europe and America parted company. Europe, for peace and political reasons, decided that religion had to subordinate itself to the state. By contrast, the emigrants to America ensured that the state did not impinge on religion. One could sum up the relationship between state and religion in the following formula: Europe needed the freedom *of* the state in order to implement freedom *from* religion, whereas the United States needed freedom *from* the state in order to implement the freedom *of* religion.[7]

The Founding of the Nation

The American understanding of history and politics was definitively shaped by the Pilgrim Fathers, who had come to the New World in order to realize their religious notions without interference, and this continues to influence the beliefs of the nation.[8] The founding of the American nation was ultimately a religious act. This is visible among other things in "civil religion"—a term that Robert N. Bellah first used in an essay written in 1967. Bellah explains this civil religion by citing the self-image of the American presidents, who essentially view themselves as the high priests of a national confession of faith.[9] No one who has seen the president of the United States holding his right hand over his heart—school children repeat this gesture every morning in a brief ceremony centered on the "Stars and Stripes"—can doubt the effectiveness of this priestly image. Even today, no American president would dare "not to be seen attending church on Sunday, or ending a State of the Nation speech without intoning a mighty 'God bless America.'"[10] The dollar bill continues to proclaim "In God we trust," and since 1954, the United States is officially "one nation under God."[11] Of central importance here is the notion that Americans are a people chosen by God—a notion that has played a substantial role since the time of the first English settlers.[12] The lack of a shared history decisively shaped the formation of the American nation. The only common denominator among immigrants was the fact that they had come to the same territory, but this territory did not mean "home" in the European sense of the word.[13] Thus, the notion of being a "chosen people of God" offered itself in the construction of an American identity. In other words, on the one hand, there was an almost unlimited religious tolerance, which would have been unimaginable in Europe following the Peace of Westphalia; on the other hand, religiosity and the profession of any religion was essentially the prerequisite for integration into the American populace.[14] The British philosopher and cultural anthropologist Ernest Gellner has discovered that even today religiosity in the United States represents more an expression of the "American way of life" than membership in a particular religious community.[15]

None of this existed in Europe. European nations were formed on historically predetermined territories by peoples with a common origin and with a common history—in many cases, a very bloody history. As difficult and troublesome as such a development might be, in historical terms there was always enough "nation-forming identification material" to avoid falling back on religious elements. If religion played a role, it was used merely to strengthen the national identity, as one could observe in the most recent Balkan Wars. In the eighteenth century, the concept of the nation was defined culturally. The French Revolution, which decisively shaped all of Europe, subsequently defined the nation as a "nation-state." One significant difference from America also lay in the fact that at the time of European nation formation, either states already existed or there were "would-be" states that had to seek a path to the formation of their own nation-states through a more or less long and frequently painful process. By contrast, the United States experienced its state formation—that is, the separation of individuals from the mother countries as well as the unification of the nation—as an almost simultaneous and unified process. But above all, and this is the most important reason for the divergent transatlantic development, in 1648 Europe reacted to the wars of religion by proclaiming the primacy of the state over religion, and the French Revolution later declared religion to be a private matter, so that a nation's religious foundation was no longer an issue.[16]

The founding of the American nation was ultimately a religious event, while a religious founding remained foreign to the European nations. Although the nation formation of the various European states differed with regard to content and chronology, the non-religious founding of the nation is something they all share in common.

Secularization

Nowhere is the separation of church and state so strictly enforced as in the United States.[17] The purpose of this measure is by no means the protection of the state from religious influences, as is the case in Europe, but rather the protection of religion from state intervention. This characteristic American order principle also has a historical explanation. "Civil religion" essentially means a close interaction of politics and religion, although not on an institutional level but rather through informal factors, such as the expressed opinions of persons of public authority, public opinion, and public and private discussions.[18] To be sure, at first immigrants from England, Scotland, and Ireland willingly implemented the principle of the state church, which they brought over from Europe. However, in the general discussion of liberation from England's paternalism, the arguments of political autonomy and those of church autonomy could soon no longer be separated. The originally political slogan "No taxation without representation," which was brought to bear against the motherland, also took root in the free churches and the sects outside the state churches. These groups gradually asserted themselves and effected the adoption of the principle of a strict separation of church and state in the constitution. Upon this basis there developed a vital variety of religious practice, and this was very much the intention. The state was prohibited from favoring one particular church or religious group over another.[19] For America, the separation of church and state means that the state does not intervene in religious practice in any way, with the goal of promoting the religious activities of Americans in order to strengthen the religious foundation of the national identity.

Europe, on the other hand, experienced the opposite development. Religious wars and cultural struggles of all kinds led to a latent distrust of the churches. I have already mentioned the historical circumstances upon which these developments were based. One can discover a broad range of politically relevant variations of the state church system—from that of the Western European countries, in which the churches are furnished with institutional and fiscal privileges, to a more strict separation in other countries, to Orthodox Christian.[20] Churches and religious communities take positions on public issues just as frequently as non-religious associations, interest groups, and parties are accustomed to doing. Despite the many differences among the European countries, there is nonetheless a basic European-wide consensus on the definition of the freedom of religion and thus implicitly a European-wide definition of the objectives in the separation of church and state, namely, in the European Convention on Human Rights. Article 9 of this convention, regarding freedom of thought, conscience, and religion, states the following: "(1) Everyone has the right to freedom of thought, conscience and religion; this right includes freedom to change his religion or belief, and freedom, either alone or in community with others and in public or private, to manifest his religion or belief, in worship, teaching, practice and observance. (2) Freedom to manifest one's religion or beliefs shall be subject only to such limitations as are prescribed by law and are necessary in a democratic society in the interests of public safety, for the protection of public order, health or morals, or the protection of the rights and freedoms of others." The restriction of religious freedom, which the second paragraph prescribes for the protection of public order, would be utterly unthinkable in the United States.

Islam does not recognize the separation of state and religion. As Gellner has demonstrated, this starting point can lead to entirely different results. On the one hand, there is Islamic fundamentalism, which has taken hold of entire nations. On the other hand, there are Islamic states that are religiously tolerant and respect the freedom of the individual. Although one cannot speak of secularization in the sense of the separation of church and state, Islam nevertheless contains a potential for the involvement of religion in integrated structures, but only if favorable conditions can be created for it.[21] Islamic fundamentalism hinders the use of this potential. However, it is important to recall that this tendency is not rooted in Islam itself; rather, fundamentalism misuses Islam in the same way that the medieval Crusaders misused Christianity and the way certain fundamentalist Protestant sects still misuse it, particularly in the Third World.

Depending on what we interpret as secularization, various states appear to be more or less secularized. If we view it only as a formal criterion of the separation of church and state, then Islamic states appear to be non-secularized, the United States fully secularized, and the European states somewhere in between. However, if the degree of secularization is measured by how strongly public events have distanced themselves from religion, then Europe appears at one end of the scale and the United States at the other.[22] And as amazing as it might seem at first, the Islamic states—which allow the state and religion to stand equally alongside each other without (as in Europe) integrating religion into state structures and without (as in the United States) subordinating state matters to religion—can be seen as lying somewhere between these two poles.

It is occasionally pointed out that fundamentalism is hostile to secularization. If one is speaking only of Islamic fundamentalism, then this statement may be accurate, namely, in the two meanings mentioned above, which can be applied to the concept of secularization. By contrast, the conservative Protestantism that makes its home in the United States and that can also take fundamentalist forms is hostile to secularization only if one understands secularization as the decline of meaning and of the social propagation of religious behaviors and convictions, as can be observed in Europe since the seventeenth century. However, if one understands secularization as the purely formal separation of church and state, then Protestant fundamentalism is in no way hostile to secularization, since it profits precisely from the strict separation in the United States, which sets no state limits for religious practice in the preservation of public order.[23] In conclusion, I want to point out once more that in the following, the term "secularization" means the separation of various areas of life from religion. If I am referring to the formal separation of church and state, and thus the final phase of this process, I will use the formulation "separation of church and state" and not "secularization." At the same time, in chapter 3, I will use "secularization" in a different sense, reaching beyond religious issues.

The Nature and Meaning of the State

Whereas a continental European speaks of the "state," an American speaks of "government" or the "administration." When an American says "state," he does not mean a structure toward which an individual person feels a sense of belonging.[24] When Americans try to describe the countrywide structure to which they belong, they say "country," "nation," or simply "America." In many cases, the term "state" will mean a federal state of the United States, but only as a formal description. However, the different meaning of the state in Europe and America goes far beyond these differences in the definition of "state." The process of the development of the political commonwealth that has characterized Europe began in the Middle Ages. There was still only a single order structure in which no distinction was made between "secular" and "religious," but the emperor increasingly competed with the pope, producing a tug-of-war between the political and the religious orders. It is to this secularization process in the Middle Ages that the modern European state owes its existence. In the eighteenth century, the French Revolution linked the state with the nation or, more precisely, the "state nation," later giving rise to the "nation-state," which equipped statehood in Europe with great weight and authority, so that statehood could now also serve as a vessel for national feelings.

In the decisive phase of the "founding of the state," developments in the United States ran in the opposite direction, as it were: the society had emancipated itself from the state, which had been represented by the mother countries, particularly England. In addition to the previously described hostility toward the state, which could be traced to the relationship between the state and religion, there was now the will to preserve the newly won freedom as much as possible and the desire not to establish a new state in the form that had just been thrown off.[25] The point was to organize things in a reasonable fashion, but the founders viewed the government that would have to be established, for better or worse, as a kind of "publicly accountable service company." It is evident that they did connect this "government" with the nation, for this first would have enhanced the status of the government. Beyond that, it would have weakened the nation, and precisely this had to be avoided at all costs, for the founding of the American nation was of decisive importance: actually, the American Revolution did not lead to the founding of a state but rather to the birth of a nation.[26] In Europe, the nations were predetermined by peoples, territories, or a shared history, and if these factors were not sufficiently apparent, they were shored up a bit using myths and education, with all the horrors to which this development would someday lead. In the United States, all the shoring up in the world would have made no difference, since the people had come together from all over the world, and this would never change. A common history was lacking, and the common territory was not historical. The great achievement was the invention of the American nation, which then appeared to the outside as a nation-state. Yet the rudimentary statehood that was accepted for purely organizational reasons was not suited to serve as a vehicle for national feelings.[27] Instead, the nation manifested itself directly, integrated into the religious context.

Today, just like two hundred years ago, Americans believe in the popular expression, "that government is best which governs least." It was not so significant whether one participated in the discussion on the form of government as an economic citizen, a member of a religious community, or as a citizen of a state. All that mattered was that its competencies be limited. In the United States, society and state were and are no longer separable. When Americans speak of the "administration," meaning the government in Washington, they are expressing precisely this relationship: they are referring to the administration of a societal matter, just like the administration of a corporation, of a religious community, or of a large association that is active in a non-economic sector. In any case, they are not referring to the administration of a state in the sense of the European concept of the state. Put differently, in America the state and society were fused in the foundation of the state, more or less in the sense that the society absorbed the state.[28] This laid the groundwork for the primacy of religion over the state.

Thus emerged the purely horizontal social contract as the basis for what America still is today and which distinguishes it from European-style states.[29] One essential transatlantic difference is already rooted in notions of the social processes upon which the organization of the commonwealth is based. In Europe, the state is a "third factor" that lies beyond the individual and his or her relationship with fellow citizens or inhabitants of the same country. In Europe today, the state—or increasingly "statehood" on various levels—serves not only the security and recognition of social tasks; rather, statehood is the order structure of society in general. Reaching far across social integration and even beyond it, statehood ensures the cohesion of society, independent of criteria such as the citizenship, residence, or origin of the individual person who is included in this cohesion.[30] In summary, we can note that the American understanding of the state is restricted to a purely horizontal social contract, whereas the European state represents a third factor that goes beyond the horizontal social contract, something that does not exist in the United States. Europe differentiates between the terms "state" and "society," while in the United States these two concepts ultimately cannot be kept distinct from each other.

Terms and Their Meanings

When people in the United States discuss their differences from Europe with regard to the understanding of the state, such discussions are usually limited to the economic sector, that is, the function of the welfare state on the European pattern. The extent to which these differences reach beyond economics is scarcely considered in either Europe or America. While the issue is sometimes addressed in scholarly publications, it rarely enters the political discussion, nor does it find its way into the bodies dealing with these questions. In the Parliamentary Assembly of the European Council after 1990, I experienced the exciting years of Europe's fresh start—the outreach first to the Central European and somewhat later to the Eastern European states, and the process that led to their membership in the European Council. Together with parliamentary deputies from all Western European countries, I traveled regularly to meet with parliamentarians as well as governmental and other authorities from these states. We discussed the current problems and explained the European understanding of the state, legal matters, and democracy. In these years I also became alert to the small nuances in this understanding that existed within Western Europe, for example, between the Scandinavian and the southern countries, between the more Germanic-influenced legal cultures and those with Romance roots, and between the continental European and the British concepts of the constitution. But there was no doubt that there was indeed such a general European understanding. The nuanced differences within Western Europe represented an enrichment and also made it possible to pay attention to the differences in the Central European countries in a more subtle way. There was also no question that this European understanding of the state was the only thing that really had to be discussed.

The transatlantic differences in the understanding of the state are relatively unknown in Europe because the same terms are used for different things on both sides of the Atlantic. One example is "republic." In the second half of the eighteenth century, after the United States had achieved independence and was preparing to "found" its "state," France had not yet transformed itself into a republic. However, the demand that it do so was already being made, the republican idea had long since been born, and there was a widespread conviction that the United States would orient itself on this idea. But the needs and problems of the American Revolution were entirely distinct from those that unleashed the French Revolution. Most of all, there was no aristocracy or monarchy to abolish; rather, the point was to find a form of government that differed from that of the mother countries in such a way that there would be no desire for a strong state. Ultimately, the Americans set out to organize not a state but rather a governmental structure. America's Founding Fathers managed this by adopting various concepts, which they proceeded to give a specific meaning that corresponded to their own circumstances and needs.[31] This is what happened to the term "republic," even before this concept and what it would come to mean for Europe could be brought to bear in France. When the French speak of their *République*, which they still do with a certain pride, they are essentially referring to a qualified statehood that ultimately guarantees their freedom.

The difference with regard to the American understanding of the same concept could hardly be greater. But there is also the opposite case, namely, that the term and its meaning do not or no longer agree with each other. In keeping with the different understanding of the state, the typically American term "non-governmental" would correspond to the European term "non-state." However, the abbreviation "NGO" (non-governmental organization)—has asserted itself on a global scale, even though it is actually accurate only for America and would have to be called "non-state organization" in Europe. The fact that the term "NGO" expresses the American understanding of the state as the only conceivable one, even though it distorts European reality, is not particularly helpful for the political identity of the countries that depend on this identity as the basis for the public order structure. Thus, in Europe it makes sense to use the term "non-state," as I do consistently throughout this text.

Before I turn to the different understandings of freedom on each side of the Atlantic, I would like to mention another difference between the American and European self-image, as this represents a point of reference for the American social contract. Here we will return for a moment to the American myth of the "chosen people of God." The United States also understands itself as constituting a "covenant" with God, analogous to the covenant that, according to the Old Testament, the tribes of Israel sealed with the Almighty. The notion of this covenant is still present today and is essential to any understanding of the American nation.[32] It is interesting that at the beginning of the emigration to the New World, the biblical idea of the covenant served both the politicians and the theologians in New England as a foundation—not under changed conditions but rather as an identical theoretical basis for both the "state" and religion. For the Puritans, the social contract and the biblical covenant were one and the same, and the citizen and believer were identical.[33] Since the purely horizontal social contract shows a primal relationship with the "contract," that is, with the contract God made with the people He selected, the Americans also have a third factor. However, this third factor is not to be found in state but rather in religious categories. Here, too, our examination of these connections leads us back to the transatlantic crossroads of 1648.

Freedom and Attachment

Aside from various previously mentioned phenomena, such as the inevitable church visits by presidential candidates, the important role of religion in the United States has not been constantly and directly visible over time. The close link between the nation and religion becomes more visible in emergency situations, such as the terrorist attacks of September 11, 2001. The point of my previous comments was not to explain American peculiarities as such but rather to understand these differences better, which become noticeable today in the transatlantic relationship. These differences reveal themselves in evaluations, behavioral patterns, and notions of what an individual can expect from life and whether he or she can lower these expectations without taking it too much to heart. This section deals with the ultimately very different understandings of freedom that prevail in Europe and in the United States. The next section will deal with the consequences that these different understandings of freedom have in the areas of justice and morality.

A Constant New Beginning

In the United States, many functions of the state as it exists in Europe are assumed by non-state associations where Americans continually come together. To be sure, they rarely describe this process as merely "coming together" but rather as "coming together voluntarily." "Voluntarism" and "non-government" are synonymous in American usage, since one's affiliation with the state is viewed as a compulsion that is to be resisted at all costs. That Americans place such stock in private associations and systematically ensure that a maximum number of functions that Europeans principally understand as public are performed by such associations is not only the result of hostility toward the state. A further historical root cause is to be found in the role that faith communities played in early American history in the guaranteeing of democratic processes and later in economic life. In a very early phase, Americans could receive permission to vote only through membership in a certain religious group, and later on such membership was regarded as an extremely important condition for credit worthiness. In fact, during certain periods of American history, faith communities basically represented the fundamental structure of social organization. Before the founding of the individual states and in view of the size and expanse of the country, they offered the only perspective of order and at times actually maintained certain functions. However, the individual had to be formally accepted into these communities, and this went beyond a mere confession of faith to mean that he or she as a person had to be regarded as morally worthy. Since the members often had to share liability for their loans, it was important to know whom one was getting involved with. These historical precedents are still alive today, since membership in certain clubs requiring formal admittance plays a much larger role in professional life in the United States than anyone could imagine in Europe.[34] For Europeans, such membership is not an indispensable condition for certain professional goals and is by no means a prerequisite for social affiliation, since clubs and associations do not assume social order functions, as is the case in the United States.

Americans' interest in private associations conceals within it another element of the American founding myth, which consists of leaving the old behind and starting all over again. The basic form of this experience was the act of leaving Europe and emigrating to America, which also contains the previously described religious component.[35] While the original immigrants came only from Europe, today they come from all over the world. But the attractiveness of the new beginning, the sloughing off of the old and the embrace of the new, has remained.[36] The state cannot be continually refounded or reorganized. Statehood, as the word stem already indicates, is static, whereby the private system of associations and clubs is dynamic. This does not mean that certain clubs are not ruled by powerful traditional rules. But new clubs and associations can always be founded, and one can always decide anew how formless or formal they should be. One can also leave private organizations, and one can join new ones as long as one is accepted into them. Those Americans who are aware that their predilection for these organizational forms is a typically American characteristic that is not self-evident elsewhere in the world generally describe it by using the word "pragmatism." "Pragmatic" is a word that one encounters very frequently in cooperation with transatlantic partners. In the meaning used here, it reveals that one wants at all times to be free to organize things anew and differently, or else together with new and different partners, should it be necessary.

A purely horizontal social contract is capable of guaranteeing the cohesiveness of the society only if it is continually renewed in a mutual pledge. This regularly occurs across the Atlantic by falling back on the American nation and its roots in religion and in the history of America. In crisis situations, such as the terrorist attacks of September 11, the renewal of the mutual pledge is especially intense, and in such moments people aver their affiliation with American society virtually on a daily basis. It is absolutely unimaginable that, in a comparable situation, parliamentarians in France, Germany, Great Britain, or another European country would come together on the steps of the parliamentary building to sing the national anthem, as American congressmen did shortly after September 11 in Washington, DC. While unimaginable in Europe, it was a natural response in the United States, and it would be utterly misguided to try to draw moral conclusions about the two societies on either side of the Atlantic on this basis. But it would be just as misguided, if not downright dangerous, to close one's eyes to such differences. Why the integration of society works differently in Europe has already been explained: in Europe it is not necessary to continue establishing the existence of the state order structure, which ultimately guarantees social integration, for it is a third factor that exists independently of relationships between individuals.

Finally, in general terms the constant new beginning also represents a basic form of American politics. Presidents of the United States have often attempted to win over the voters through a fundamental new beginning in the form of a "new covenant," which, on the one hand, bases itself on the founding act of the nation and, on the other, is a "covenant with God," even if this is not stated explicitly. Examples of this include President Roosevelt's "New Deal" or President Johnson's "Great Society." Even President Clinton opened his election campaign in 1991 by promising a "New Covenant" between the people and the government. Candidate Clinton's first programmatic speech of 23 October 1991 included the following passage:

> More than 200 years ago, our founding fathers outlined our first social compact between government and the people, not just between lords and kings. More than 100 years ago, Abraham Lincoln gave his life to maintain the union that compact created. More than 60 years ago Franklin Roosevelt renewed that promise with a New Deal that offered opportunity in return for hard work. Today we need to forge a new covenant that will repair the damaged bond between the people and their government, restore our basic values, embed the idea that a country has a responsibility to help people get ahead but that citizens have not only the right but the responsibility to rise as far and fast as their talents and determination can take them, and most important of all, that we're all in this together.[37]

Key Term: Pledge of Allegiance

What links these phenomena together is the pledge of allegiance. Anyone who attempts to understand the various transatlantic differences will eventually be confronted not only with the fact that the phenomenon of the pledge has a very central function in American society, but also that it is a key aspect of the difference between the European and American understandings of society. Thus, the phrase "pledge of allegiance" becomes a key term for the explanation of transatlantic differences, particularly in connection with an individual's affiliation with society, that is, in connection with social integration. In America, social affiliation is always based on a pledge, while a European's affiliation with society represents a "pledge-free" affiliation. Or, looked at another way, in Europe the individual belongs to society simply because he or she exists, while across the Atlantic mere existence does not lead to affiliation. Viewed this way, one can look across the Atlantic and contrast the concepts of "affiliation through existence" in Europe and "affiliation through pledging" in the United States. Americans demonstrate their agreement with certain objectives by joining an association or a club. In individual terms, too, they proclaim their acceptance of a wide range of ideals reaching far beyond religious matters, where the word "pledge" is normally localized. People commit themselves to values, the family, and always "freedom," or they commit themselves to economic success by striving for it themselves and by seeking corresponding models to emulate, such as the archetypal rags-to-riches millionaire.

An important role is played by the adoption of the "American way of life." The previously mentioned sociologist Schmuel N. Eisenstadt traced the often speedy adoption of the "American way of life" by immigrants to the way the latter wanted to commit themselves visibly to America in order to belong to it as soon as possible.[38] According to this view, this phenomenon could be particularly traced back to the fact that American society has always been one of immigrants. This is particularly evident to European observers in the everyday pledge to "America," a word which expresses an entire worldview. Non-pledged people are difficult to classify. But Americans want to be able to classify people in order to know whom they are dealing with. This can also be traced back to immigrant society.

The same difference can also be described the other way around by using the term "exclusion," which can be seen as the opposite of "affiliation." Europeans who deal with the social conditions in the United States regularly notice that relatively more Americans are socially excluded than in Europe: the proportion of those who live on the margins of the poverty level is greater than in Europe, homelessness and abject poverty are taken for granted, and the difference between rich and poor is obviously greater. To take another example, there are more prisoners, and the ongoing executions represent the final act in the exclusion process, the "quintessence of exclusion." How can such a wealthy country, where values and religion are discussed publicly and play such an important role, afford to have so many excluded people and treat them in this way? However, this question is problematical, if not downright wrong, because it is based on a European concept of humankind. To find the answer, we must dig deeper and proceed from the concept of humankind upon which American society is based. Americans are not really acquainted with exclusion since there is no collective to which one could belong existentially and thus from which one could be excluded. The perspective is reversed when Americans attempt to involve themselves actively in society. There is essentially no passive affiliation. Instead, there is only active access to society, and this is achieved by a pledge to an idea, an activity, a community, or a professional activity where one can point to success. Thus, the term "exclusion" cannot encompass the situation in the United States. This does not mean that the economic conditions that have led Europe and the United States to different social conditions should not be compared. But this comparison shows that what Europeans would call exclusion basically amounts to "non-acceptance in society" in the United States, since the perspective is inverted.

In conclusion, it is important to clarify what I have meant by the word "affiliation" in this section: it is a matter of social affiliation and not formal citizenship. Citizenship is regulated internationally by individual states, and thus it is made clear who has certain rights and duties with regard to a particular state and under what conditions, whereby the rights particularly also include participation in the formulation of political demands and objectives. It is thus a purely organizational question, namely, the regulation of the legal relationship between the individual and the state to which the person has a particular relationship, through origin, residency, or other circumstances.

Social affiliation, however, extends far beyond citizenship. The question of political affiliation asserts itself just as much for persons who do not possess citizenship of the country in which they find themselves at a certain time. It is also relevant for stateless persons—particularly when it has an existential foundation in the European sense—and for every person everywhere, precisely because the United States is a perfect example of how persons without citizenship can nevertheless achieve social affiliation. But in Europe too, social affiliation must be viewed separately from citizenship: to the extent that statehood plays a role in social integration, it does so outside the question of citizenship. In summary, we can say that anyone who wants to "belong" in America first has to do something, and, second, has to prove that he or she wants to belong. Europeans have the same opportunities to be active in various areas of life, publicly and privately, professionally and within the family. They also have the same possibilities to participate in common activities of all kinds. Ultimately, everyone is free to commit themselves to the widest variety of things. But there is a big difference compared to the United States: in Europe, one's affiliation with society does not depend on doing or proving anything, since this affiliation is ultimately an existential one.

Attachment to Principles

When mass demonstrations in the streets of Belgrade in October 2000 made it clear that the population of the Federal Republic of Yugoslavia was putting an end to the regime of Slobodan Milošević, the international public soon made its voice heard regarding this event. Alongside the European Union and Russia, President Clinton also staked out a position, demanding that Milošević resign and denouncing his regime in the most contemptuous terms he could come up with. Of course, he omitted the fact that Richard Holbrooke, the American envoy to Yugoslavia, had once come courting the selfsame Milošević in order to create the conditions for the conclusion of the Dayton Agreement. Milošević served as one of the principal signers of this agreement, and I have always considered myself fortunate that the appendix to that document, which created the legal basis for my institution, did not bear the signature of the Yugoslavian president because this amendment to the agreement was regarded as an internal matter of the Bosnian state. With its strategy, Washington had significantly contributed to the state of affairs that had allowed Milošević to last for so long. This is undisputed.

For those who had actively experienced the Balkans, such positions raised a few questions: Did President Clinton not remember the years that went before? Were his advisers unaware that, against such a background, this position appeared cynical? Here too one must dig down deeper to find an answer, because these questions are incorrect, from an American perspective. Based on a European understanding of principles, they ignore a fundamental difference between European and American traditions. "Continually starting over again" involves not only continually adapting problem-solving methods, but also throwing old principles overboard and replacing them with new ones. The constant new beginning, which is so essential to American thinking, leads to another evaluation with regard to an action's short-term and long-term consequences. Short-term success and consequences are much more important to

Americans than long-term ones because they rely on finding some way to correct the long-term consequences later on. By the time long-term consequences have transformed themselves into short-term ones, the situation will be clearer, and the problem can be solved with dynamic action—that is, by adapting the strategy in time. That is the American philosophy, which has apparently paid off throughout history. That is why the "lack of principle" in one's choice of allies appears so only from a European perspective. In American English, such an approach is called "dynamic" or "pragmatic," which in European eyes appears as a further definition of US pragmatism. Its first meaning, as we have seen, is the will to be free at all times to organize things in a new way, or to associate with new and different partners whenever that should prove necessary. This second meaning shares an inner connection with the first one, and it consists of not at first paying attention to the long-term difficulties that an action could bring about as long as the short-term goal can be attained.

What from a European perspective looks like an unprincipled choice of allies has been a common thread over recent years. Saddam Hussein was Washington's blue-eyed boy in the struggle against Iran before he transformed himself into a thug. The Taliban were armed by the United States to fight the Russians in Afghanistan before they advanced to become Public Enemy Number One. It was the Americans who before the war against the Federal Republic of Yugoslavia chose the UÇK (Kosovo Liberation Army) as the sole representative of the Kosovo Albanians, a choice that later proved to be less than optimal. All of these allies had one thing in common during their alliance: they were just as "pragmatic" as the Americans. In the business of politics, the Americans approach those groups that think in a similarly pragmatic way with downright instinctive certainty. Conversely, their path leads them with equally instinctive certainty past all those forces that, alongside the achievement of a certain objective, also consider the maintenance of certain basic ideas or principles to be important. In the process, the Americans are only in the rarest of cases aware of what these principles might be. In their search for partners, they intuitively regard the groups or persons in question as "complicated," since they embody something with which the Americans are simply not acquainted and that they cannot comprehend. This disjunction can basically be expressed in terms of the category mentioned before: these groups or persons are not pragmatic enough for the Americans. A diplomat told me that at conferences on the situation in the Balkans, Richard Holbrooke used to relate the bon mot that the Europeans created structures and the Americans solved problems. This statement nicely sums up the American perspective. It is also true from the European perspective, but more in a symbolic sense, which could hardly have guided the inventor of this transatlantic comparison. When Holbrooke mentioned structures, he was apparently referring to organizational structures. But what distinguishes the European approach even more from the American one are the "thought structures" upon which strategy development is based. European thinking tends to include consideration of medium- and long-term consequences. If they appear too negative, the strategy is hastily dropped, even if short-term success is a likely outcome. This difference is in no way due to Europe's greater morality but rather to a painful and burdensome history that has brought modern Europe to view today's European thought structures as being more beneficial in the final result.

Nor is Europe immune from relapses into oblivion regarding its own history. The behavior of the Western European states at the start of the Balkan crisis is one such example. The Balkans are a prime example of how much bitterness an approach lacking in basic values and principles can cause among a population, for an ethnonationally wounded society cannot help but perceive such events as particularly cynical. To be sure, one must make one proviso, which once again points back to a fundamental transatlantic difference. All politics is occasionally confronted with the question of whether "the end justifies the means." Those who reject this notion demand the preservation of certain principles, especially in politics. I have already mentioned several historically determined reasons that have led Europeans to assign a greater degree of importance to loyalty to principles than Americans do. One important concept in this connection is the nation. For the American public, strategies that appear unprincipled to Europeans are often not seen as unprincipled because they are subject to an absolutely key principle—namely, the maintenance of American interests. Not only in Congress but at all levels of the population, the mere assertion that something is "in America's interest" serves as a magic word that can be used to justify actions. Moreover, this magic word justifies practically all imaginable means.[39] If the Europeans do not possess such magic words, once again this is not due to the Europeans' higher morality: on the contrary, and most emphatically, it is due to a guilt-ridden history. In Europe, this ultimate justification by appealing to national interest had to be overcome and replaced with the will to cooperate.

Democracy and Politics

Democracy is also one of the terms used in the unchallenged assumption that it means exactly the same thing on both sides of the Atlantic. A glance at history places this assumption at least partially into question. In Europe, the French Revolution replaced the king—who until then, partially in concert with the aristocracy, had issued the laws—with the "sovereign people." Although only male citizens were granted the right to elect the law-giving assembly, at least they were entitled to do so, and thus also to decide by whom they wanted to be ruled. The republic took the place of the monarchy. That is why "popular sovereignty" played a central role in the invention of democracy in Europe. I have already mentioned that the needs and problems that instigated the American Revolution were entirely different from those that brought about the French Revolution. The American Constitution never had the function of replacing the absolute ruler with the sovereign people; rather, its role was to create minimal structures in order to ensure the continuation of the American nation after it had freed itself from its mother countries. A powerful state was to be avoided, and in the future it should not be possible for things to develop that way. Thus, in this situation it is understandable that the framers of the Constitution of the United States not only distrusted the elected representatives of the people but also the people themselves. That is why the Constitution lacks the principle of popular sovereignty.[40] American history is, so to speak, a grand and continuously successful attempt to prevent the emergence of a political power that could speak in the name of the people.[41]

From the beginning, the Founding Fathers considered it to be immensely important to create a system that could effectively protect the country from the will of the majority.[42] Thus, in the constitutional debates, the protection of all kinds of minority interests had been a central concern whose roots reached back to the protection of religious communities and sects in the earliest times. Over the course of the American Revolution, a solution was found by which jurisprudence would be placed on a higher level than democracy: every outnumbered minority can appeal to the Supreme Court and refer to the Constitution in combating laws passed by the parliamentary majority. In Europe, democracy is clearly linked to parliamentarianism, while in the United States it is much more closely linked to the legal system. In Europe, democratic identity lies in the election of parliaments, to which citizens are entitled in their status as part of the sovereign people. In the United States, democratic identity lies in possessing rights that are guaranteed by a constitution and that one can litigate over as an individual or as an attorney for minority interests. Thus, the law and the judiciary are granted a function entirely different from the one that holds sway in Europe: due to the lack of state identity, the affiliation of the individual to the United States manifests itself less through elections and legislation than "primarily through the exclusion, assertion, and imposition" of individual rights, so that "the institution of the court becomes the highest and final guarantor of individual security and *civil* recognition."[43]

Of course, there are constitutionally guaranteed rights in the European states, too, and these rights can be litigated employing a broad range of methods. But Europeans subordinate this phenomenon to the law and the judiciary. And conversely, popular sovereignty has certainly been an issue in the United States, particularly during the American Revolution.[44] But the point of the discussion was how to prevent this popular sovereignty from claiming the sole right to speak in the name of the people. In particular, a parliamentary majority should not be readily given the right to do so. Basically, popular sovereignty was exercised for the first time with the adoption of the Constitution, and since then it has been used in the rare cases when the Constitution has been amended. Otherwise, the written Constitution clearly takes precedence over the democratic process: while the US Constitution can be amended, the hurdles are so high that this happens very rarely. The height of these hurdles expresses the lack of trust the United States places in its people. Americans prefer to rely on the Supreme Court rather than on the people.[45]

But it is also interesting that the concept of sovereignty turns up again in an entirely different context that would be wholly unimaginable for Europe. Speaking in the context of the American Declaration of Independence, Robert N. Bellah, who, as we have already seen, introduced the term "civic religion" in the United States, discusses the sovereignty of God, which is placed above the entire society: "It is significant that the reference to super-political sovereignty, to a God who stands above the nation and whose objectives represent the yardstick by which the nation is measured—indeed, by which the nation itself is justified—has since become a permanent characteristic of American political life."[46] With regard to the concept of sovereignty too, the investigation of these connections leads back to the transatlantic crossroads of 1648.

To this is added something else, namely, the Americans' lack of an understanding of politics in the European sense. In the United States, various standpoints are reflected in the struggle for justice, and this struggle is largely fought in the courts, partly by individuals and partly by the various social groups who represent their minority interests. The European tradition of democracy fights such battles in the parliaments and in the many activities that serve to gain influence on events in these state institutions and gain minorities within them. This gives elections an extraordinary importance. By contrast, the American tradition of democracy is focused on articulating individual and minority rights. While the minorities manifest themselves more or less in the shape of lobbyists hovering around the seats of government, they appear more frequently and often more effectively in the courts. That is why the two political parties in the United States are so similar and the conflict between them is far less important than between the political parties in the European states. The fact that this situation is intentional is shown by the numerous failed attempts to establish a new third party alongside the two large American parties: the electoral system is apparently conceived in such a way that this is not possible, not even with the expenditure of vast sums. Of course, there are also transatlantic commonalities. For example, the American Congress passes a budget, just as the parliaments of the European states have budgetary debates and pass corresponding resolutions, just to name one example. And conversely, in Europe too laws can be challenged before a wide variety of courts. This tendency is on the upswing. However, this cannot hide the fact that the term "politics" is not understood the same way on both sides of the Atlantic because there is a different emphasis, one that has existed since the revolutions that occurred over two hundred years ago. Politics, as it is understood in Europe, basically does not exist in the United States because no one ever wanted it.[47]

In summary, we can note that across the Atlantic the conflict over the distribution of power occurs directly—horizontally—within society, and only partially in the government, while in Europe this conflict occurs within the political process, whose central political arena is none other than parliament. In the United States, the actors in these conflicts are minorities of all kinds, whose interaction and counteraction prevent the emergence of majorities. In

Europe, by contrast, such conflicts lead to political majorities that ultimately have to consider minority interests in order to emerge in the first place. In essence, Europeans fight over laws, while Americans fight over rights.

Concepts of Freedom

First of all, I need to mention the broad areas where "freedom" means exactly the same thing on both sides of the Atlantic: the rejection of dictatorial forms of state and government, the rejection of totalitarianism. But these matters are not at issue here. Instead, I will now attempt to present some general remarks on claims of personal freedom. What do individuals expect from life? In which areas could they lower their aspirations? Which freedoms would they abandon in favor of others that are more important? With regard to the understanding of freedom, we want to compare something that can be boiled down to a collective self-image. A collective self-image in the sense of a social backing also exists, precisely in those societies that function in a highly individualistic way and in which individuals do not need this backing or expressly distance themselves from it. Ralf Dahrendorf has compared the Anglo-Saxon, Rhenish, and Asiatic models of society and—using rather simplistic terms—has characterized them as follows: the Anglo-Saxon model emphasizes competitiveness and political freedom but sacrifices social cohesiveness; the Rhenish model emphasizes political freedom and social cohesiveness but fights for competitiveness; finally, the Asiatic model emphasizes social cohesiveness and competitiveness but to some extent sacrifices personal freedom to the social control of state administration.[48] This portrayal is already several years old, and since then there have been changes. But one thing that has not changed is the dependence that this description illustrates: freedom and attachment always retain a balanced relationship with one another. When someone claims that he or she lives entirely without attachments, this merely means that attachments are being experienced in another area that is being excluded from the discussion at hand. That is why one can approach differing concepts of freedom only by examining freedom and attachment together.

The following thoughts deal with affiliation and the responsibility that attends it. In the United States, people reject affiliation and the responsibility it entails with regard to things that they did not decide on themselves. Freedom means that one does not want to be pulled into things one has nothing to do with. And freedom means that one wants to keep on choosing affiliation and responsibility, either in confirmation of what one had already chosen beforehand, or by leaving behind what one previously had and heading for new horizons. Stated in admittedly banal terms, in a certain sense, every individual wants to emigrate to America and thus be allowed to cast off his or her previous ideological ballast, even if this already occurred long ago, perhaps even generations ago, in geographic terms. Freedom "from the state," which is intended as much as possible to ensure that a person is not compelled to assume any responsibility for situations not of his or her own choosing, corresponds to the embrace of "voluntary union" in private associations, which certainly represents an attachment. I have already mentioned further aspects of the American claim to freedom, such as the freedom from being subordinated to the decisions of congressional majorities by ensuring that politics occurs mainly in competition between minority interests. And we can see it in the previously mentioned freedom from attachment to principles, to the extent that respecting them prevents the achievement of short-term results. However, these attachments include religion. Family attachments are also important: the pledge to one's family is discussed much more frequently in the United States than in Europe.

Europeans, by contrast, embrace affiliation and the responsibility that attends it in matters about which they have not made an active decision, namely, in the area of the state in the broadest sense. In this area, Europeans in their historical development have accepted an attachment. This attachment expresses a person's existential affiliation with society together with responsibility for persons or conditions not of one's own choosing. Why do Europeans accept this attachment, or, stated in even more banal terms, what freedoms do they seek? First, it is the freedom not to have to make pledges. In the previous section, we already saw how far in Europe the freedom *from* religion extends back in history and to what extent it is connected with the freedom *of* the state. But European "freedom from pledging" goes much further. Statehood is the only structure that can guarantee this freedom. Statehood does not demand any identification, any faith in the state, and certainly no pledge to it. Citizens or persons who submit themselves to a statehood whose civil rights they do not possess may certainly have reservations toward this statehood or an inner doubt, an intellectual distance. They must merely respect the rights and duties that the law provides in the relationship between them and this statehood. In return, Europeans know very well what they risk if they submit themselves to statehood in the broadest sense: for them the state, seen historically, is "the final reserve, whose potential guarantees the unity of society."[49] Two hundred years ago in France, earlier in England, and later in other countries—but ultimately following the same pattern everywhere—Europeans have freed statehood from the hands of monarchs; they have taken it into their own hands and have made it into the guarantor of freedom. The fact that various European states later had to be liberated again from the clutches of dictatorships and totalitarianism has not weakened the primal experience of the French Revolution; rather, it has strengthened it. The statehood of the European Union, which has not yet discovered its form, bears witness to the lessons that Europe has learned from its recent past. However, the path that will lead to a viable form for this new statehood, a statehood that can live up to the high demands on popular sovereignty first set by the French Revolution, will be a long one.

When trying to grasp the mental parameters of a specifically European understanding of freedom, it is helpful to include the concepts of "foreign" and "foreignness." Americans possess an identity by virtue of their origin, but they leave it behind to become Americans. This occurs through one's pledge to the "American way of life." There is scarcely any foreignness in US society, since every person (or his or her ancestors)—aside from the scattered natives who survived this invasion—immigrated at one time, so that the difference persists only in one's land of origin, which everyone has somewhere. By contrast, in Europe foreignness exists in many forms and for various reasons, all of which amount to an important transatlantic difference: a European who emigrates to a foreign country is not compelled to establish affiliation by making a pledge to a new society; rather, he or she retains the option of remaining foreign, an individual in a foreign society. This is possible because the foreigner is also included in an existential affiliation, independent of the citizenship of the country in question. Affiliation with the foreign society, which one does not join and to which one does not commit oneself, is a very great freedom.[50] But the freedom to remain foreign is possible only if social affiliation is made possible without adaptation or explicit pledges, for it rests only on the individual's existence in a certain place.

The extent to which the transatlantic difference is rooted in the realm of freedom and attachment becomes clear when we look at a person's geographical attachment to the soil. Although Americans rarely leave their continent, they nonetheless frequently and easily change their place of residence within the United States.[51] Americans scarcely understand the concept of geographical attachment. Instead, geographical mobility is a very important element of their understanding of freedom, with the well-known foreign policy effects that this has on the country's dealings with oil-producing nations, which often differ strongly from those of other nations. With such a concept of freedom, it is extremely difficult for Americans to understand why entire populations in Europe insist on living in regions where their forebears had lived, and why in these regions families and clans unquestioningly persist in maintaining or rebuilding, and in any case living in, houses whose cornerstones were once laid by their ancestors. This attitude is tied to an explicitly geographical understanding of history. The tragic events in the Balkans provided worldwide renown to the so-called Battle of Kosovo Polje, where the Turks repelled the Serb army in 1389. This site, which is located in modern-day Kosovo, has been used continually as a symbol for Serb national consciousness. Thus, it was easy for Milošević in 1989 to use his more infamous than famous speech to unleash the Balkan Wars of the 1990s by referring to that battle, which had been fought exactly 600 years earlier. Compared with the United States, the bond to the soil is a typically European phenomenon.

Let us return for a moment to history, which has left a powerful mark on these issues. American freedom derives from the primal experience of an individual act, namely, the act of individual emigration, the abandonment of European statehood. European freedom derives from the primal experience of a collective act, namely, the act of assuming control by the sovereign people: the people took collective control of statehood and transformed it into the guarantor of this freedom. Thus, as far as one's place in the individual and collective sphere is concerned, the primal experiences of achieving freedom on both sides of the Atlantic go in two directions which, viewed in symbolic terms, are diametrically opposed to each other. Europeans generally accept their placement into historical and current parameters that have something to do with the collective, and this is precisely what Americans do not accept. Conversely, individual attachments to the family, to religion, and to other "voluntary" communities play a large role in the United States. In Europe, freedom in the individual sphere, the freedom not to pledge allegiance, that is, not to make attachments, is much greater. We can summarize these differences as follows. The basic social structure in the United States is an exclusively individual one: Americans form "voluntary communities" so that freedom and the pledge of allegiance can be balanced. The basic social structure of Europe contains an additional collective element: Europeans can afford the freedom to organize their lives on an individual basis, free from pledges and attachments to "communities," with the result that attachment and freedom are nevertheless balanced.[52]

In conclusion, let me illustrate the tug-of-war between attachment and freedom in their differences on both sides of the Atlantic with a few more examples. Here I would like to mention the many park-like "gated communities," in which abundant living space, schools, hospitals, churches, shopping centers, and sports facilities have been established, surrounded by high walls, and guarded around the clock by specialized security services. Within such compounds the inhabitants are provided with all they need to make life pleasant. They leave the protected area only to earn money: high performance motorways guide them from parking ramp to parking ramp, so that the inhabitants of such facilities are scarcely confronted with the "outside" world. Invented in the United States, this institution can now be found scattered across the world. It is most prevalent in regions with high numerical and economic gaps between rich and poor. It explicates the transatlantic differences with regard to freedom and attachment since it is based on a clear hierarchy between various assets. The denizens of this protected area defend their freedom not to be confronted with any affiliation—and the responsibility it entails—that they have not actively chosen themselves. This lifestyle links freedom to the self-chosen group in order to protect it from collective attachment. Those who reject this lifestyle (we have to assume that these are persons who can afford it in economic terms, so that this represents a genuine freedom of decision for or against this lifestyle)—because they would experience being closed in behind high walls and living under constant surveillance as a lack of freedom—demand a hierarchy of the same assets in a reverse order. They accept daily confrontation with attachment and the responsibility it entails, even though they have not actively chosen it. Such a lifestyle appears to them less odious than the "tyranny of intimacy" in a protected zone.[53] It takes major and minor collective attachments in stride so that it does not have to tie freedom to the self-chosen group. This example is intended merely to clarify the tug-of-war between attachment and freedom in connection with self-chosen and non-self-chosen situations. It would be incorrect to assume that the life-style in such gated communities corresponds to the general aspirations of American society.

Law and Morality

Even the most superficial examination of legal notions in Europe and the United States—and that is all we have space for here—must first take a brief look at the difference between the continental European and the Anglo-American legal systems. Expressed in simplistic terms, the former is a legal system based on laws and the second is a legal system based on decisions in individual cases. It is worth noting that the two forms have increasingly come to resemble each other in recent years. If the United States does not recognize statehood as a third factor, this is not due to the difference between the two legal systems, which is obvious if we look to Great Britain. The British Parliament is often called "the mother of all parliaments," since the parliamentary system was invented in England. Unlike in the United States, the political identity of the British is intrinsically linked to the institution of Parliament, which has nurtured a pow-erful state-political identity. While the judges see to the further development of the norms set by Parliament, this is not viewed as a political activity, aside from exceptions of the kind that can occur on the European mainland as well. Britain and the United States differ greatly in their understanding of the con-stitution, which is scarcely surprising considering that the British emigrants to the New World consciously sought to detach themselves from their motherland. The fact that England does not have a written constitution is merely an external indication of this difference. At the time when England was "constituting" itself, that is, when it was seeking its path toward its modern-day political order, the sovereignty of Parliament took center stage. In the United Kingdom, Parliament is still considered to be sovereign, naturally as the representative of the sover-eign people. According to the will of the "constitutional revolution," the lower House of Commons, the upper House of Lords, and the Crown were henceforth required to work together. And the only form in which Parliament could express itself was through legislation. There was thus no fear whatsoever of majority decisions or the necessity of being able to correct parliamentary decisions, as was the case in the American Revolution. So in the context of the topic under discus-sion here, there are vast differences between Britain and the United States.[54]

Legislation and Jurisdiction

When looking at modern day legal practice, continental European lawyers who deal regularly with America notice two things. First, treaties worked out by American lawyers are always much longer than treaties on the same subject drafted by Europeans according to their own customary forms. Second, American lawyers proceed differently from European ones when they are confronted by a new problem. These two differences reveal a logical inner connection. The continental European approach consists first in considering how to classify the problem within the legal order, what legal areas are affected, and to what extent matters are regulated there; what leeway the legal order provides for private agreements; and whether conflict regulations are provided for. European lawyers will first attempt to figure out "where the problem really belongs." An American lawyer, by contrast, immediately goes about looking for identical or similar cases in order to approach the matter from this angle. If a European colleague asked him to classify the problem within a larger context, he might well reply that he is concerned with solving the problem and not classifying it. He wants to proceed "pragmatically."[55] The considerably longer treaties he drafts—on any given issue they can amount to up to 10 times more pages than the continental European fashion calls for—are one result of this approach. Since individual problems cannot be classified within a larger context that might provide certain answers for newly arising questions, all conceivable situations have to be anticipated and regulated in the treaty. When concluding a treaty, an American lawyer wants to leave nothing to chance, and by chance he means that he does not want to leave anything to the trial and the judge's decision. Thus, every treaty becomes something of a "comprehensive legislative act, but only for this concrete case."[56]

European lawyers also do not leave things to chance, but they can rely on much clearer general legal rules and conflict regulations in laws from which they can respond to newly arising questions. American legal regulations are much more closely concentrated on procedure. Americans are convinced that as long as the procedure runs correctly, then the result will be correct as well. Thus, in all areas of life, even beyond the narrow framework of the law, the concept of "fairness" plays a very important role, whereas this category has been much less important in Europe up to the present. This is certainly not meant to imply that legal procedures in Europe are not "fair," but rather that the manner in which matters are regulated justly is fundamentally different in Europe. Fewer procedural rules are necessary since there is a certain density of regulations with regard to content.[57] This is also one of the reasons why the American judicial system is so much more expensive than the European one. And this is in turn one reason why an American lawyer simply cannot afford to draft shorter treaties. Another reason lies in the fact that everything that is not expressly forbidden is permitted, and an American lawyer is well advised to think through everything that might someday occur to the other party.

This basic attitude reminds us of the previously mentioned bon mot on the occasion of the Balkan conferences, according to which the Europeans create the structures and the Americans solve the problems. In Bosnia, Americans frequently asked me—even appealed to me—to proceed "pragmatically." Here again is the term "pragmatism," now in another meaning. I have already commented that the first meaning of this term is the will at all times to be free to organize things anew and differently or together with new partners, if needed. The second meaning is the will not to consider the long-term difficulties that an action could bring about as long as the short-term objective can be reached. The third meaning of "pragmatism" lies in the desire not to proceed from certain premises or a superordinate structure, but rather to deal with matters on a case-by-case basis. The legal system also illustrates the notion of American freedom, according to which it should be possible to organize everything anew or differently if this should turn out to be necessary for whatever reason. Legal security is above all anchored in procedures. With regard to content, Americans want to have the freedom to develop the law from one case to the next.[58]

One recent example of this is the controversy over the legal status of the captured Taliban and al-Qaeda fighters, whom the American armed forces brought to their base at Guantanamo Bay in Cuba. From the point of view of international law, there are only two types of status for captured combatants: first, there is the legal status of captured combatants, who become prisoners of war; second, there is the status of civilians captured during war, who are not regarded as prisoners of war as determined by the courts. Since the United States was greatly interested in interrogating the captives, which is not permissible with prisoners of war, and because it did not intend to determine their status as non–prisoners of war through the courts, the American government promptly invented a new legal status for them as "unlawful combatants," which no one had ever heard of before. The status definitions in the Geneva Conventions serve legal security in the sense that all persons captured in conflicts are encompassed and protected by the rights defined in the conventions. When a new status is invented to avoid being forced to guarantee these rights, this impinges on humanitarian international law and, moreover, legal security. It is particularly remarkable that this statement did not come from a private lawyer representing the interests of a particular party but rather from the government itself. In the United States, the law is a political matter. As such it is intended to serve political purposes and is understood by everyone in that way.[59]

As far as legal security is concerned, it is also important to point to the class-action lawsuits that to a large extent embody the American understanding of law. Things that are fought for politically in Europe, such as the claims of ordinary people or underprivileged persons, are fought for in the courts in the United States. The instrument of the class-action lawsuit does not entirely fit into the European system: in Europe, competing interests are not brought into equilibrium in a legal procedure in front of a court, but rather in a political procedure through legislation. When Europe is nevertheless confronted with class-action lawsuits, this is because European firms with branches in the United States or with assets located there can be sued in American courts. The class-action lawsuits against German companies in the forced labor issue are particularly instructive in this regard. I do not intend to comment on the facts of the matter, let alone on the circumstances surrounding it, since the guilt it entails cannot be expiated with cash payments. For an understanding of the transatlantic differences in the understanding of law, it is particularly instructive to note how, based on their European understanding of law, the sued firms in Germany demanded a certain legal security, since after paying up in one case they had reason to fear further lawsuits in others. The United States, however, was not in a position to guarantee legal security, likewise on the basis of its legal system. The maximum that could be reached in this regard was a declaration by the American president calling on the country's courts to halt pending lawsuits against German companies regarding the compensation of forced laborers and not to permit new lawsuits since this lay "in the interests of US foreign policy." As a result, this declaration was called a "statement of interest" and did not bind the courts. With every fiber of its being, American legal thinking resists such pledges, and it has to do so, for otherwise it could no longer exercise the political function for which there is no substitute in this country. Conversely, European legal thought strives for legal security with every fiber of its being, for this security can only be anchored in the legal order. When ultimately the German Bundestag ensured legal security for the sued companies, so that the necessary conditions for the payment of funds to the affected parties could be fulfilled, this went beyond the normal bounds and represented an attempt to maintain the European understanding of law against the entirely alien system of class-action lawsuits.[60] From a European perspective, it looked as if people were being forced to "buy legal security."[61] From the American perspective, legal security does not exist in this form through the legal system, so that the procedure appeared to be absolutely standard and normal.

In this context, it is important to point in general terms to the significance of damage payments. The sums that are awarded in such cases are many times higher in the United States than in Europe. Here we can also discern the lack of what Europeans would see as systematic legal thought, combined with the notion that everything that is not expressly forbidden is permitted. Seen close up, the system of potential liability replaces that of the European legal system, from which certain rules of behavior are derived. In the end, these two systems achieve the same result—namely, the result that certain actions are avoided—but they achieve it in entirely different ways. Stated very simply, within the European legal tradition, the motive for refraining from performing an action lies largely in the fact that the action could impair or injure someone in an unacceptable manner, whereas the motive in the American legal tradition largely kicks in at the other end, namely, in the realization that an action could become extremely expensive if one were to be sued for it. Of course, people are sued for damages in Europe too, and it goes without saying that in the United States people naturally refrain from performing actions because of a direct awareness of their harmfulness or danger. Here we are merely dealing with a comparison of the two mechanisms. In Europe, the menacing sword of Damocles represented by damage suits is not especially important because an individual has the possibility to deduce proper behavior from the legal order, whose basic parameters are generally known.[62] The United States does not actually have a legal order in the European sense, since law is a matter for specialists. Americans only know that "the law" is extremely important, and they frequently appeal to this concept, but usually only in the sense that the law guarantees them personal freedom and a "fair" trial. They are less certain about what "justice" and "injustice" mean, and how far this freedom extends. It is enough for them to know that everything that is not expressly forbidden is permitted. This is precisely the reason why the sword of Damocles represented by damage suits has such great and objective meaning within American society in the maintenance of a certain order. Once again, we can see Europe achieving a certain objective by focusing collective ideas and America achieving an objective through an individual consideration of advantages and disadvantages. We have already seen this distinction in connection with the relationship between freedom and pledges of allegiance.

We can summarize the transatlantic differences in legal understanding by saying that the European legal system tends to strive for what amounts to a peace treaty, whereas the American system represents an adversarial culture. In the European tradition, law is a certain framework within which the individual legal person moves and upon which he or she can rely, whereas the American legal tradition ensures that the law always remains changeable. In Europe, the political authorities argue over legislation, while in the United States, we can witness a struggle over rights that is waged in the courts by individuals or minority groups.

Different Moral Paths

We can see one effect of this transatlantic difference in the powerful impact of moral notions on American court decisions. Here, too, the cause can be located in historical factors. In Europe, the Enlightenment separated law and morality once and for all. A consensus arose that only an individual person's actions should matter in court. It was of no significance what these persons were thinking at the time or whether they understood the meaning of the legal order, just as long as they obeyed the law externally. This regulation also worked the other way around: the state guaranteed an individual's security— namely, of life and limb, which was about all it amounted to in the seventeenth century—but even this guarantee existed independently of the moral attitudes of the person in question. Thus, not only the virtuous person possessed a dignity as a human being and enjoyed the protection of the state, but also the non-virtuous person, whatever one might consider a non-virtuous person to be. The penal responsibility was also to be handled according to strictly legal and not moral criteria. To this day, the question of whether the offender is "good" or "bad" is not permitted to play any role. However, it is evident that law and morality actually are connected, and the French Revolution set out clear guidelines for Europe on how to ensure that the legal order can live up to moral criteria despite the separation of law and morality. In principle, the Revolution gave each male citizen two roles: one as part of the "sovereign people," which made him able to elect to the legislative assembly that person who would best bring his moral notions into the laws; the second as a "legal subject" or "legal person" who was to obey the laws, which affected the female half of the population.[63] We have already seen in the last section how in the United States the separation between the citizen's twin roles as popular sovereign and legal subject was not conducted the same way as in Europe. Political identity is experienced more through an active approach in the courts and less through representation in the government. That is why in the United States morality takes a direct path to legal application before the courts, while in Europe it asserts itself primarily in the legislative process.[64]

The European process of implementing moral notions through legislation tends to include more and more persons. At the dawn of democracy only male citizens were entitled to elect the legislative assembly, and in some places the right to vote was even dependent upon income. This condition was later removed, and the circle of eligible voters was expanded continually until women received the right to vote. Today one can observe a tendency whereby people residing in an electoral district are becoming increasingly active in the democratic process, even though they do not or do not yet hold citizenship. Popular sovereignty contains an inclusive tendency. The American process of implementing moral notions runs counter to this, at least to the degree that these notions flow directly into legal application in the courts. This becomes particularly clear to the extent that—from a European perspective—the judiciary functions as a substitute for politicians, whereby interest groups become involved in individual cases and take them to court in order to gain social recognition for themselves and their moral notions. We have already seen how much more expensive it is to conduct trials in the United States. This is not to say that the enforcement of moral notions through litigation is exclusive. But compared with the European tradition as presented here, we can say with certainty that the latter is definitely more inclusive. Here we can see a parallel to the transatlantic differences regarding affiliation, as discussed in the last subsection. In Europe, affiliation is ultimately an existential matter, whereas in the United States, it can be acquired only by "doing something for it." Of course, participation in the democratic process also requires that an individual person develop an opinion and contribute it, even if only by participating in regular elections. But this is nevertheless far less demanding, and certainly far less expensive, than going through all the courts.

The contrasting transatlantic paths through which moral notions enter into law can be traced to the previously mentioned differences in the understanding of the state. Because Europeans view the state as a third factor, they entrust the law to this state in the form of a systematic order. Since the sovereign people acts as such through its parliamentary representation in the legislative assembly, it contributes its moral notions to the legislative process. In this way the state is endowed with an intrinsically ethical quality.[65] In the United States, the reverse situation prevails: since the social contract is entirely horizontal, the law is developed in a direct relationship between individuals. Because the American conception of society has painstakingly avoided allowing anyone to speak in the name of the sovereign people, it appears logical that moral notions are discussed both directly in the courtroom and publicly in the discussions surrounding trials. The separation of law and morality, which the Enlightenment brought to Europe, is difficult to achieve under these circumstances. This becomes clear, for example, in the way that Europe and the United States deal with the death penalty. In Europe, the death penalty is clearly viewed as being irreconcilable with human rights, whereas across the Atlantic it continues to be imposed and carried out.

The voices raised against the imposition of the death penalty in the United States argue almost exclusively in procedural terms: it is claimed that even the minute possibility of a legal error should compel the courts to refrain from imposing this punishment. Thus, the now-famous group of students who are struggling against the death penalty meticulously search for procedural errors. Thanks to their findings, they have been repeatedly successful in freeing convicts from death row. However, the fundamental and essentially political question of whether the state has the right to put a person to death because of criminal offenses is not up for discussion. And yet the attendant circumstances that turn up in the media—how the victim's family members applaud the perpetrator's death, sometimes telling the media that they hope that the perpetrator will die as painfully as possible—give rise to further comments. American criminal law is much more strongly informed by the idea of revenge than European law. Stated simply, criminal proceedings have three participants: the offender; the prosecution, which represents the state's power to punish in the name of the collective; and finally the person who has been wronged by the offense. In the European tradition, the law and the state's power to punish take center stage, while certain legal regulations even provide for the possibility of referring the injured party to a civil court to resolve his or her damage claims. The injured party has no greater right than any other citizen to exert influence on the perpetrator's punishment and must limit itself to the legal representation of its damage claims. The fact that in recent years various laws have been passed to provide for state compensation to the victims of criminal offenses is only marginally concerned with these issues. On the one hand, this again expresses the fact that Europe gives greater emphasis to the collective aspect, whereas across the Atlantic the individual aspect is dominant. On the other hand, the strong presence of the idea of revenge reveals the same Old Testament component that we have already seen in connection with Americans' belief that they are a "chosen people of God."

There is no need to repeat the historical reasons that explain why a person must be considered morally worthy to be accepted by the community. The consequence of such individually defined affiliation is the emergence of non-affiliated persons, and this necessarily leads to the fundamental moral categories of "good" and "evil." The execution of an offender is also a symbol that one is not only combating "evil itself," but exterminating it forever. The campaign against the death penalty in the United States is conducted on a purely procedural basis, since a content-centered, ethical line of argument would meet with little response. The constant need to distinguish between "good" and "evil" is too deeply anchored in the "American soul." Incidentally, this is also one of the reasons behind the need for pledges, which represents a key factor in explaining a number of transatlantic differences. It is hardly coincidental that the European Enlightenment led to the separation of law and morality and that in the United States this was not the case, at least not with this clarity.

In the understanding of the American nation, the "goodness" for which this country stands has played a central role from the beginning. The basis for this moral component remains religious, and today this is often expressed in moral categories. If "goodness" is part of the national self-image, then there must also be "evil," since the two categories are dependent on one another. Toward the outside, evil is continually identified with persons and states, thus preserving the national mission, which is to impose goodness upon the world. While one does not need to look at the events following September 11, 2001, to see these mechanisms in action, nevertheless they were particularly obvious during those months. The same mechanisms are mirrored within the country itself. Since "Americanness" is also defined by being good, one must constantly be careful to distance oneself from the country's less-than-good inhabitants. In Europe, by contrast, evil in this sense does not exist: here the enactment of penal norms remains a political process, as long as the norms have not gone into effect. As soon as they have become a positive law, then the criminal guilt they address remains morally neutral. And since evil in this sense does not exist in Europe, neither does goodness, let alone a sense of mission in the world.[66] In summary, we can note that the Europeans have fashioned vessels for morality, first bundling it in legislation, and then turning it over to the state in the form of a legal system. The United States does neither, at least not explicitly, which is why the individual is directly exposed to the moral claims of other individuals or groups.

International Law

International law is the system of laws that for several centuries has regulated the legal relations between peoples—whereby "peoples" are meant in the sense of the modern-day nation-states and not as ethnic groups—and still regulates them today. In international law there is no legislator. Even the General Assembly of the United Nations cannot enact international law; however, it continually suggests conferences at which delegations from the individual states conclude international treaties with one another. Thus, international law consists of treaties between two or more states through which an individual state subordinates itself to an international order. The treaty is first signed and later on—after approval by the responsible authority in the individual country, which is usually the parliament—it is formally ratified. From this moment on, it is valid for the state in question. Depending on constitutional provisions, it is either automatically regarded as national law or else transformed into national law through a parliamentary decision.

Whenever they attend conferences designed to hammer out international treaties, European delegations are first struck by the sheer size of the American delegations, which is not solely due to the country's size and influence.[67] Countless specialists are on hand to deal with all imaginable practical questions that might pop up. Furthermore, European participants at such conferences report that the Americans play a much more aggressive role in the negotiations than would normally be the case in Europe. Both elements basically only reflect national legal understandings on both sides of the Atlantic: the Europeans are trying to create a system, whereas the Americans are concluding a special treaty. Over the last several years there has been an increasing tendency to create a sort of preliminary step toward a "world legal system" in various subareas, particularly within the framework of conferences that have been convened by the United Nations or one of its special organizations. Not only trade relations have been globalized. There are also numerous problems that threaten human beings and the natural environment throughout the world and that can only be tackled globally. Thus, the previously mentioned tendency is heading in a direction that corresponds more closely with the legal conceptions of the European delegations than those of the Americans. This explains at least to some degree why over the last few years a great many states have agreed to a new international order in the form of treaties under international law, while the United States together with a few outsiders has remained on the sidelines.[68] Americans cannot accept the way that international law is increasingly developing into a "supranational" legal order since they have a much harder time thinking in terms of legal systems than Europeans. Many commentaries on this reserved stance particularly cite the great power concentration in the United States, which makes it possible and even desirable for the only remaining "superpower" of the Cold War to behave this way. Although this analysis is correct to some extent, it falls short since the behavior of the United States is due just as much to its legal understanding.

Another reason can be derived from its understanding of sovereignty. Treaties under international law that tend toward a supranational legal order demand that individual states give up some of their sovereignty in favor of a supranational legal order, often linked to the transfer of competencies to an international court or arbitration authority. Such a relinquishment of authority is extremely difficult for the United States—it is certainly more difficult than for the European states. The reason for this can also be found in the concentration of power, but here too this analysis falls short. As already mentioned, the United States Constitution lacks the principle of popular sovereignty, so that American history represents a grand and successful attempt to prevent any one political force from claiming to speak in the name of the people. The number of competencies that the individual is prepared to relinquish to the state is kept to an absolute minimum, and this occurs in the name of "personal freedom." The situation is quite the opposite in Europe. States existed long before the Enlightenment propagated the idea of individual freedom, and the first guarantees of freedom came from the legal orders that developed within the framework of these states when sovereignty still lay in the hands of kings and princes. When the people later seized sovereignty from the hands of the aristocracy, this sovereignty ceased to be limitless. Instead, the law provided it with a framework to protect the freedom of the individual. In other words, even then it was clear to every reasonable person in Europe that the individual had to relinquish his or her limitless primal freedom to the state if some sort of order was to be possible—an order that would provide protection and freedom to the individual. For Europeans, the first, original, and individual relinquishment of sovereignty in favor of the state is considered so natural that this idea no longer even exists in anyone's consciousness as a separate category. This "shared sovereignty" represents the historical foundation upon which it first became possible in the French Revolution for the people to wrest sovereignty from the king. And it is precisely this core component of European intellectual history that generations upon generations of immigrants to the New World have rejected in the name of a "new freedom," which approaches the same question from a perspective diametrically opposed to the European one.

The increasingly more apparent rejection of shared sovereignty by the United States has historical roots that can be traced back to the way Americans have long regarded in negative terms the relinquishment of sovereignty by the individual in favor of the state. All social classes regularly bring their entire energy to bear on minimizing this phenomenon. The rejection of the individual's relinquishment of sovereignty is so powerful in the "American soul" that it also limits America's ability to relinquish sovereignty under international law, for how can something be possible on a large scale that is impossible on a small scale?[69] The intellectual historical roots for America's behavior toward international law are significant. Even if the United States should lose its powerful political domination, its historically influenced difficulties with shared sovereignty will remain an effective problem. This phenomenon particularly affects Europe: the old continent contributes a diametrically opposed historical understanding to the international community. This has become increasingly more important in recent decades in that shared sovereignty represents a principle in the development of the European Union that underpins the entire notion of peacekeeping.

Regarding the creation of a sort of preliminary stage of an international legal system in various sectors, which the United Nations is promoting in conferences or in its special organizations, it is also important to mention the role of morality. The political motives behind the convening of such conferences can be traced to the moral desire to strengthen international peace, international welfare, and the international protection of human beings and the natural environment. Who could doubt that a sense of horror at the events of World War II has been the driving force behind European integration within the framework of the European Union? However, in the notions of how such motives should be implemented—that is, how to move from morality to action—we see again the old transatlantic differences. If the European representatives tend to conclude binding treaties under international law, they do so because they wish to move from morality through the legal system to action, in the certainty that all participants are attempting the same thing within a certain legal framework, or at least should attempt it. By contrast, Americans prefer the path that leads from morality directly to action, for they do not want their "pragmatic" approach to be obstructed by consultations, let alone by treaties under international law. Here, too, one can observe the different paths of morality on both sides of the Atlantic.

The fundamental difference between Europe and the United States becomes particularly evident in each side's dealings with international law, namely, that for the old continent, law represents a peace order, whereas across the Atlantic, law and the judicial system have a political function. This became very clear in the example of the International Court of Justice, whose charter was approved in Rome on 17 July 1998. At first, the United States drove a hard bargain in Rome and attempted to design the court to be as weak as possible.[70] Later on, it signed the charter in order to be involved in the development of the detailed regulations. It did so with the same objective, although with an open admission that it was unlikely to ratify the charter. In the end, the United States formally withdrew its signature from the charter. From a European perspective, it appeared dishonest and inconsistent for the United States not to ratify the international treaty on the International Court of Justice after acting as one of the chief promoters of the creation of special war crimes tribunals for the former Yugoslavia and Rwanda within the framework of the United Nations, and also after exerting massive pressure on states to deport certain accused parties to The Hague. Across the Atlantic, however, scarcely anyone could imagine that a trial of a defendant of American nationality would not be decided in a political sense, namely, in the sense that his or her nationality would be incriminating. To a large majority in the United States, the fact that their country will not join the International Court of Justice appears not only legitimate but even as the state's duty toward its citizens, who are to be protected against unjust—in the sense of "violating US law"—treatment and unfair prosecution. This stance is thoroughly consistent, as seen in the controversy regarding the procedural guarantees toward the captured Taliban and al-Qaeda combatants who have been brought by American troops to their base on Guantanamo Bay. Just as Americans take for granted that they will not receive a correct trial before a "foreign" court because they assume that a completed military action will be held against them as an immoral act, they also take for granted that the prisoners have morally disqualified themselves by virtue of their participation in military action in Afghanistan. Thus, to them it appears justified not to allow these combatants the procedural guarantees that apply to American citizens.[71] This example illustrates not only the political understanding of the legal system, but also once again the direct path of morality, as already discussed above.

In summary, we can see that the behaviors of Europe and the United States with regard to the development of international law are so very different that if one were to establish a worldwide scale of acceptance of international law, Europe would be found at one end and the United States at the other. Today, it is becoming increasingly illusory to speak of "the West." Up until the fall of the Berlin Wall, it was essential not to analyze these connections. In fact, for Europe it was a question of survival. Perhaps today a more questioning attitude is equally essential.

Human Rights

In no other area has the different meaning of international law for Europe and the United States become so clear so soon as in the field of human rights. After the United Nations proclaimed the Universal Declaration of Human Rights on 10 December 1948, Europe immediately went ahead and passed the European Convention on Human Rights in 1950. This document was not satisfied with the mere political enforcement of these rights but provided for individual complaints within a legal procedure. The European Social Charter, dealing with the social rights that had been left out of the European Convention on Human Rights, followed in 1961. In 1966, within the framework of the United Nations, the two human rights pacts on civil and political rights, on the one hand, and economic, social, and cultural rights, on the other, were passed, whereby the former set of rights also provided for individual complaints on an optional level. Then in 1969, the Inter-American Human Rights Convention followed, also allowing the possibility of individual complaints and encompassing North and South America. Alongside the legal enforcement mechanisms for human rights—and, in chronological terms, usually before the legal mechanisms—political instruments have been implemented. On an international basis, the UN Human Rights Commission deals with political enforcement. Each year it wrangles over whether individual states should be reprimanded by resolutions for human rights violations. The political enforcement of human rights is also promoted in bilateral contacts between states, while the legal enforcement can occur only multilaterally, since this requires the participation of a certain number of states. The fact that these states have equal status distinguishes the legal implementation measures from the political ones, where powerful states have more weight than others. On the European level, equality is particularly expressed by the way each state sends a judge to the European Court of Human Rights.

A further difference between the two types of enforcement concerns the equal treatment of human rights violations by various states. In the legal sector, this equal treatment is guaranteed to the extent that all individual complaints must be judged according to the same rules and that the same conditions hold true for their submission. One can hardly expect a state that repeatedly violates human rights to be successful in preventing its citizens from submitting complaints. In the political procedure, however, equal treatment is in fact possible, although there is a danger that a powerful state will more easily disregard a verdict.[72] In the political procedure, the states always attend to their own interests, which occasionally leads to situations that no longer entirely live up to the basic idea of human rights, for example, when economically developed states hold back from accusing less developed states of violating human rights only because they do not wish to risk future business with these rising economic partners. For purely technical reasons, this danger is practically non-existent within the framework of the legal enforcement mechanisms. Nevertheless, human rights must be enforced with both types of mechanisms—both the more effective legal and the political method.

The differences between Europe and the United States in their dealings with human rights first appear in purely formal terms. Today, no state can become a member of the Council of Europe without having relinquished sovereignty to the European Court of Human Rights, which has two major effects: the question of whether a human rights violation is ruled on is decided within the framework of certain procedural conditions solely by the complainant, who turns to the court; and whether a violation has actually taken place is decided solely by the court. Neither process can be influenced by the governments of the contractual states, as they appear merely as adversaries before the court. By contrast, for reasons that have already been presented, the United States has consistently refused to subordinate itself to any protective mechanisms with individual complaints under international law. It has recognized the facultative protocol in the UN pact concerning individual complaints with regard to civil and political rights just as little as the protective mechanism of the Inter-American Convention on Human Rights.

In the area of political enforcement instruments as well, preferences are very different on both sides of the Atlantic. The United States prefers bilateral agreements over multilateral ones since they better allow it to act "pragmatically," as it understands this term. The European countries have moved some distance away from bilateralism in the field of human rights because for them the European Union often speaks with one voice. There are various reasons why the United States, unlike Europe, clearly prefers political enforcement of human rights to legal enforcement, some of which have already been mentioned: first, there is the general legal understanding, and, second, the different approach to international law. As a third element, we must look at how for the United States the issue of human rights does not, strictly speaking, belong in the category of law at all, but rather in the category of foreign policy. And this in turn has to do with the fact that Americans do not see human rights as an international concept but rather as a national one, which they wish to export into as many other countries as possible. This becomes very clear when one considers the United States' elaborate domestic system of legal mechanisms designed to protect constitutionally guaranteed basic rights, compared to its consistent rejection of international protective mechanisms based on individual complaints.

When I was working in the field of human rights in Bosnia, I noticed the differences in this sector for the first time. We originally began our activity, which consisted of dealing with complaints by individuals, in a consciously formal manner. At the same time, countless internationals across the country were engaged in human rights "monitoring." Their task was to investigate human rights violations and to report on them, either to an international organization or to a national government, or even to a non-governmental organization, depending on who had sent them to Bosnia in the first place. What both activities had in common was the attempt to engage in a dialogue with the authorities or their subordinates who were blatantly disregarding human rights, whereby the monitoring methods were less formal but more comprehensive. While we may have been formally equipped with more state authority in our dealings with these institutions, we nevertheless worked much more selectively. Apart from certain exceptions, we wanted to receive a complaint, whether in written or oral form, in order to be able to confront the state authority with straightforward facts. Among other reasons, we chose this clear strategy because the informal approach was backed up by what seemed like an endless supply of monitors. This would not have been the case with a more formal approach, for which we, in contrast to the monitors, had sufficient competency on the basis of the Dayton Agreement. Unfortunately, another thing the two activities had in common was that they were rarely successful, particularly at the beginning, and required great perseverance in their attempts to persuade people to remove their ethnic spectacles. Many people involved in monitoring informed the affected persons of the possibilities of referring complaints to our institution, and conversely many tips by the monitors were very helpful in our efforts to process the complaints, particularly when trying to evaluate the chances for opening dialogues with local authorities. In any case, the two sides kept each other informed to the extent that we were not bound to discretion by our regulations in an open complaint procedure.

In this connection, I became acquainted with a first practical difference between European and American human rights culture. While the Bosnian authorities would ask me why we were expecting different behavior from them and where the legal basis for it could be found, Americans frequently referred to the US Constitution, specifically to the first 10 amendments, which contain the actual guarantees of basic rights. A Swede, a Spaniard, and certainly a "Republic-conscious" Frenchman would never dream of basing an argument on the Swedish, Spanish, or French constitutions, for the simple reason that these constitutions do not apply to Bosnia. However, this is apparently not the case for the US Constitution. It is hard to know whether the Americans somehow failed to recognize the international instruments that were implanted into

Bosnian law by the Dayton Agreement or whether they viewed the phenomenon of "freedom" as a strictly transatlantic invention (as if references to the
US Constitution would make a greater impression on the Bosnian authorities)
or whether it was a combination of both.

The United States also rejects international supervision of its own human
rights behavior through individual complaints within the framework of international organizations because for it, the notion of human rights represents a
national concept. Americans assume that there could be no better protection
of the individual than that provided for in the US Constitution and its amend-
ments, whereas for Europeans, human rights are definitively an international
concept. Furthermore, in the United States these rights represent a much more
political concept than they do in Europe, where they are largely defined in
legal terms. Americans understand human rights as something that the individual fights over with the government in what is understood as a political
arena. Europe goes one step further in its understanding of human rights: the
state commits itself with regard to the community of states and assumes active
responsibility to ensure that an individual's human rights, particularly those
of a weaker individual, are not violated. This results in a difference in the way
that Europe and the United States approach structural development assistance
for states in crisis regions. Americans place considerable importance both on
making the individual powerful enough to fight for his or her rights and on
setting up a functioning judicial system to which the individual can turn for
support. They assume that the "state" will then develop automatically from
these elements. For European development workers, these sectors are also
part of their responsibility; however, they place additional significance on the
growth of an administrative culture of the rule of law. In other words, they
not only develop the individual but also the state. To be sure, there are also
development workers of European origin who have already adopted American
notions of law and the state. Perhaps they view this approach as more "pragmatic," and they may well be right. Particularly in a post-war situation, it is
easier to convince people of the "struggle for rights" as a basic social structure.
It requires somewhat more time and patience to explain the advantages that a
rule of law understood as a peace order can bring, and to show the paths that
can lead to it.[73] We will return to the Bosnian example in the next chapter.

One ostensibly unspectacular event can serve to illustrate a further, profoundly national component. When the American president spoke in the
media a few days following the terrorist attacks of September 11, calling on his
countrymen to behave correctly toward their fellow citizens of Arab descent,
he did not base this appeal on the human dignity of these persons, but rather
on the fact that they were "Americans."[74] Of course, it would be wrong to
take this to mean "American = human; non-American = non-human." Nevertheless, the president's statement was not accidental and points to something that we have already discussed in the last two sections. Many Americans
consciously or unconsciously assume that personal freedom was first born

within the framework of their nation and therefore that their country is best able to administer and protect this freedom. Thus, there is no dishonesty, let alone presumptuousness, whatsoever in their occasionally using "American" and "human being" as synonyms in connection with the notion of freedom. For many Americans, the pledge to "freedom" also amounts to a pledge to "America."[75] For European observers, this American identity is understandable only against the background of the myth of the "chosen people." But it is precisely at this point that the American national soul experiences the fusion of an understanding of freedom that opposes the relinquishment of individual sovereignty with a national identity that opposes shared sovereignty under international law.

The transatlantic differences in the field of human rights have begun to reveal themselves in practice only since 1989, and have done so very slowly. Until this point, the United States had also recognized the European understanding of human rights, as this "European-packaged" concept made it all the easier to exert pressure on the Eastern Bloc. There is no doubt that this pressure was absolutely essential, which is why no one can blame Western Europe for paying so little attention to transatlantic differences in this area.

Should We Grow Together or Stay Apart?

The transatlantic differences presented in this chapter are by no means comprehensive. Instead, I have made a selection according to the criterion of how important these phenomena are for developments both within East Central Europe and in the interactions between Western Europe and East Central Europe. Beyond that, my selection is restricted to those areas that I described at the beginning of this chapter. And yet all the differences recounted here have something in common: they all have their roots in the history of ideas and can be traced to historical facts. Not only do these differences have rational explanations, but also these explanations make them rationally intelligible. And this in turn is a precondition for a meaningful treatment of these differences. It is only through rational analysis that we can recognize and weigh the advantages and disadvantages of the divergent thought patterns on both sides of the Atlantic as we seek to discover the points where we can learn from one another and where these differences are best left alone.

Sadly, the debate over transatlantic differences—to the extent that it is even perceived as such—is often characterized by powerful emotions and reduced to a question of faith. Faith and the pledge of allegiance, which are so important in the American national understanding, also appear to play a large role in the debate over these differences, and Europe's faith-resistant rationality has a hard time being heard. This is all the more remarkable since the practical argument over these differences usually takes place in Europe and not in the United States. Many Europeans who deal with transatlantic differences seem to adopt American thought patterns by quickly moving the discussion to the level of the pledge—namely, choosing sides either for or against the United States. It would be more helpful if they would assume a position of detachment, for which Europe has a great variety of thought patterns at its disposal. The debate over transatlantic differences has very little to do with faith or morality, but with rational analysis. This shows that in questions regarding whether the two shores should grow together or stay apart—and in formulating an answer to this question from a European perspective—precisely those basic categories come into play that, stemming from the history of ideas, represent an important transatlantic difference.

The first signs of this phenomenon could also be observed in Bosnia. As I mentioned in chapter 1, the international activities in this country, at least in the first years following the conclusion of the Dayton Agreement, were strongly dominated by the United States. Thus, the numerous internationals who populated Bosnia in those days were saying that Bosnia represented the "fifty-first state," or at least an American colony—note that it was an American colony in Europe. Since the United States justifiably viewed the Dayton Agreement as its own achievement, and because America is a matter of faith, "Dayton" too became a matter of faith. And those who did not repeatedly express their pledge to "Dayton" risked having their personal dedication questioned. But over the years this pledge grew more and more difficult, the reasons for which will be discussed in the next chapter.

Notes

1. Stephen Kalberg, "Strukturierte Missverständnisse: Unterschiede der politischen Kultur in Amerika und Deutschland," *Europa oder Amerika? Zur Zukunft des Westens*, special ed., *Merkur* 9/10 (2000): 948.

2. A description of this development can be found in Herfried Münkler, "Bleiben die Staaten die Herren des Krieges?" in *Politisches Denken: Jahrbuch 2000*, ed. Karl Graf Ballestrem, Volker Gerhardt, Henning Ottmann, and Martyn P. Thompson (Stuttgart, 2000), 16–34.

3. Otto Kallscheuer, ed., *Das Europa der Religionen: Ein Kontinent zwischen Säkularisierung und Fundamentalismus* (Frankfurt am Main, 1996), 22.

4. Ernst Vollrath, "Die Trennung von Staat und Kirche im Verfassungsverständnis der USA," in *Gott und Politik in den USA: Über den Einfluss des Religiösen. Eine Bestandsaufnahme*, ed. Klaus-M. Kodalle (Frankfurt am Main, 1988), 218.

5. Schmuel N. Eisenstadt, *Die Vielfalt der Moderne* (Weilerswist, 2000), 57.

6. In an article commemorating the 350th anniversary of the Peace of Westphalia, Heinz Schilling wrote the following: "For the European state system, 'peace through law' meant an order supported by the still young international law based on a fundamental equality of law and status between states. From then on, one

power's pursuit of absolute dominance, whether in the sense of a universal monarchy or as a sustained, unbalanced hegemony, was regarded as illegal. Attempts to achieve such dominance were also undertaken after 1648, starting with Louis XIV's expansionist wars beginning as early as the 1660s. However, they stood in contrast to the continent's notarially certified legal culture as set down in the Peace of Westphalia, and further encountered energetic resistance on the part of the other states." *Neue Zürcher Zeitung*, 24–25 October 1998.

7. The First Amendment of the US Constitution, which guarantees freedom of religion, is expressly understood as freedom *for* religion and not as freedom *from* religion. President Ronald Reagan's statement that "the First Amendment was not written to protect the people from religious freedom" is particularly memorable in this regard. Quoted in Erich Geldbach, "Religion und Politik: Religious Liberty," in Kodalle, *Gott und Politik in den USA*, 250.

8. Kurt R. Spillmann discusses the reasons why a relatively small group of immigrants managed to exert such a sustained influence: "It was this small group of rigorous Puritans, who sought their path through reality with an externalized covenant theology along with an externalized eschatology, or who *sought to create a reality that matched their ideology*, that provided the core of the American nation and, thanks to the closed nature of their religious system and the force of this self-aware ideology, also provided the crystallization point of a new nation." Spillmann, *Amerikas Ideologie des Friedens: Ursprünge, Formwandlungen und geschichtliche Auswirkungen des amerikanischen Glaubens an den Mythos von einer friedlichen Weltordnung* (Bern, 1984), 41 (emphasis added).

9. This essay is prefaced by an analysis of President Kennedy's inauguration speech. Regarding the president's oath of office, Robert N. Bellah writes: "This oath is the oath of office which includes the pledge to preserve the Constitution. He swears it in front of the people (you) and God.... Although the will of the people as expressed in electoral majorities is meticulously institutionalized as the sole genuine source of political authority, it is deprived of its ultimate meaning. The will of the people itself is not the measure of right and wrong. There is a higher measure against which this will is measured; it is possible for the people to be wrong. The President's pledge encompasses this higher measure." Bellah, *The Broken Covenant: America's Civil Religion in a Time of Trial* (Chicago, 1992), 22ff.

10. Otto Kallscheuer and Claus Leggewie, "Deutsche Kulturnation versus französische Staatsnation? Eine ideengeschichtliche Stichprobe," in *Nationales Bewusstsein und kollektive Identität: Studien zur Entwicklung des kollektiven Bewusstseins in der Neuzeit*, ed. Helmut Berding (Frankfurt am Main, 1994), 124.

11. Gustav H. Blanke, "Das amerikanische Sendungsbewusstsein: Zur Kontinuität rhetorischer Grundmuster im öffentlichen Leben der USA," in Kodalle, *Gott und Politik in den USA*, 129.

12. The phenomenon is discussed in depth in Spillmann, *Amerikas Ideologie des Friedens*, 39ff. Bellah dedicates an entire chapter to the topic "America as a Chosen People" in *The Broken Covenant*, 36ff. An interesting tidbit of historical evidence can be found in Otto Kallscheuer, *Gottes Wort und Volkes Stimme: Glaube, Macht, Politik* (Frankfurt am Main, 1994), 119: "The first designs for the Great Seal of the United States (by Benjamin Franklin and Thomas Jefferson) were intended to represent the USA as 'God's new Israel.' Moses raises his staff to part the Red Sea, in which

the enemies of freedom drown: God leads the chosen people through the desert with pillars of cloud and fire."

13. See Thomas Fleiner-Gerstner, "Multikulturelle Gesellschaft und verfassunggebende Gewalt: Staatslegitimation und Minderheitenschutz," in *Die multikulturelle und multi-ethnische Gesellschaft. Eine neue Herausforderung an die Europäische Verfassung*, ed. Thomas Fleiner-Gerstner (Fribourg, 1995), 53.

14. David Martin describes the meaning of religion as follows: "Religion could thus be effective in two ways. For one thing, it could release the ecstatic enthusiasm which then called a vast number of voluntary religious communities to life, all of which competed with one another and thus had to focus on their respective markets. In addition, it could legitimize the endeavors and destiny of the American people as a whole in such a way that the ideal could never be refuted by harsh realities. Religion—and that means almost every religion—was thus viewed positively as an indisputably *pro-American activity*." Martin, "Europa und Amerika: Säkularisierung oder Vervielfältigung der Christenheit—Zwei Ausnahmen und keine Regel," in Kallscheuer, *Das Europa der Religionen*, 167ff. (emphasis added).

15. Ernest Gellner, *Postmodernism, Reason and Religion* (London, 1992), 5.

16. In a comparison between what they describe as American and French civil religion, Heinz Kleger and Alois Müller present this difference: "Biblical notions ... turn out to be the matrix of the Americans' political self-interpretation and, in alliance with the secular myth of progress, they remain to this day the religious-political dynamic of the sense of *national* mission. [For France], however, the religious tie obstructs the constitution of the citizen. The individual must be liberated from the tutelage of the church and be empowered to enjoy cultural freedom by the *state*, particularly in the form of the uniform educational system." Kleger and Müller, *Religion des Bürgers: Zivilreligion in Amerika und Europa* (Munich, 1986), 68 (emphasis added).

17. Such a description can be found under the title "McJesus Worldwide, Inc.," in Claus Leggewie, *Amerikas Welt: Die USA in unseren Köpfen* (Hamburg, 2000), 123ff.

18. The Puritans in the New England colonies made just such a demand: "Religion, at least that part of it which joined the citizens to one another and with God, should also be politics and statecraft, and statecraft should also be religion." Blanke, "Das amerikanische Sendungsbewusstsein," 187.

19. A description of this development can be found in Vollrath, "Die Trennung," 222ff.

20. Kallscheuer describes the common denominator of these different situations in Europe as follows: "In Europe [the Christian churches] are to a large extent furnished with considerable institutional and fiscal privileges and serve a sort of semi-official moral supervisory role. However, they must constantly justify their constitutional and actual range of action against a global public that has grown distrustful after the various cultural struggles of the past two centuries." Kallscheuer, *Das Europa der Religionen*, 17.

21. Ernest Gellner, *Bedingungen der Freiheit: Die Zivilgesellschaft und ihre Rivalen* (Stuttgart, 1995), 25ff.

22. In this regard, José Casanova describes the United States as the least secularized society of the modern era. Casanova, "Chancen und Gefahren öffentlicher Religionen: Ost- und Westeuropa im Vergleich," in Kallscheuer, *Das Europa der Religionen*, 182f.

23. "What can justly be called the unifying mission of secularism has a sanctity all its own." Agnes Meyer, the wife of the editor of the *Washington Post*, cited in Klaus-M. Kodalle, "Zivilreligion in Amerika: Zwischen Rechtfertigung und Kritik," in Kodalle, *Gott und Politik in den USA*, 43.

24. Wolfgang Fikentscher notes that in the United States, the term "state" has never meant "the aggregation of the American people into a unity defined by public law." Fikentscher, "Staat vs. Government—eine Beobachtung zum Thema Kulturpersönlichkeit," in *Staatsphilosophie und Rechtspolitik: Festschrift für Martin Kriele zum 65. Geburtstag*, ed. Burghardt Ziemske, Theo Langheid, Heinrich Wilms, and Görg Haverkate (Munich, 1997), 1408.

25. Dick Howard describes the situation at that time as follows: "The Americans' independence—their revolution, if you will—came down to the fact that the members of society wanted to pursue their own interests and had liberated themselves from the tutelage of the state without giving thought to institutions or politics. The ideological component of this lay in the pretense of a self-sufficient society. Political intervention, which was equated with state intervention, was not desired. People were expected to be satisfied with society as it was." Howard, "Demokratische Republik oder republikanische Demokratie? Die Bedeutung der amerikanischen und der Französischen Revolution nach 1989," in *Das Recht der Republik*, ed. Hauke Brunkhorst and Peter Niesen (Frankfurt am Main, 1999), 170.

26. The Declaration of Independence of 1776 was the high point of the American Revolution. The Federal Constitution was adopted on 17 September 1787. Cf. Dick Howard, *Die Grundlegung der amerikanischen Demokratie* (Frankfurt am Main, 2001), 29ff.

27. The term "publicly accountable service enterprise" is used by Willi Paul Adams, who also demonstrates why there was no use for the term "state" in the "inflated German sense of the word" in either the "recently United States or, therefore, in the text of the Constitution or the Federalist Papers," simply because "government" and "nation" were not fused together. Adams, "Verfassungstheorie und Verfassungspraxis der amerikanischen Gründergeneration: Von der konstitutionellen Monarchie Grossbritanniens zum republikanischen Bundesstaat," in *Bürgerreligion und Bürgertugend: Debatten über die vorpolitischen Grundlagen politischer Ordnung*, ed. Herfried Münkler (Baden Baden, 1996), 296f. Regarding the Federalist Papers, see note 31.

28. Birger P. Priddat describes this as follows: "In the American tradition, the state is an organ of society." Priddat, "Gerechtigkeit oder Fairness: Der Staat in der Zivilgesellschaft," *Europa oder Amerika? Zur Zukunft des Westens*, special ed., *Merkur* 9/10 (2000): 1028.

29. Ulrich K. Preuss explains the term "horizontal social contract." Preuss, "Der Begriff der Verfassung und ihre Beziehung zur Politik," in *Zum Begriff der Verfassung: Die Ordnung des Politischen*, ed. Ulrich K. Preuss (Frankfurt am Main, 1994), 16ff. The term "horizontality" is also used to describe the transition in the historical process of secularization in which the transcendent founding of the state—for example, by the authority of a divinely understood monarch—was definitively replaced by the self-organization of citizens who, without supernatural authority, would thenceforth decide how they wished to be governed (see, e.g., Günter Frankenberg, *Die Verfassung der Republik: Autorität und Solidarität in der Zivilgesellschaft* [Frankfurt

am Main, 1997]). I use the term in the latter sense, whereby the horizontal social contract as presented here exists both in European and American thought. Across the Atlantic, however, only this social contract exists, and not the state as something that goes beyond it. If the term is used in the sense of secularization, then one could justifiably ask whether this horizontality actually exists in the United States. This explains the preceding discussion of secularization.

30. Preuss describes the connection between the horizontal social contract and the limited authority of the government as follows: "In the contract-theoretical tradition of Locke, who, in contrast to Hobbes and Rousseau, already attributed the natural state with all the essential qualities of a society differentiated by property and contracts, and thus for which the social contract is in no way concluded for the sake of protecting the natural elementary needs of individuals, the word 'people' did not mean the unity of a collective person which had been bonded together for the needs of all, but rather the 'endless diversity of a crowd whose dignity lay in their pronounced diversity.' The power attributed to 'the people' thus did not exist in the sum of the 'natural' forces of individuals living in the natural state of all ties and its transference to the authority now embodying this power; instead, it materialized in the originally legally bound authority of a 'government' that was transferred by individuals who already formed a society through mutual legal obligations, and thus who do not establish a government out of a state of nature. The experience of the American colonists and their diverse pacts and 'covenants' make it plausible that their first notion of a 'social contract' was a horizontal agreement based on reciprocity, through which they joined together as a community (in both a religious and secular sense) and overcame the weakness arising from their individual isolation by establishing reciprocal obligations; the triumph over the state of nature was created by the security expectations of the law, which thus assumes the existence of a power that guarantees it. And this security of law is on the one hand based on the law-producing, mutual trust of those who have embarked upon a shared and dangerous undertaking. Thus, social power does not emerge from a concentration of the natural power of the individuals in a sovereign, but rather in the transference of previously formed, reciprocal powers to a 'government'; its authority thus cannot be viewed as limitless from the start." Ulrich K. Preuss, *Revolution, Fortschritt und Verfassung: Zu einem neuen Verfassungsverständnis* (Berlin, 1990), 32.

31. The development of this new interpretation and its justification can be read in detail, namely, in the Federalist Papers, which are actually a commentary on the Constitution published by Alexander Hamilton, James Madison, and John Jay in 1787. See Hamilton, Madison, and Jay, *Die Federalist Papers,* trans. Barbara Zehnpfennig (Darmstadt, 1993). This polemical collection of essays was in favor of the Constitution as put forth by the Federalists and, like them, ultimately asserted itself. Barbara Zehnpfennig speaks of a genuine "reinterpretation of terms," and describes this as follows: "Republican equality is transformed into a modified form of elite rule; federalism becomes the justifying theory for the strengthening of central power; the diversity of opinions and lifestyles, i.e., pluralism, becomes an instrument for what is fundamentally a monistic objective." She also includes an explanation of this reinterpretation highlighting individual points. Zehnpfennig, "Die Federalists zwischen Gemeinwohl und Partikularinteresse," in Münkler, *Bürgerreligion und Bürgertugend,* 304f.

32. The book by Robert N. Bellah in which he laments the decline of American civil religion bears the title, *The Broken Covenant: America's Civil Religion in a Time of Trial.*

33. Adams has the following to say about the New England colonies: "[T]he English bridgeheads ... were not crown colonies at first, but rather private enterprises approved by the Crown.... [A]ssemblies of elected representatives of the large landholders ... represented further organizational forms that urged or forced the interplay of English colonial rule, English business practices, and American settlement and economic conditions. This secular impulse to participate in self-government as a shareholder ... was intensified by religious conviction: for the Puritans there was no question that the community of the faithful had to be largely autonomous in questions of church administration and that every full-fledged member of a congregation had the same voice, for example, in the election of a pastor. The symbols providing the legitimacy of the social contract and the biblical covenant were inextricably linked in the person of the citizen and the believer." Adams, "Verfassungtheorie," 285.

34. In his 1906 book, *The Protestant Ethic and the Spirit of Capitalism*, Max Weber described the historical connections in depth. On the meaning of clubs and associations for professional and commercial advancement, see Weber, "Die protestantischen Sekten und der Geist des Kapitalismus," in *Die protestantische Ethik I: Eine Aufsatzsammlung*, 8th ed., ed. Johannes Winckelmann (Gütersloh, 1991), 286ff. The following is an example of the mutual liability for debts: "From an account by a German-born nose and throat specialist who had established himself in a large town on the Ohio and told the story of the visit of his first patient. Lying down on the sofa on his doctor's instructions so that he could be examined with the nasal speculum, this patient sat up once more and commented with dignity and force: 'Sir, I am a member of the *** Baptist Church in *** Street.' At a loss to understand what significance this fact could have for a nasal ailment and its treatment, [the doctor] confidentially asked a well-known American colleague about the matter and received the smiling reply that it only meant: 'Have no worries about the *fee*.'" Weber, "Die protestantischen Sekten," 281 (emphasis added).

35. Eisenstadt describes how the notion of starting over again and leaving the old behind has a religious component: "[The American] founding myth ... describes America as 'new' and pure, as holy.... The idea of the 'newness' of the American experience led to a specific conception of history, of collective time. It emphasized the common—historical—origin of the American myth and of the American people. But this historical origin meant a discontinuity, the severance of the European tradition, and this did not entail the notion that the American vision would continue to develop in a historical process." Eisenstadt, *Die Vielfalt der Moderne*, 58f.

36. In an entirely different context—namely, with regard to the factors behind the Americans' relatively high internal mobility—Hans Joas emphasizes the discovery that this mobility was not so much a consequence of individualism alone, but also "a result of very different tendencies ranging from the push from one's previous home to the pull towards another." Joas, "Gemeinschaft und Demokratie in den USA: Die vergessene Vorgeschichte der Kommunitarismus-Diskussion," in *Gemeinschaft und Gerechtigkeit*, ed. Micha Brumlik and Hauke Brunkhorst (Frankfurt am Main, 1993), 58.

37. This quotation can be found in Kallscheuer, *Gottes Wort und Volkes Stimme*, 138ff.
38. Eisenstadt, *Die Vielfalt der Moderne*, 50. The process of achieving conformity through "Americanization" also has historical roots, which are described in depth in Spillmann, *Amerikas Ideologie des Friedens*, 161ff.
39. Cf. note 59 regarding the status of the captured Taliban and al-Qaeda militants in the Guantanamo Bay detention camp in Cuba.
40. Following is the formulation Preuss has used to explain the absence of the notion of sovereignty in the US Constitution: "The notion of an unconditional and unshackled sovereignty of the nation and the people was thus alien even to the radical republicanism of the Anti-Federalists, even more so to the drafters of the Constitution, who regarded the possibility of a unified collective will and the logic it entailed with extreme distrust. In state and constitutional-theoretical terms, they had no need for such a hypothesis, for their Constitution was aimed at a public power that would protect the citizens' freedom—and at the end of the eighteenth century this meant the freedom of the propertied classes—as effectively as possible; a historical mission of public power that went beyond individual legal protection, and the notion that this power was, in effect, the incarnation of a prudential common will, was alien to them, in fact, it even appeared downright threatening, and thus they assiduously made sure that the formation of the political will would remain as fragmented as possible in order to prevent the suppression of the propertied minority by the majority of the unpropertied. In structural terms, this constitutional conception aimed at the guarantee of freedom expressed itself in the fact that 'the' public power, i.e., the unity of a center, did not exist in the American Constitution; from the beginning, it was based on the foundation of a pronounced federalism and constituted various powers and regulated their mutual relations in the sense of a system of 'checks and balances,' so that the notion of a sovereign met with no response in the Constitution. Thus, the pathos of popular sovereignty, which in Europe has been bound up with the idea of collective reason along with social and moral progress ever since the French Revolution, is lacking." Preuss, *Revolution, Fortschritt und Verfassung*, 32f.
41. Howard expresses this as follows: "Political life in the United States appears ... as a constant self-transformation of the economic society, a sort of permanent revolution that is protected by constitutional mechanisms guaranteeing that none of the political powers can claim to embody the popular will and impose measures in its name." Howard, *Die Grundlegung*, 49f.
42. The thesis that "'173 tyrants [the elected representatives of the state] can exert just as much oppression as a single one' and that America did not go to war merely to replace a hereditary tyrant with an elected one" goes back to Thomas Jefferson in his *Notes on the State of Virginia*. Howard, *Die Grundlegung*, 298.
43. Preuss, "Der Begriff der Verfassung," 19 (emphasis added).
44. The question of how to express this popular sovereignty in a way that would not endanger the fundamental issues of the American Revolution is discussed in the Federalist Papers, the previously mentioned constitutional commentary by Hamilton, Madison, and Jay.
45. Eisenstadt also attributes the American solution to the fact that it was difficult to localize the bearers of the general will: "Primordial affiliations—founded on territory, descent, or language—were poorly developed. Nevertheless, a civil religion

developed whose various premises always stood in a tense relationship with one another. In this situation, parts of society began seeing jurisprudence as the arena in which the general will, the *volonté générale*, could be formulated. In revolutionary and post-revolutionary France *la République française* or *la patrie* could, so to speak, be inserted in the place of the king and be presented as the bearer of the *volonté générale*. In the United States this was not possible on account of the negative attitude toward the government and the state, as described above." Eisenstadt, *Die Vielfalt der Moderne*, 73.

46. Robert N. Bellah, "Zivilreligion in Amerika," in Kleger and Müller, *Religion des Bürgers*, 50. See also note 9.

47. Hannah Arendt noted with regret how Americans have transformed political principles into social "values." Arendt, *Über die Revolution* (Munich, 1974), 285.

48. Ralf Dahrendorf, "Weltmarkt und Sozialökonomie," *Kapitalismus als Schicksal? Zur Politik der Entgrenzung*, special ed., *Merkur* 9/10 (1997): 821.

49. Preuss, "Der Begriff der Verfassung," 19.

50. This freedom is, for all intents and purposes, described in America and for America. Richard Sennett discusses the opportunity one gains of encountering other people "without feeling the compulsive desire to get to know them as persons." Sennett, *Verfall und Ende des öffentlichen Lebens: Die Tyrannei der Intimität* (Frankfurt am Main, 1983), 428.

51. See note 36.

52. A critical overview on the concept of community in the United States and Europe can be found in Walter Reese-Schäfer's text. He distinguishes between the terms "community" and "society" in a manner going back to the sociologist Ferdinand Tönnies. Community is based on the "'special social power and sympathy' that holds people together as members of a whole. Society, by contrast, is a circle of people who live and work peacefully alongside one another but who are nevertheless 'essentially separate.'" While this distinction applies to a portion of the theme discussed here, it does not go far enough. Reese-Schäfer, *Grenzgötter der Moral: Der neuere europäisch-amerikanische Diskurs zur politischen Ethik* (Frankfurt am Main, 1997), 418ff.

53. See note 50.

54. Preuss points out that on the institutional level, the contrast between the British and American constitutional models could hardly be more drastic. Preuss, "Der Begriff der Verfassung," 15.

55. In a legal context, "pragmatism" is a philosophical school that has exerted great influence on American legal thought. Wolfgang Fikentscher describes it as the attempt "to determine a person's position in society and in the world in general by reducing it to the simplest possible level and making it as realistic as possible." Fikentscher, *Methoden des Rechts in vergleichender Darstellung, Anglo-amerikanischer Rechtskreis*, vol. 2 (Tübingen, 1975), 279.

56. Winfried Brugger describes this peculiarity of American law as follows: "Systematization and inner consistency [are] alien to American legal thought." Brugger, *Einführung in das öffentliche Recht der USA* (Munich, 1993), 83.

57. The failure of the United States to recognize the International Criminal Court is justified by various American lawyers on the basis that the procedural guarantees for defendants do not meet the high demands of American law. See also note 71.

58. There is a difference between England and the United States in this regard as well. Fikentscher describes English jurisprudence as "one of the most traditional, respected, reliable, predictable, and exemplary" systems, which takes "the top position in the world on the basis of these criteria." Differences from the United States are particularly evident with regard to predictability. Fikentscher, *Methoden des Rechts in vergleichender Darstellung*, 149.

59. The executive director of Amnesty International USA attempted to show that the humane treatment of these prisoners was in the essential interests of Americans. This inspired a reporter from the *Neue Zürcher Zeitung* to comment that this appeared to be the only way to raise America's awareness of the problem. *Neue Zürcher Zeitung*, 21 January 2002.

60. The Bundestag's decree was particularly aimed at persuading the companies to contribute their share to the compensation of the victims.

61. Otto Graf Lambsdorff, the German government's chief negotiator, used this expression in an interview. *Der Bund*, 3 June 2000.

62. The debate over this European legal tradition is not particularly topical at the moment. It appears to have made itself heard for the last time in the legal political discussion a quarter century ago, and not in a transatlantic context but rather in a confrontation with a tendency in Europe that "never tires of depicting the prevailing legal system or law in general as irrelevant or even despicable." Thus, one has to go back several decades to find formulations of the European legal tradition, for example, the following one, which arrives at a downright apocalyptic conclusion: "A sufficiently broad and intensive legal attitude appears to be the precondition for any meaningful intellectual work with legal questions. As soon as one no longer views (shared) law but rather the opinions and interests of a special group or of his own person as a standard of behavior, no one is interested in rational solutions for legal questions. To be sure, there is also no more legal community, but rather violence, chaos, and at most the unrestrained rule of whoever is the strongest at the moment." Franz Bydlinski, "Rechtsgesinnung als Aufgabe," *Festschrift für Karl Larenz zum 80. Geburtstag*, ed. Claus-Wilhelm Canaris (Munich, 1983), 6f.

63. Corresponding to these two roles, the first French declaration of basic rights is called the Declaration of the Rights of Man and of the Citizen (Déclaration des Droits de l'Homme et du Citoyen), according to which human rights are related to one's role as a person subject to the law and to one's role as part of the sovereign.

64. Klaus Günther has described the relationship between the citizen and the legal person in detail and arrives at the following definition: "The democratic constitutional state depends on the *regulated and institutionalized, general and equal exchange* [emphasis added] between the roles of citizen and legal person, not by their fundamental blend of virtuous active citizen or their absolute separation in the roles of the lawgiver who is exempt from following the norms (*princeps legibus solutus*) and the passive subject." Günther, "Welchen Personenbegriff braucht die Diskurstheorie des Rechts? Überlegungen zum internen Zusammenhang zwischen deliberativer Person, Staatsbürger und Rechtsperson," in Brunkhorst and Niesen, *Das Recht der Republik*, 97. On the participation of non- or "not yet" citizens, cf. chapter 3, note 74.

65. This quotation on the European understanding of the state can serve as an illustration: "Whoever recognizes the personal dignity of an individual human being

must also realize that the individual on account of his social nature experiences the full development of his personality in the encounter with the other … and in community, whose most comprehensive organization is the state. In this view, the state is not the condition for the development of the individual's personality, and yet it is the framework for the public and plural life of the human being who codetermines his fate. The *state's claims of order and the attitude of the individual* therefore *stand in a reciprocal context*; they should lead to a legal attitude in which legality and humanity can join hands." Herbert Schambeck, *Ethik und Staat* (Berlin, 1986), 170 (emphasis added).

66. Under the title "Zwei Gasthäuser in jeder Straße. Soziale Bindung ist eine gute Sache. Eine 'gute Gesellschaft' sollten wir uns aber nicht wünschen," Ralf Dahrendorf points to the authoritarian problem that sets in as soon as social cohesion (in the sense of "being good") is demanded directly from the individual. *Die Zeit*, 5 October 2000.

67. The German Foreign Office issued a publication on such a situation during the negotiations in Dayton, which ultimately led to the conclusion of the peace agreement for Bosnia and Herzegovina. Wolfgang Ischinger, "21 Tage Dayton," *Deutsche Aussenpolitik 1995*, 29f.

68. An overview of the international obligations in the field of human rights and international jurisdiction that have not been upheld by the United States can be found in Carsten Stahn, "Gute Nachbarschaft um jeden Preis? Einige Anmerkungen zur Anbindung der USA an das Statut des Internationalen Strafgerichtshofs," *Zeitschrift für ausländisches öffentliches Recht und Völkerrecht* 60 (2000): 634f. To this list must be added the Child Protection Convention and the Convention on the Elimination of All Forms of Discrimination against Women.

69. In his text *Toward Eternal Peace* in the late eighteenth century, the German philosopher Immanuel Kant had already established a link between the process by which an individual gives up his natural state of "lawless freedom" in order to found the state, and also the process by which states leave their "international" natural state in order to cooperate. Kant viewed the first process as obligatory and the second as voluntary, which differs little from present-day reality. Kenneth Baynes, "Kommunitaristische und kosmopolitische Kritik an Kants Konzept des Weltfriedens," in *Frieden durch Recht: Kants Friedensidee und das Problem einer neuen Weltordnung*, ed. Matthias Lutz-Bachmann and James Bohman (Frankfurt am Main, 1996), 325ff. An example for an appeal of this kind to the "American soul" can be found in chapter 4, in the section "The Role of Statehood," subsection "'Civil Society.'"

70. The United States' approach is described in detail by Stahn, "Gute Nachbarschaft um jeden Preis?"

71. The promoters of the law to protect the American armed forces, which was introduced to the American Senate and sought to ban all cooperation by US authorities with the International Criminal Court, primarily cite the danger of politically motivated charges against American soldiers engaged in global missions. Christian Schmidt-Häuer, *Die Zeit*, 7 February 2002.

72. However, this cannot be ruled out in the final phase of its legal implementation. Once a human rights violation has been registered in a legally binding manner, the measures to be taken against the convicted state are in turn incumbent upon

the political organs of the respective international organization, since a worldwide "enforcement authority" in the form of a police force does not exist. Nevertheless, a legally equipped enforcement mechanism guarantees a higher degree of legal equality than a merely political procedure.

73. At the end of his activity as the High Representative in Bosnia, Petritsch pointed to the "American skepticism toward our usually unspectacular and protracted efforts to develop a civil administration," adding that this skepticism had noticeably increased since the terrorist attacks of September 11, 2001. *Neue Zürcher Zeitung,* 27 May 2002.

74. At the same moment, the British prime minister issued a similar appeal to his countrymen, although with a strongly European justification that emphasized human dignity.

75. Klaus Stüwe points out that for many Americans, "I am an American" means the same thing as "I stand up for democracy." He also quotes the political scientist Samuel P. Huntington—who proposed the theory of the "clash of civilizations"—as stating that being an American was an ideal and not a fact. Stüwe, "Eine Zivilreligion als Integrationsideologie? Das amerikanische Beispiel," *Stimmen der Zeit* 57 (1997): 461, 464.

Chapter 3

The "Western Europe/East Central Europe/ United States" Triangle

Since 1989, East Central Europe has been caught in the grip of a rapid transformation that no one in the mid-1980s, in either the West or the East, ever could have imagined. The East Central European nations turned to Western Europe, and in many places after the upheaval, unanimous calls could be heard to join the European Union and NATO as quickly as possible. It goes without saying that people made no distinction between Europe and the United States, since both of them represented "the West," which had been kept from East Central Europeans by force for such a long time. How could people in this part of Europe have made a distinction when even Western Europeans did not do so? After all, the constellation of the Cold War did not allow a discussion or even awareness of transatlantic differences. To the extent that such differences exist, there soon arose a sort of competition between European and American values, which the two competitors have not perceived as such. The term "triangle" does not imply any sort of geographical dimension, but rather East Central Europe's struggle with the conflicting values of the West, the activity of Europe and the United States in their development aid to East Central Europe, and the central question regarding to what extent European and/or American values are being adopted by East Central Europe.

In the following I intend to speak in general terms of East Central Europe with a complete awareness that the situation varies among the states in a region that extends from the far north to the Mediterranean and that emerged as a result of the divergent histories of these countries. In some of them, the question

Notes for this chapter begin on page 111.

of adopting new values is less topical since, during the period of the totalitarian dictatorships, they maintained their own identities and developed further, whereas in other countries this question is more important. Some of these nations will soon become members of the European Union, while for others this remains a long-term prospect. If I nevertheless use the general term "East Central Europe," then I do so because it is impossible to make distinctions on a nation-by-nation basis when dealing with questions of values. Even if specific issues do not concretely manifest themselves in a certain country of East Central Europe, there is nevertheless usually an opinion regarding these problems that arises because of events in other countries. Beyond that, the discussion on old and new values, as well as the adoption of the same, represents an important basis for the cooperation of the European Union with the candidate nations in which all participate in the same way. In their dealings with the transatlantic differences, the East Central Europeans are faced with very different understandings of the state, the nation, religion, morality, law, and democracy. This is—or was—most palpable in Bosnia, particularly in the years before the implementation of the Dayton Agreement, when American influence clearly dominated European affairs. Nevertheless, this phenomenon affected all of East Central Europe, for Bosnia was merely the country where this "triangle" manifested itself most noticeably. The thought patterns that became established in Bosnia, whether shaped by Europe or America, have also influenced opinions in other East Central European states. European and American values compete all across East Central Europe for the simple reason that the communist dictatorships had discredited statehood throughout the entire region. However, it is precisely this statehood that represents a cornerstone of the transatlantic differences. East Central Europe as a whole is faced with the question of whether its citizens should lean more toward adopting European or American patterns. There are no more East Central European islands left in the "Western Europe/ East Central Europe/United States" triangle.

Bosnia in the Transatlantic Tug-of-War

It is highly probable that the desperate situation in Bosnia and Herzegovina in 1996 immediately after the war, as described in chapter 1, could have been handled more quickly and sustainably by using an approach with distinctly European premises with regard to the state and the nation. This assertion concerns only the civilian sector. I do not deny that a strong military presence was necessary. On the contrary, state building and the re-establishment of the rule of law could not begin until the weapons had been silenced, and without the powerful international military presence, these objectives would never have been achieved in such a thorough fashion as they in fact were. The military action occurred within the framework of the North Atlantic alliance, and if the United States had a relatively powerful position here, this was due to

NATO's internal structures. I do not intend to discuss this area, nor do I intend to challenge the relevant conditions in Bosnia. In any case, NATO's situation has changed considerably since 1996.

The Dayton Agreement

Anyone involved with the development of state structures, the re-establishment of statehood, human rights, and other aspects of law who has spent some time in Bosnia cannot help but arrive at the conclusion that, at least in the field of human rights, the Dayton Agreement contained contradictions that should have been avoided. For example, the agreement created no less than three institutions, all of which were authorized to make final and binding decisions in cases of certain human rights violations. Not only did this lead to the danger of contradictory decisions, but there were also many instances in which complainants simply referred their case to another authority if a different one had decided a previous, similar case against their interests. In these circumstances, it was extremely unclear what was valid and who had the final word. Such a situation is not exactly conducive to re-establishing the rule of law in a "lawless and stateless" society. Conversely, other authorities were lacking. Although the European Convention on Human Rights had been declared to be the directly applicable law of the land, people were apparently still not well enough acquainted with its content to be able to establish supreme jurisdiction in civil and criminal cases on the level of the entire Bosnian state, as demanded by the Convention. It had been left to the European Commission for Democracy through Law, the so-called Venice Commission, working within the framework of the Council of Europe, to draft an expert opinion on this point, which urgently recommended the rapid creation of such a court.[1] There was no international legal supervision of such questions, aside from the various internationals who attended to the institutions of the Bosnian state in a judicial function. As mentioned at the beginning, the European Convention for the Protection of Human Rights may have been the law of the land, but it had not been ratified under international law, nor could it be ratified as long as Bosnia was not a member of the Council of Europe. But without the ratification of the Convention under international law, the European Court of Human Rights in Strasbourg had no jurisdiction over Bosnia. Arguing among other things that this jurisdiction could prove to be a hindrance to Bosnia, the United States repeatedly intervened in the Council of Europe to prevent Bosnia from joining it precipitously.[2]

When I first began my work, I accepted the inconsistencies in the Dayton Agreement as inevitable. I too felt the great relief that my Bosnian colleagues experienced when NATO (finally) intervened. We were relieved that the Dayton Agreement was concluded at all and that the international community was so numerous in Bosnia. It had apparently been extremely difficult to move the estranged parties to accept the agreement; their long-standing attempts to obstruct its implementation spoke a clear language. As far as the military aspects were concerned, along with other sectors with which I was not involved, this judgment still stands. The structural contradictions and legal inconsistencies, however, soon cost us a great deal of time, which we could have better used to process complaints. We thus needed to hold many meetings with other institutions in order to clarify overlapping competencies and other structural inconsistencies through mutual agreements. Fortunately, the previously mentioned Venice Commission was soon asked to draft a report designed to bring some order into the bewildering array of institutions. In the first years, I traced the inconsistencies in the Dayton Agreement to the fact that great pressure must have been applied during the negotiation phase. As shown by the documentation later published by the German Foreign Office, this assumption proved entirely accurate, although this element by no means explains everything. For the Americans, Dayton was so dominated by the military aspect that, from the point of view of the German delegation, the groundwork for the agreement's civil implementation was not given the attention it should have received. It also appears as if the civilian aspects of the treaty were largely determined by military actors.[3] Thus, it is hardly surprising that in this respect the Dayton Agreement contained contradictions and inconsistencies that were not taken seriously enough by the United States. At first it never occurred to me to think that such an approach might be considered perfectly normal on the other side of the Atlantic—and to ask why.

But first let us go back to the basic structure of the state of Bosnia and Herzegovina as it was set up in Dayton. In principle, the Bosnian Serbs and the now at least provisionally allied Bosnian Croats and Bosniacs had fought against one another until the Serbs were driven back onto a territory that made up 49 percent of the entire state. Then in Dayton an interstate frontier was drawn, which, with only minor corrections, corresponded to the line between the estranged troops. On one side of this frontier lay the Federation of Bosnia and Herzegovina, on the other side lay the Serb Republic, and both of these component states formed the state of Bosnia and Herzegovina. The "ethnic cleansings" had led to a situation in which the Serb Republic was largely inhabited by Bosnian Serbs and the Federation was largely separated from Bosniacs and Bosnian Croats. The latter two groups were also separated territorially. This did not have to happen. In January 1993, a peace proposal, the so-called Vance-Owen Plan, was presented. This measure sought to overcome nationalist thought through the creation of ethnically mixed regions. It failed, just like later plans, because not all of the important international powers stood behind it, and the warring parties knew this. In particular, the United States was not prepared to send troops to Bosnia in order to implement the proposed plans.[4] This changed only when the United States ensured, through the conception of the Dayton negotiations, that it would be able to leave its own mark on the events.[5] There is no doubt that individual European states also prolonged or even promoted the struggles in Bosnia by "[climbing] into old trenches and coddling their allies from World War I or World War II."[6] However, later events in the Balkans showed that the European states quickly accepted the consequences of these events and steered clear of further historical relapses.

I did not write these lines to raise questions of guilt. To do so would be not only presumptuous but also meaningless. Instead, I am concerned with understanding, or learning to understand, matters in order to derive pointers for future situations. With regard to the issue under discussion here, we can note that throughout the Balkan crisis, the military parameters presaged those of the civilian sphere, as well as the political options. In the military sector, the United States clearly dominated events. However, the subordination of the other sectors to the military led to a situation in which Europe had to conform in its political and civilian sectors. The powerful American shape of the latter did not simplify the peace efforts in Bosnia. Looking back, "Operation Dayton" came to be seen by Europe as "a bitter lesson in international crisis management, as it was in alliance politics."[7] To trace this bitter lesson solely to international power relations, to an at least intellectually understandable behavior on the part of the sole great power to emerge from the Cold War, falls short as an explanation. The experience that Europe ended up gaining also concerned the various transatlantic differences, as presented in the previous chapter. Europe has an interest in dealing with this side of the bitter lesson, since the transatlantic differences will still be present if the dominant power of the United States—for whatever reason—should one day shrink. In the following we will take a closer look at some elements in this context.

The Relationship of Law and Politics

The contradictions and inconsistencies in the civilian aspects of the Dayton Agreement were not accidental. They reflected the American view of the relationship between law and politics, as presented in the preceding chapter. These contradictions and inconsistencies accommodated the host country and created in Bosnia the foundation for an approach that Americans would probably characterize as "pragmatic." The documentation of the German Foreign Office shows the depth of disagreement between the United States and Europe about the status and the competencies of the supreme civilian representative of the international community in the country itself: whether he would be subordinated to the military sector, whether he could be a European (the post of high representative had always been filled by a European), and which positions in his office should be filled by Europeans and which by Americans. The United States was particularly concerned with such questions and less with possible inconsistencies in the legal underpinnings. After detailed research, a journalist described the method by means of which the United States apparently already intended to dominate the events in Bosnia during the Dayton negotiations and which Americans then made liberal use of: "So far the Europeans have paid the lion's share of the reconstruction in Bosnia, but the Americans are in charge everywhere. In every office—this is how the Europeans see it—there is 'the American' without whom nothing happens. He is the boss, or else he has a key position as the boss's representative."[8]

The fact that many of these Americans viewed themselves not as members of the international community—for example, as the staff of an international organization—but rather as agents of Washington, to which they sent regular reports and from which they received their instructions, can be illustrated by the example of a high functionary of the Office of the High Representative. He apparently assumed that, as part of the office staff, he could use stationery displaying not only the office's letterhead but also, prominently, the federal department in Washington that had deployed him to the office in Sarajevo for a certain period of time. *Se non è vero, è ben trovato.* Over the years, many such anecdotes circulated in Bosnia. They were based on real events and were gleefully passed around among Europeans in the international community. The chief of mission in an international organization that places particular importance on independence from the states that support it financially told me that he once received a telephone call from Washington with the good news that he was to be given a staff member, and that this person was already on his way. The chief of mission graciously thanked the State Department, immediately rented an office in the vicinity, greeted the new arrival very cordially, and presented him with the happy news that he was always delighted to welcome observers from the capitals and had spared no efforts to provide nearby office space for such cases.

The less matters were brought into a certain order from the beginning, the more latitude there was to develop things on the spot and thus for individual states to influence things through a large deployment of personnel and other resources, which were purposefully made available as the states saw fit. This led to what from a European understanding of law and politics looked like an imbalance, since, first of all, it was entirely unclear just what the order of things was to be, and, second, it was impossible to rely on any order at all. In other words, politics took the place of law. At the same time, a seemingly marginal factor—one that today is apparently commonplace in regions under international crisis management—became important. This is the simple fact that most internationals who are sent on "missions" do not stay very long in certain regions. Particularly in the first period following the conclusion of the Dayton Agreement, many internationals spent three or perhaps six months in Bosnia, and only a few spent more than a year in the country. We were confronted with the negative consequences of this constant coming and going in the adjustment of structural contradictions and legal inconsistencies. We frequently noted that at meetings with other institutions in which overlapping competencies and the clarification of other structural inconsistencies were at issue, new faces suddenly surfaced: internationals who understood previous agreements or who knew how things had been handled in the past were no longer active in the institution. Those who constantly want to "begin anew" and place great value on pragmatism in the American sense of the word are not troubled by such situations—quite the contrary. However, under such conditions it is extremely difficult to reacquaint a "lawless and stateless" society with the phenomenon of the rule of law as understood by Europeans and the calculability that is essential to state structures. During the second half of my stay in Bosnia, virtually every discussion with representatives of the Bosnian state, the component states, and other public agencies ended with a complaint about the constant game of musical chairs among the international dialogue partners, since, due to my long presence, the Bosnians understandably thought I was an appropriate person to approach about this matter. It goes without saying that this situation was deliberately exploited by those persons in the country who had no interest in the progress of the peace process because it would have narrowed their previous ethnonationalistic power base.

As an institution, we were on occasion directly confronted with short-term political actions that did not pay sufficient attention to the long-term establishment of structures under the rule of law. I recall one example in the first year of our activity when the return of displaced persons was practically impossible, especially across the border between the two component states, since those who sought to come back were often forcefully prevented from returning to their villages by those who had seized control of their empty houses. Someone had the idea of creating a body that would deal with such cases and decide on them quickly. The procedure's objective was to set a process of return into motion. This was an extremely important matter for the peace process. However, the promoters of this procedure also had the idea that I should serve as a member of this body. My American deputy at the time—who had spent a large portion of her professional career in Europe and was well acquainted with European human rights culture—dealt with this idea at first and was utterly astounded. Precisely those cases could be sent to us in a later complaint procedure if it was claimed that a human rights violation had occurred—which, at that time, sadly, could not be ruled out. How should we have been able to deal with such cases if I, as the addressee of such complaints, had already been involved in the case in a different function in a different body of which I was to be a member? This undertaking would practically have turned my institution, which at the time was still fighting for a minimum of respect, upside down. We therefore rejected the request with the pretext that there was an incompatibility between the legal foundation contained in the Dayton Agreement and our institution. Such short-term actions, which took little consideration of long-term negative effects, showed how great the pressure in the international community was to demonstrate short-term results. This pressure came from the United States in particular.[9]

One result was that "famous"—although "infamous" would be a more appropriate term—cases were always dealt with by many organizations at once. As already mentioned, numerous international and non-state organizations were active in the field of human rights "monitoring," whereby certain redundancies naturally could not be avoided.[10] When we were dealing with a case that had gained some publicity, international and non-state organizations also dealt with the case, which only helped us in constructive cooperation. When I published my final report, which generally contained recommendations on how the registered human rights violations could be eliminated or compensated, and how similar violations could be avoided in the future and by what means, the missions of international organizations declared their support for my findings in the press, at least for the occasional, highly publicized cases. In this phase we arrived at the second half of my tenure, when the institution already enjoyed a certain standing. At the same time I began to make some distinctions; in my own activity and in my organization's strategy, the promotion of the rule of law always took first place. The rule of law, which protects all persons equally—and, only in second place, the ability of the individual to protect him- or herself from violations—is the most effective protection against human rights violations and thus forms an important basis of human rights culture. But in my cooperation with the international community, I was still relatively cautious in expressing this conviction, for I had become reconciled with the fact that Bosnia was first going through a phase dominated by an understanding of human rights that was based on American notions of law, the state, and politics, and which would later be replaced by a more European-oriented understanding. I therefore always viewed my activity in this country as the groundwork for that later time. I made sure to express my sincere thanks for the media's support of my recommendations when I subsequently encountered the respective head of mission or the responsible staff members.

What I did not mention, and what I tried to suppress in my own thoughts, was the fact that I actually viewed such actions as problematic, since they weakened the standing and effectiveness of my recommendations as a whole by creating an imbalance. What of the remaining 99 percent of the cases for which public support by the international community failed to materialize? If we had been less successful in clearing up certain cases, then were my recommendations in these cases less important or even wrong? It was clear that no one working for the internationals ever thought of such an interpretation. But the public and potential complainants could not help but gain the impression that my recommendations were effective or worthy of being taken seriously only if they were publicly supported by all those who had international renown and status. Thus, it was easy to draw the conclusion that there was little sense in turning to our institution with a complaint without having first lined up a certain amount of publicity and international support—that is, law enforcement with a political spin. In reality, precisely the reverse was true: the more publicity a case received, the less the responsible authorities could afford to reverse a human rights violation on my recommendation or to pay compensation, particularly if it was an ethnically motivated violation, and this was nearly always the case. In cases without great publicity, it was considerably easier to convince flawed authorities of the need for the rule of law because they had less to fear from the reactions of those who still wore ethnic spectacles.

Law and Power

The experience of the negative consequences of the politicization of law, as expressed in the last example, was a constant companion of my work in Bosnia. It was clear to me from the beginning that the Bosnian authorities had to be led away from an ethnic understanding of law—which ultimately meant an ethnonationalistically imbued political understanding of law—and then, in painstakingly detailed work, to be convinced of the value of the rule of law, for that was the essence of my work and why I had come to this country in the first place. However, the fact that part of the international community also assumed a political understanding of law, which in legal thought ultimately provided no alternative to the local conditions, bothered me more and more. Many of the phenomena that could be observed in Bosnia concerned the relationship between law and politics, as well as the circumstance that this relationship could easily transform itself into a relationship between law and power as soon as politics fell into the hands of powerful actors, whether as a result of great power behavior or through the force of arms or both. The Bosnian side of this connection has already been presented in detail in the first chapter. As far as the transatlantic side of this situation is concerned, it would be a mistake to examine it solely with regard to the behavior of one great power. The chief problem in the transatlantic relationship does not lie mainly in the distribution of power, but rather much more fundamentally in the role of law in the limitation of power. Even if the transatlantic relationship were to approach a balance, this fundamental, intellectual, historical difference would remain.

Looking back, the situation in Bosnia under the Dayton Agreement appears as a reflection of the situation in which international law has found itself since September 11, 2001.[11] After the terrorist attacks, the United States has been confronted with a large group of states that encompass nearly "the rest of the world." Today, Washington makes it perfectly clear that it is not prepared to permit the emergence of an international legal order to which this great power would be forced to adhere.[12] If there are to be international agreements, then it must be only in the sense of a "provisional legal situation" that can be changed continually, for example, through the inclusion of new "willing" coalition partners.[13] The legal situation in Bosnia seemed equally provisional to me. It was very dependent on the politics of the international community and only became tangible through the activity of the latter. To some extent, such an approach was inevitable, and at the beginning I had great understanding for it. It was only when conditions remained "provisional" after months and years that I began to have doubts and started to ask myself whether there was a concept behind these arrangements that had at first seemed so bereft of any concept.

At that time, my personal perceptions of this issue were not particularly interesting to others, except for a small circle of specialists. However, in the wake of September 11, the relationship between power and law became much

more topical, which in turn had effects on Bosnia that confirmed my perceptions. Ulrich Ladurner has described such a situation in the following terms:

> Do you remember Bosnia? That is the small Balkan state where, not so long ago,
> murder was the order of the day. The West looked on for years and did nothing.
> When in 1995 it finally decided to end the killing with bombs, it did so in the name
> of its values: democracy, human rights, the rule of law. Since then, billions of euros
> have flowed to Bosnia. They have served to reconstruct a functioning state. Justice
> in Bosnia was once more to be administered by independent courts. Last Friday, a
> court released six Arabs who were suspected of having worked with al-Qaeda. The
> evidence was not sufficient to continue holding these men who had been in prison
> since October. While the American authorities said they possessed evidence, they
> did not wish to turn it over to the court in Sarajevo. The judges then made the only
> possible decision: they released the six Arabs. Nevertheless, a few hours later the
> suspects found themselves back behind bars. American soldiers had picked them
> up and presumably flew them to Guantanamo. Hundreds of people in Sarajevo
> demonstrated against this action. Even the highest legal authority in the country,
> the Chamber of Human Rights, protested. It did no good. The Bosnian authorities
> turned two blind eyes to the questionable action. Faced with the choice between
> law and power, they chose power. That of the United States. This is a disastrous les-
> son for Bosnia. After all, the West wanted to teach the little state the exact opposite:
> law goes before power.[14]

Ethnicization and Individualization

Another consequence of the Dayton Agreement was the actual ethnicization
of the country. Looking back historically, it cannot be ruled out that this ethnicization will be identified as one of the chief causes of the slow normalization of public life in Bosnia in spite of the massive deployment of human
and financial resources. The construction of the Bosnian state already bore a
kernel of ethnicization within it and represents the cementing of the result of
"ethnic cleansing." But it did not stop there. Instead, the ethnic thought model
found its way into the basic constitutional structure of the entire Bosnian state,
through which ethnicization runs as a central theme. Examples include the
lesser chamber of the Bosnian parliament and the state presidium. In accordance with the Dayton Agreement, the House of the Peoples is made up of 15
deputies: 10 from the Federation and 5 from the Serb Republic. The constitution prescribes that the 5 deputies from the Serb Republic must be Bosnian
Serbs; of those from the Federation, half must be Bosniacs and the other half
Bosnian Croats. The three-headed state presidium is set up according to the
same pattern, namely, 1 Bosnian Serb from the Serb Republic, as well as 1 Bosniac and 1 Bosnian Croat from the Federation. A Bosnian Serb who lives in the
Federation or a Bosniac or Bosnian Croat living in the Serb Republic cannot
run for these offices, and, as far as both bodies are concerned, they are excluded
from passive voting rights.[15] As a counterweight to this ethnicization, the

constitution of the entire state adopted comprehensive guarantees of human rights, complemented by the previously mentioned instruments of international law that were integrated into the law of the land. In practical terms, the pronounced protection against discrimination within the framework of these guarantees became especially active in the regulations favoring refugees and expellees, by which these persons were expressly guaranteed the right to return to their original place of residence. The human rights guarantees were apparently intended as an equalizer for the basic, ethnically oriented structure that continued on into the constitutions of the two component states.[16]

This construction massively hindered the promotion of human rights. As already mentioned, we were tirelessly engaged in explaining that a person possessed human rights solely on the basis that he or she had been born a human being, and not on account of some special characteristics, such as ethnic background. This proved to be extremely important, since we were continually confronted with the argument that someone felt that his or her human rights had been violated as a Bosnian Croat, a Bosniac, or a Bosnian Serb. On the one hand, this view could be traced back to the monolithic ethnic identity presented in chapter 1. On the other hand, the basic ethnicizing structure of the Dayton Agreement practically forced itself on the Bosnian population. It was primarily the guarantees of human rights that created a counterweight to this basic structure. This could not fail to overtax the Bosnian population, whose judgment in such matters had already been traumatized and weakened by the events of the war years.

Elections were held soon after the signing of the Dayton Agreement; in fact, elections were held over and over again, and they did not have a particularly pleasant effect on our work. In the months preceding the elections, it was harder than usual to convince state authorities or individual staff members of the meaning of the rule of law. If they belonged to a nationalistic party, during these months they took special pains to demonstrate that they had no intention of taking off their ethnic spectacles. And among our dialogue partners, the representatives of these parties were in any case the ones from whom we encountered more resistance. Naturally, democracy had to return to Bosnia, but it would have been better if this had occurred under different conditions. At least in the early years, due to the basic ethnicizing structure, presidential and parliamentary elections on the various levels could not help but lead to the victory of the ethnonationalist-oriented parties. The United States sought to counteract these parties by utilizing its influence, and this may have been a contributing factor to the frequency of elections and the way the international media contributed to the inaccurate impression that peace in Bosnia was merely a question of the correct election results. In Dayton, the American architects had apparently assumed that the population would identify itself so strongly with its "liberators" that it would automatically vote "correctly," or else that the desired behavior could be produced by bringing American influence to bear.[17] This proved to be an illusion, since the problems of this "lawless and stateless" society lay deeper.[18]

Basically, the Dayton Agreement brought with it an individualization of responsibility for interethnic co-existence. This resulted from the combination of the two elements I have already described. Individuals did not have an opportunity to help create better opportunities for this co-existence through their participation as citizens; on the contrary, they learned that certain structures had been created within the state organization along distinct ethnic lines. As "legal persons," however, individuals enjoyed all the guarantees and rights designed to enable them to avoid restrictions resulting from the basic ethnicizing structure and to settle down at their original places of residence, even if in the meantime members of another population group had exclusively or in their majority settled there and actively opposed such a return.[19] The country's inhabitants were expected to achieve on the individual level—namely, by returning to their original places of residence—that which the Dayton Agreement prevented on the structural (and collective) level of the state: the re-establishment of interethnic co-existence as it existed before the war. On the one hand, through various human rights guarantees, individuals were provided with the best conditions to re-create their interethnic co-existence. But on the other hand, a profound ethnicization had been created that transformed this intention into an illusion, at least in the first years following the end of the war. This approach overtaxed the population, and the human rights culture as a whole was affected. Each thwarted return now appeared mainly or exclusively as a violation of human rights. It was indeed a violation, to the extent that it represented a denial of the freedom of movement. But it was also primarily a consequence of state organization. Human rights culture is in danger of being weakened when human rights are instrumentalized—if not to say misused—by, as it were, staging an inflation of human rights violations.

We must be somewhat cautious in viewing the ethnicization of Bosnia through the Dayton Agreement in light of the transatlantic differences. It would be too facile to ascribe this ethnicization directly to the United States and its lack of understanding for the European notion of statehood. After all, the negotiators present in Dayton were themselves the people who—partly out of conviction, partly for reasons of survival, but partly also against their better judgment and for purely power and political reasons—had actively driven their people into the monolithic ethnic identity. Under these conditions, it would have been unthinkable to have entirely excluded ethnic criteria from the negotiations. Nevertheless, within the framework of this chapter on the Western Europe/East Central Europe/United States triangle, it makes sense to take a brief look at the differing transatlantic perspectives, whereby we will look at only three aspects: first, the purely horizontal American social contract and, by contrast, the European state as a third factor reaching beyond the horizontal social contract; second, the numerous minorities as actors in American politics, whose interaction is intended to prevent the emergence of majorities, while in Europe political debate leads to majorities who are ultimately expected to take minority interests into account so that they can come together in the first place; and third, politics, which in Europe takes place as a struggle over laws and which in the United States is partially replaced by the struggle over rights. It is evident that a European understanding in these areas would have represented a more effective alternative for the "lawless and stateless" society that emerged from the war in Bosnia. After all, the point was to help people remove their ethnic spectacles and replace their identity as members of an ethnic group with a civic identity. This confrontation of the interests of various groups—particularly those of ethnic population groups—could not be viewed as especially promising since it repeated exactly the pattern of the preceding war.

Unfortunately, the Dayton Agreement was based to a much larger extent on American thought patterns than on European ones. Thus, a basic ethnicizing structure in the construction of the entire state, along with comprehensive guarantees for returnees, essentially failed to provide people with the possibility to create multiethnic co-existence through civil effort, pointing them instead toward a struggle for their individual rights. European thought patterns would have made it possible to proceed from the assumption of group interests. However, beyond that, they could have gotten past these group interests to derive further interests, because Europeans have experience with shared sovereignty and are also acquainted with the third factor, which ultimately stands for the state or statehood. As far as the international community was concerned, what would have been needed was a clearly presented concept for a public order structure as an alternative to the thought patterns of the war. This would have been a structure that would have served as a reliable orientation. But it is unlikely that anyone was thinking about such matters at the time. For many people in Bosnia, Dayton meant the silencing of the weapons, which at the end of 1995 represented the greatest gift that anyone could have imagined. The gratitude people felt for this gift was most noticeable in the first months of 1996. There is no doubt that the international community was unanimous in its objective of silencing all the weapons, and rightly so.

The transatlantic differences in the understanding of the state, law, politics, and democracy had already played a role in the realization of the Dayton Agreement. The European delegations ultimately agreed to a construction that was strongly oriented on the American understanding of these areas, and they did so, let us remember, with regard to the reconstruction of a country located in Europe. If the peace conference had taken place on the European continent, matters would have proceeded differently, at least in this regard. If we look back with a certain historical distance, and particularly from the perspective of the events following September 11, we can perceive a certain irony in the way that the Europeans, for whom a conference venue in the United States had been unimaginable at first, were forced to give in on this point because this was the only way that the participation of the American armed forces in the military operation in Bosnia could be guaranteed.[20]

Community and Statehood

As far as the Western Europe/East Central Europe/United States triangle is concerned, Bosnia is fortunately not representative of the specific context that has focused world interest on this country. Nowhere else in the Balkans did the collapse of the old order, which had held sway since 1945, lead to such a long war between ethnic population groups. In another regard, however, Bosnia can be seen as the tip of an iceberg spanning all of East Central Europe. The European and American thought patterns that encountered one another in Bosnia also compete with one another in other East Central European states. Bosnia is merely the country where the triangle has manifested itself most distinctly. In the following I will present various forces within this triangle that affect East Central Europe as a whole.

Even if the revolutions in the East Central European states, which began in 1989 with the fall of the Berlin Wall, have been characterized as soft or "velvet," they were nevertheless genuine revolutions. If one attempts to classify them within the triangle, they can be compared with both the French and the American Revolutions. The difference between these two events has been presented in chapter 2 and can be summarized as follows: the American revolutionaries sought to reduce the state in the form represented by the mother countries as much as possible, while in the French Revolution, the people seized control of the state and based their new-found freedom on it. The communist regimes that were ended by the revolutions of 1989 made use of a party-dominated state apparatus that vastly restricted the freedom of the individual. In this way, the state—in the sense of actual statehood—had been discredited throughout East Central Europe, with the logical outcome that the revolutions of 1989 would come to be seen as "revolutions against the state."[21] To the extent that these revolutions can be compared with historical events, they show a greater similarity to the American Revolution than to the French Revolution.[22] The revolutions of 1989 were also prepared by the various dissident movements in the East Central European states. These movements did not reconstruct the primal European experience of achieving freedom, which consisted of the sovereign people assuming sovereignty, collectively taking control of sovereignty, and transforming it into the guarantor of its freedom. In view of the actual power relationships and the omnipresence of the state and party, this perspective simply did not exist. Instead, the aim of these movements was to strengthen the resistance of individual persons so that they could defend themselves against an understandably hated statehood. They were ultimately successful. This process is much more similar to the individual act of liberation on the American pattern, which European statehood had left behind. And yet, at the moment of the revolutionary breakthrough, the collective aspect of the primal European pattern was also clearly expressed, for example, in the proclamation, "We are the people," as a result of which the rulers of the time had to step down. Nevertheless, the

European pattern—precisely 200 years after its birth—could not assert itself, since the collective idea had been stretched to the limit for decades. Or, if we want to express it in the categories of freedom and attachment that we have been using so far, individual attachments to the family, to religion, and to self-elected non-state and non-party communities had been so powerfully and violently suppressed for decades, and an individual's commitment to such communities was linked to such enormous disadvantages, that such attachments could not fail to appear to many people in East Central Europe as the very essence of freedom and democracy.

Community and Nationalism

Individualism was born in the late Middle Ages when the freedom of the individual confronted the prescribed "divinely ordained" order. This individualism has informed Western societies for centuries, particularly all those that form the triangle under discussion here: Western Europe, East Central Europe, and the United States have an identical basic structure. However, differences have existed in the way in which individual freedom confronts attachments ever since the non-attached new freedom brought about the chaos of the wars of religion. In somewhat abridged form, one could say that at that time Europe chose statehood as a social integration, whereas the United States chose "community."[23] True, the Americans also created a nation-state after they freed themselves from their mother countries in Europe, but the integration of the individual was carried out by self-chosen communities. Hans Joas points to one difference between Europe and the United States, namely, the way that in Europe the transition from "community" to "society" is theoretically conceived as a two-phase process, whereas Americans think of it in terms of three phases. The organic medieval village community, into which a person was born, was first replaced by the artificial "better" community of individual immigrants, for example, in the "ethnic 'ghettos' of large American cities."[24] An example of the still unbroken orientation of the public order structure to communities is communitarianism, a political and philosophical school of thought that, especially since the 1980s, has contrasted unimpeded individualism with the demand for more public spirit. The communitarians view an alternative to the modern atomization of the individual in the form of communities, which they to some extent romanticize as the very essence of virtue.[25]

The public order structure that guarantees the society's cohesion is state-based in Europe and primarily community-based in the United States. East Central Europe lies beneath a matrix of various levels of historical influence: an older European history is confronted with the second half of the last century, in which the state fell into profound disrepute. Thus, the communal thought pattern is not only treated in the European sense as one of various possibilities of private social attachments, but also in the American sense as a public order structure that takes the place of the state. This historically determined ambivalence becomes particularly significant when it is viewed in the context of the phenomenon of nationalism, as the previously mentioned philosopher and cultural anthropologist Ernest Gellner describes it. His definition first runs as follows: "Nationalism is a form of political thought based on the assumption that social attachment depends on cultural agreement." That is why nationalists seek to bring the political boundaries of nation-states in line with the cultural boundaries that they themselves define. In the process, nationalism always arises where "a *society* adopts the language of a *community*; this means that a socially mobile, anonymous society suddenly acts as if it were a hermetic, cozy community."[26] Since we are speaking of the Western Europe/East Central Europe/United States triangle here, we need to make one immediate clarification: nationalism is not an East Central European phenomenon. Western Europe has been just as afflicted by this specter and still cannot claim to have banished it entirely. To be sure, after World War II, all of Europe believed it had taken charge of the problem of nationalism, and the continent was all the more horrified when this monster reappeared in the last decade of the twentieth century and demanded tribute in Southeastern Europe.

Everyone who has observed the mechanisms of nationalist agitation in this region knows that Gellner's analysis goes straight to the heart of the phenomenon. Within this context it may be possible to point to some reasons why from the beginning the Americans may not have been the right doctors to liberate or "heal" the war-traumatized society in Bosnia. From a European perspective—and let us say also from a purely state-philosophical perspective—the Americans themselves were afflicted at least to some extent with the very same illness they were trying to cure.[27] From their own perspective, the Americans viewed themselves to be fit as a fiddle, and viewed objectively they really were, since they rely on a public order structure that they in turn know and that is much more of a community-based structure than a state-based one. That is why the notion of guilt is inappropriate here. What is needed today is by no means a debate over guilt but rather over rationality. The point is to understand that in many areas Western Europe and the United States base their actions on vastly different premises, a fact that few suspected during the Cold War. At this point, however, I do not intend to refer back to Bosnia but instead to address the entire Western Europe/East Central Europe/United States triangle head on. It would be problematic not only for East Central Europe if this region adopted the concept of community in the American sense as a public order structure that takes the place of the state. Such an adoption would undoubtedly have effects on Western Europe and thus on the development of the entire continent. There are various reasons why Europe cannot relinquish statehood as its primary public order structure guaranteeing the cohesion of society. However, we can end this section by stating that it is not possible to confront nationalist tendencies effectively on this basis alone.

The Return of Religion

Regarding religion, it is time for another clarification. The Balkan Wars—particularly the war in Bosnia—were not wars of religion, even if the Bosnian conflict was occasionally perceived as such by the international public, since the three ethnic population groups that were fighting each other belonged to different religious communities. Instead, religion was deliberately used for ethnonational agitation in order to further amplify the inherited cultural-communal identity through the addition of an inherited religious-communal identity.[28] The impression that the Bosnian war was a religious one was also intensified by the fact that mosques as well as Orthodox and Catholic churches were the preferred targets of armed attacks. This should not be explained by a certain population's special affinity with religious matters, but rather by the simple fact that since ethnic population groups were being attributed to different religions, the destruction of a house of God was the quickest, most unmistakable, and symbolically most unambiguous way of demonstrating that the ethnic group in question had no further business in a particular area. The Bosnian population had never been very religious, as we have already seen in chapter 1 in connection with ethnic blending, notably in urban environments. In view of developments since September 11, 2001, it is important to point out that the Islam of the Bosniac population had always been a notably secular version, and it remains so to this day.[29] It is a typically European, enlightened variety of Islam, and the fact that it has existed for centuries is important for the further development of this continent. Sarajevo has always been a symbol of this European wealth.

When speaking of the return of religion, a distinction must be made between religion as a private matter and religion as a public order structure guaranteeing social integration. In Europe, values that the individual derives from religion in private affairs find their way into the public order structure through a special process that is primarily state-based. The process is the same as for moral value judgments or other convictions, whatever they are based on, whether it be faith, experience, or reason. The individual must contribute his or her conviction to the public discussion. He or she must, as it were, "translate" it into a language that can also be accepted by people who reject religion as such.[30] In this way, these values reach the level of the public order structure, where, however, they are confronted with other values that also have been translated from their respective areas into a general language so that they can be expressed in law. In Europe, there is no way to make religious, moral, or other value judgments directly binding on other persons except through law. Legislation serves as a sort of filter for the demands placed on individuals. These demands can become binding for an individual only in his or her capacity as a person subject to the law if they have gone through the process in which the same individual could participate in his or her capacity as a citizen.[31] This in turn is the precondition for the demand that an individual legal person obey those legal regulations that he or she may reject as a citizen and, by reject-ing them, may be placed into a minority and made inferior. Because of this process, the demand that one obey legal regulations is not a moral, let alone religious, duty but merely a legal one. This is basically identical to the process of secularization. The fact that Europe has organized itself in such a way can be traced back to the centuries-old process of secularization in which the state order has been separated from religion, all the while ensuring that, on the one hand, religious structures would subordinate themselves to state structures and, on the other, the individual would possess religious freedom. In a broader sense, one can view the process of translating religious values onto the public level as a form of secularization that must be performed continuously in order to contribute values to the level of public discussion.[32]

We have already examined conditions across the Atlantic. Just as moral notions flow directly into social debates in the United States, so do religious values. In this way, religion also attains the status of a public order structure, for which there is a definite need. Unlike Europe, the public order structure is not primarily state-based but rather community-based, and it eagerly joins forces with religion, since both share the same historical origin in the reli-gious communities. This is also the reason why there is a certain receptivity for the American pattern in East Central Europe. In the communist coun-tries, religion was scorned, and those who wished to practice it anyway could expect discrimination and harassment. Thus, a relative receptivity to religion as a public order structure is essentially the flip side of a relative hesitation to accept statehood as a primary public order structure. These two phenomena have historical roots in East Central Europe: an older and centuries-long char-acteristic of East Central Europe is entirely European, but it is currently being overlaid by the processing of the events of the past half-century.

These considerations lead us back to the intellectual parting of the ways in 1648, when Europe chose freedom *for* the state in order to assert freedom *from* religion, while the United States instead committed itself to freedom *from* the state in order to assert freedom *for* religion. Religious freedom is the area where, as far as the history of ideas is concerned, the United States has made intensive international efforts to make its view universally valid. For example, the US State Department regularly commissions reports listing deficiencies in the free practice of religion in all the countries of the world, and European states are repeatedly cited. In the Western Europe/East Central Europe/United States triangle, the relationship of church and state might well represent the field of action par excellence where the United States today intervenes in East Central Europe and also directly in Western Europe. One example is the law on religious sects passed by the French Parliament in June 2001, which enables the authorities to proceed against religious bodies that challenge human rights and basic freedoms. Even before it was passed, the draft law led to a debate in the US Senate, where fears were expressed that the law would infringe on religious freedom, that is, another human right. Nor is it accidental that France is particularly sensitive with regard to the sect issue and wishes to see matters regulated clearly. As a result of the French Revolution, this country is characterized by an extremely clear state political identity that does not tolerate half-measures. The controversy on the sect issue also illustrates the different understandings of human rights on both sides of the Atlantic; indeed, the sect issue goes straight to the heart of the transatlantic differences with respect to the history of ideas. Europe allows churches, free churches, and sects to function within the framework of the public order protected by the state; it has deliberately not gone nearly as far as the United States in the separation of church and state because it wants to keep the churches integrated within a state framework, which by no means should be taken to imply that the European churches all have to be state churches. Thus, in the question of the separation of church and state, European and American notions are diametrically opposed. The American methods of gaining influence in East Central Europe have been highly aggressive at times. As if it were the most natural thing in the world, American religious sociologists assumed that the events of 1989 had finally brought about the preconditions for the definitive separation of church and state *à l'américaine*. As we can read in a 1996 omnibus volume from an international congress on religion in Europe: "Although it may take some time before the American model asserts itself generally in Europe, there are increasing indications that, despite its historic 'exceptionalism,' it best agrees with the complex structures of the modern era as a result of its separation of church and state, its free practice of religion, its voluntary denominations, and its religious pluralism."[33]

Let us first clarify the meaning of religion. "Re-ligio" means "tying back," that is, the anchoring of the individual in value concepts. Many positive inspirations for intellectual historical development are derived from the field of religion and from practically all religions worldwide. For example, Catholic social teachings have provided impulses that, alongside other important influences, have found expression in the European models for the social market economy. In addition, concepts advocating a careful treatment of nature go back to processes dealing with "the Creation" within the framework of the ecumenical movement. In Islam, too, one can discover remarkable approaches, as in the Asiatic religions.[34] It is a welcome sign that impulses of this sort are being adopted in private religious practice, and in this sense a return to religion can have thoroughly positive effects.[35] However, for Europe this positive effect changes entirely when attempts are made to insert such influences directly without performing the translation that, so to speak, transports the impulse from the private to the public sphere—for this amounts to a demand to adopt the value in question *as a religious one*. This continent cannot accept religion as a public order structure, which guarantees the cohesion of society. Here I will draw the same conclusion regarding religion that I did in connection with communities as a substitute for the state order structure—namely, that if religion were to be received in the American sense as a public order structure taking the place of the state, it would be problematic not only for East Central Europe. Such a reception would doubtless also have repercussions on Western Europe and thus on the development of the entire continent.

As we have already seen, there is an affinity within the public order structure based on the notion of community and nationalism. Against this background, the correspondence between nationalism and religion was not accidental, for at one time nationalism assumed the place of religion in Europe.[36] There are parallels between certain manifestations of religion and the emergence of nationalistic movements: one such parallel is expressed in the way nationalism "works by means similar to those of the church and takes on sacral-liturgical forms. People salute the national flag as they would the Holiest of Holies, they sing the national anthem like the *Te Deum*, they gather for mass meetings as on religious holidays, they stage processions to national shrines like the faithful to pilgrimage sites."[37] A further element that nationalism shares with the so-called revivalist religions is the national "awakening" that Gellner describes as follows: "To those for whom human fulfillment is linked to the attainment of a national consciousness and its successful political realization, a national awakening means far more than a spiritual awakening; indeed, for them it is a kind of spiritual awakening in its highest form."[38] It is precisely in this phenomenon that we must seek the roots of the emergence of monolithic ethnic identity in the first place, as presented in chapter 1. This "awakening"—that is, a person's sudden realization of what he or she is and apparently always has been, without having previously understood this in such clarity—and the liberating simplicity that this insight suddenly brings with it (because there is now only one measure and a single task that one must concern oneself with) are shared by both nationalism and revivalist religions.

Across the Atlantic, the revivalist religions play a significant role that reaches far beyond anything known in Europe.[39] Once again, we must turn to Casanova, our author with the American perspective on possible religious developments in East Central Europe, who explains: "In view of the general demoralization and moral collapse, as well as the secularized wasteland produced by decades of communist rule, we should not underestimate the significance that the resuscitation of the traditional theological virtues (faith, love, hope) and the cardinal virtues (justice, intelligence, moderation, and courage) can have. If a religious revival led to a moral revival in the private sphere, this would have only beneficial effects on the public sphere." And further: "Under the conditions of the modern era, an individual's religious commitment, even if he or she adheres to an orthodox religious tradition, always involves a reflected, personal, and free choice. Viewed this way, modern individual religiosity, at least with regard to structure, is always an implicit rebirth, an adult conversion. Thus, the pietistic revival experience is paradigmatic in a certain sense. Here too the decisive question is whether the Eastern European religions will undergo such an evangelical transformation."[40] As inappropriate as such expectations from beyond the Atlantic are for Europe, they are nevertheless useful in understanding various aspects of what has unfolded since the terrorist attacks of September 11.

Racism, Xenophobia, and Violence

There is still one area to be discussed wherein Western Europe cannot claim to have a significantly better vantage point than East Central Europe. Racism, xenophobia, and nationalism are closely related phenomena. Their starting point is to some extent the same, namely, the uprooting of individual human beings through the increasing individualization that has been advancing inexorably since the sixteenth century. The great initial loss of security in the "divinely ordained" medieval order has been followed ever since by countless further losses of security. Individualization means the liberation of the individual, but the freedom won in this way always has two sides, which is why in the preceding chapter we saw it placed in relation to the attachment that the liberated individual organizes in turn, or seeks to have organized by others, and which provides him or her with identity. The loss of identity can lead not only to nationalism but also to racism and xenophobia. At the moment when individuals begin to fall through the mesh of the social net—or even beforehand, as soon as they fear that such a thing might happen—they seek guilty parties and find them in persons who are "different" from themselves. They could be members of a different nation who believe in a different religion or have a different skin color, and misogyny is doubtless a part of this too. Non-existent or vanishing social integration provides the breeding ground for racism and xenophobia and is a factor in their occurrence, although not the only one. Nationalism, which can also be embraced by affluent and socially integrated persons, is always accompanied by xenophobia and often by racism as symptoms. Generally speaking, the more broadly based an identity is, the less it leans toward racism and xenophobia.[41] A monolithic ethnic identity, as depicted earlier, cannot help but lead to both phenomena.

Racism and xenophobia exist on both sides of the Atlantic, and yet the two phenomena do not mean the same thing within European and American societies. In this context, we must return again to the general mechanisms through which foreignness is integrated or not integrated. The traditional American integration mechanism is the "melting pot." According to this idea, when immigrants come to the United States, their previous identity is supposed to be "melted down" into an American identity. I have already mentioned the often very rapid adoption of the "American way of life" by immigrants, which goes back to the way they seek to commit themselves visibly to America in order to achieve affiliation as quickly as possible.[42] I have also mentioned foreignness, of which there are many forms in Europe. In Europe, with its cultural compactness and variety, such a "melting" was never demanded, and between the European countries, the notion of remaining foreign in a different country has a centuries-old tradition. In the past decade, immigrants from Eastern and

Southeastern Europe, just like those from other continents, were expected to do more for their integration, particularly when their immigrant group attained a certain magnitude. However, this tendency is already being challenged since members of the second generation of such immigrant groups are apparently organized in such a way that while they certainly maintain a foreign identity, they have also learned how to integrate themselves into the European target country and combine this with a local feeling of belonging.[43] Conversely, the American melting pot idea is increasingly being frustrated by the deliberate maintenance of ethnic identities that go beyond the previously traditional but small-scale neighborhood cultures of urban districts—such as "Chinatown" or "Little Italy"—and make ethnically defined group claims in the social distributional struggle.[44] However, these are not experienced but rather instrumentalized ethno-identities. We can, nevertheless, notice great differences in the way that racism and xenophobia are manifested in Europe and the United States.

One important transatlantic difference can be seen with regard to violence, which continually appears in connection with racist and xenophobic activities. The fact that the acceptance of violence is much greater in the United States than in Europe has historical roots and can to a large extent be explained by the transatlantic differences we have already discussed.[45] The most illustrative factor in this context is the individual relinquishment—or sharing—of sovereignty, which in Europe has led to the guarantee of individual freedom. By contrast, American freedom is primarily gained in an individual act that is ultimately contrary to the individual relinquishment of sovereignty. One element of US identity, which should not be underestimated, is the conquest of the continent from East to West, which required, on the one hand, individual mobility—at the time, horses and wagons—and, on the other hand, a willingness to defend oneself. This nation was created, as it were, through "individual effort and individual hardship." Even if this historical aspect has absolutely no meaning today, now that living conditions have been transformed beyond all recognition, nevertheless certain elements have been preserved, and they continue to play a large role in the national identity.[46] Americans' absolute demand for individual mobility can be traced back to this experience, as can private gun ownership. Both are hallowed in the United States as a kind of religious-national value concept and can be understood only against this background. As far as mobility is concerned, the religious-national value concept has considerable foreign policy consequences, for example, in America's dealings with oil-exporting countries. As far as private gun ownership is concerned, the effects are of a primarily domestic political nature: the American gun lobby sees to it that the laws are not changed, even though the corresponding discussion always reappears whenever an excess of private gun violence occurs. It is not only that Americans are more trigger-happy than other peoples. The generally greater acceptance of violence also goes back to these connections. We can also observe the effect of this basic attitude on foreign policy, particularly since the terrorist attacks of September 11.[47]

The American model of social integration cannot be applied to Europe because there is no pure immigrant society to be found in Europe. Nor is European society founded on a territory in which the indigenous population has been pushed back so far that their history and uniqueness enter the social debate practically only under the topic of culture. Europe's peoples live with a centuries-old history in territories delineated from one another. Their national identity does not emerge through the melting of nationalities, but rather through more or less successful attempts to integrate the nationalities within their own nation-states and within a civic identity. The European manifestation of racism and xenophobia cannot be viewed separately from the development of the nations in Europe, which is the topic of the next section.

Western Europe Following the Cold War

When the competition that is going on between Western European and American thought patterns in East Central Europe is discussed in public, the debate usually occurs in the context of economic structures. One frequently used example is the Russian Federation and its abrupt transition from a state-run economy to a powerfully deregulated economic order, which occurred with the help of American advisers and without significant European influence. While the dimension discussed here has an economic connection, the debate usually goes beyond purely economic factors and touches on the general relationship between individualism and statehood. During the Cold War, the United States was the epitome of "freedom against the state," whereas from the Western point of view, the Soviet Union stood for "the state against freedom." Today, many observers and commentators interpret the Western European development during the Cold War as having been imposed by external compulsion, which was unavoidable due to the constant maneuvering between the two blocs. In reality, Western Europe profited from the way it could remain true to its already centuries-old intellectual historical tradition in the shadow of the two great protagonists of the Cold War, largely unbeknownst to the world public. The European sixteenth century had given birth to individualism and individual freedom. In the seventeenth century, individualism passed through its obligatory teething troubles when, particularly in the wars of religion, it first led to an almost complete disconnection from public order, to chaos, and therefore also to severe threats to individual freedom. Europe reacted by subordinating religion to statehood, but also by linking it with the individual freedom of conscience. In this way, statehood and individualism were brought into balance.

One decisive aspect of this statehood was also the element of inclusivity: each person enjoyed freedom of conscience and was included in the state's guarantee of security. The French Revolution later took place upon this basis. In this phase, Europe for the first time experienced an antithesis that did not come from foreign or even "savage" peoples, but from "their own" people, who had immigrated to America, although in the first decades or for almost a century, this antithesis was not necessarily perceived as such. In the United States, a nation-state had come into being in which the relationship between statehood and individualism was dealt with differently: statehood was limited to an absolute minimum, and individualism was everything. Thus, it came as little shock to Europe when somewhat more than a century later the exact antithesis saw the light of day, namely, in the shape of the Russian Revolution of 1917. Here the relationship between statehood and individualism was dealt with the same way, but in the reverse: statehood was everything, and individualism had to submit to it. The Cold War permitted Western Europe to continue its own tradition under these conditions, namely, to maintain the balanced link between individualism and statehood, which mutually inform one another in the way that, on the one hand, the state guarantees individual freedom and, on the other, individual freedom makes the state, conceived of in this way, possible in the first place. The development of the social market economy in large portions of Western Europe goes back to this intellectual historical background. It is the economic expression of a philosophy whose effects reach far beyond the economic sector.

With regard to security policy and economic policy, and in the world's political perception, Western Europe was an undisputed member of the Western war party during the Cold War. It was within this framework that the intellectual historical demarcation occurred to East Central Europe, whereby Western European "free inclusivity" faced off against an "unfree inclusivity." Alongside the intellectual historical antithesis in the East, Western Europe continued to live with that other antithesis in the West, which is much older and in which Western European "free inclusivity" was confronted with a "free exclusivity." In terms of intellectual history, the triangle discussed here actually already existed during the Cold War, only at that time it represented a tradition with an orientation in which the concepts were arrayed, East to West, in the following order: "unfree inclusivity," "free inclusivity," "free exclusivity." The differences between the two former concepts are once again based on the categories of affiliation and responsibility, as presented in the preceding chapter. In the United States, affiliation and the responsibility attending it are rejected with regard to things that the individual has not specifically decided on. The correlative on the lack of affiliation is represented by active access, which individuals bring about themselves. In Europe, there is existential affiliation, and, as a counterpart to it, there is a sense of responsibility for situations that one has not actively decided upon but rather into which one has been placed through historical and contemporary parameters. And these situations are ultimately concerned with the collective.

The end of the Cold War brought with it the disappearance of the Eastern antithesis, and this has brought changes to Europe's intellectual historical development. The debate over the much older and still existing antithesis in the West can no longer occur in the shadow cast by the Eastern antithesis. That is why the debate over the antithesis in the West is not only more visible but also demands

a different and new form of awareness in Europe. This is not the place for specu-
lation regarding Europe's development in security policy and in other types
of cooperation in the transatlantic sector. And yet, in view of the intellectual
historical development, an answer is possible. Recent history has shown how,
following the end of the Cold War, Europe has become the natural antagonist
of the United States, and it is evident that this intellectual historical dimension
could one day become a determining factor for the development of security
policy and other types of cooperation within the transatlantic relationship.

The Future of the Nation in Europe

The Balkan Wars confronted not only East Central but also Western Europe
with its own history in a way that challenged a great deal of what Europeans
had viewed as certain for decades. There, on the boundary between the two
parts of Europe that had been separated from each other for so long, historical
breaks appeared that, however, have always codetermined the continent's identity.[48] We now have the opportunity to gain a better understanding of the history and identity of all the participants and, above all, can learn to relate them
to one another. In the following we will leave aside the transatlantic dimension
for a while and return again to European history.

The Alliance between Republic and Nation

The modern European nation-state goes back to the French Revolution. As
already mentioned, during the Revolution two elements forged an alliance
that had very different historical roots, namely, the republic on one side and
the nation on the other. We need to examine these two highly unequal alliance partners for a moment. The European republic is a form of government.
In the Middle Ages, people's positions had depended on their social status,
which was viewed as divinely ordained and from which there was practically
no escape. The Enlightenment confronted this state of affairs with a philosophy
that was individualistic, universalistic, and egalitarian: "The duty or fulfillment
of man was no longer derived from his social status but rather from that of
all of humanity," as Gellner puts it.[49] On the basis of this philosophy, the state
was to become a matter for everyone, a public matter, described by the Latin
expression *res publica*, and this represented the birth of the republican idea. The
French Revolution put this idea into action, although only for the male seg-
ment of the population. The concept of the nation—the other ally—had already
existed among the Romans, and over the course of history "nation" meant very
different things in different places.[50] For our purposes, the decisive development got underway in the eighteenth century in the Romantic era, a reaction
to what people perceived as the "cold" logical arguments of the Enlightenment.
Accordingly, this idea of the nation was infused with a cultural content.

Under the title "'Roots' vs. Reason," Gellner describes this development in the following way: "[There] are two central points in which Romanticism contradicts the ideas of the Enlightenment; while the latter still emphasize reason and human universality, the former attempt to place feeling and uniqueness, i.e., *cultural* peculiarities, into the center of attention. Of course, both negations were closely linked. While the precepts of reason are universal (what makes them valid is the fact that they are *always* valid for *everybody, everywhere*), emotions are ascribed to certain communities (cultures); these are thus associations that come about and are maintained on the basis of shared sentiments; these sentiments are shared only by the members, not by outsiders."[51] Originally, the concept of the nation as created by Romanticism entailed neither an ethnic nor a political interpretation; it was merely defined culturally. It is important to recall this in order to understand these developments properly. As Friedrich Schiller wrote in a letter: "The German Reich and the German nation are two things.... Separate from the political sphere, the German has established his own value, and even if the empire were to fall, German dignity would remain unchallenged. It is a moral quantity; it dwells within the culture and character of the nation which is independent of its political fate."[52] Thus, in its early stages, nationalism was anything but aggressive. Let us go back to Gellner: "Early nationalism [tended] toward modesty and shyness, as seen in Herder's defense of the charms of popular culture against the arrogant and presumptuous imperialism of the French court or English commercialism, or the bloodless universalism of the Enlightenment. The initial return to the totem pole or, rather, to the village green was defensive, akin to a timid apology."[53]

Just as the Enlightenment brought forth one of the two allies, namely, the republic, Romanticism created the other ally, namely, the culturally defined nation. "Republic" describes a form of government, while the culturally understood nation essentially describes an identity. Despite their differences, an alliance emerged between them. This alliance was sealed in France, where, in a revolutionary act, the previous power wielders—the king, the aristocracy, and the clergy—were overthrown and replaced by the Third Estate, namely, the people with their democratic rights.

Thus, the country and the people were established as distinct entities. However, that apparently was not enough, for the toppling of the king brought with it the disappearance of the previous figurehead of the state with which people had identified themselves. The state and the king had been one, and the state had been represented not only through the king but also "in" the king.[54] The dethroned king had, so to speak, pulled the state down with him, even though the revolutionaries certainly did not intend this. The Enlightenment ideas, however, were too abstract to serve as a form of identification. The previous estates had been replaced by the individual, and the new ideas of reason demanded universality. As a result, neither one served as a form of identification with France in its new form. A new identity had to be created, and it was discovered in national identity. Or, stated differently, the nation served the republican idea as a sort of vessel that facilitated the emergence of an identity.[55] For this to work, however, this vessel had to be redesigned, that is, it had to be transformed from a "culture nation" into a "state nation," whereby, on closer inspection, it became a "citizen nation."[56] This alliance is the reason why the democratic movements of the time also became nationalist movements.

Although Romanticism at first provided only the identity-creating vessel for the nation-state, it later provided a more substantial contribution. This occurred particularly in the wake of the Napoleonic Wars, which, while spreading the enlightened ideas of the French Revolution across all of Europe, nevertheless ensured that the cultural concept of the nation would rise up in resistance to French domination.[57] The historian Hagen Schulze describes the interplay of the Enlightenment and Romanticism within the national idea as follows: "[The] two national ideas, the subjective political notion of the French Revolution and the objective cultural notion of German Romanticism, enriched each other, intersected each other, and provided the modern era in Europe with a constant keynote. In a period of continual uprooting and existential crisis, of the loss of the past and euphoria over the future, the idea of the nation provided three things: orientation, community, and transcendence."[58] The nation-state had been born as a child of the Enlightenment, and yet in subsequent years it did little credit to this philosophy. Due to the excesses of nationalism, the European nation-states in the first half of the twentieth century brought other peoples far beyond the confines of their own continent to ruin. Western Europe reacted to the catastrophes of the two world wars with the establishment of a new peace order, which was in turn largely based on Enlightenment ideals. With the revolutions of 1989, Europe has become a whole, and the incipient peace order is facing a new challenge. Europe may now have another chance—finally—to reconcile Enlightened and Romantic thought. Even if this should succeed, it must never forget the victims of the most recent Balkan Wars, which have once again suddenly and terrifyingly reminded Western Europeans that this reconciliation is a precondition for continued work on the European peace order.

The State and the Nation in Western and East Central Europe

In East Central Europe, the term "nationality" still describes one's state affiliation, while in Western Europe, it serves to characterize a person's formal citizenship status. This difference can be traced to the different course of history in the two sections of Europe. Following the discovery of the term "nation" as an intellectual historical thought model, and after the terms "republic" and "nation" were linked to the nation-state, the term "nation" underwent a further development, depending on whether the inhabitants of an already-existing state created their nation or whether a "stateless" people invoked its common origin. In Western Europe, nation formation occurred either within the framework of already existing states, as in England and France, or else, later on, in new states materializing from the merging of various principalities or other territorial unities, as in Germany and Italy. Both developments led to nation-states in which a state's people lived in a certain territory, joined together in the vast majority of cases by a common language and a common culture. In France and England, the idea of the nation encountered a state that had existed within more or less clear borders, so that the state nations mentioned in the preceding section emerged directly. Particularly in Germany, but elsewhere as well, the culture nations remained, since national identity—for lack of already existing states—attached itself to nationally conceived poetry, painting, education, and art in general. Only a century later did these culture nations become state nations.[59] However, throughout Western Europe the ultimate result was nation-states after the pattern of England and France, whereby today the term "nation" means the same as the term "state" with regard to territory. States and nations had been brought into agreement. The adjective "international," which today is understood in the same way worldwide, expresses this Western European understanding of the nation by using "state" and "nation" interchangeably: an "international" phenomenon is one that affects several states. Essentially, it means "interstate."

Although in Western Europe nations and states agree in principle, the term "nation" also calls up very different associations within Western European hearts and minds. For example, people in France and Germany do not understand the same thing when they hear the word "nation," even though the nation-state formally means the same thing to both. To a great degree, this has to do with the fact that practically a century lies between the founding of each of these nation-states. Basically, the original German understanding of nations forms the foundation for the still valid meaning of this term in East Central Europe, since the creation of the German nation occurred in a "stateless" condition—that is, first as a culture nation—and the transition to the state nation led to an adaptation at a later date to the modern-day Western European understanding. In East Central Europe, the emergence of culture nations was the standard, for here the great empires of the Turkish Osmans, the Austrian Habsburgs, and the Russian Romanovs continued long beyond the period when the Western European nation-states developed. These empires were all multicultural, multilingual, and largely also multireligious, creating cohesion among the various peoples with means other than common culture, from the granting of greater or lesser autonomy, on the one hand, all the way to violent suppression, on the other. Since the founding of states—that is, the formation of state nations—was not possible in this environment, Romantic notions emerged in which the boundaries of the imagined state nation could be effortlessly envisioned as encompassing even the most distant members of one's own people. Since such dreams could not be easily concretized within the existing empires, such imaginary frontiers met with no resistance, and thus countless territories were multiply "occupied" by various peoples and populations in thought. This had disastrous consequences, namely, when at a later period attempts were made to put such dreams into practice, for which the recent wars in the Balkans provide appalling evidence.

Since the state nation did not develop in East Central Europe, the nation lived on in the form of the culture nation over such a long period that to this day, the term "nation" is classified not in state terms but rather in cultural terms. The example of a Croatian student of Serb background at the University of Zagreb lucidly illustrates this situation: while he recently recorded his citizenship and nationality for his student ID as a Croatian citizen, he nonetheless described his nationality as Serb.[60] Today, the East Central European states fundamentally orient themselves on the Western European understanding of the nation-state. Nevertheless, we should recall that in this part of Europe, the terms "state" and "nation" have not grown together. In East Central Europe, "nation" remains a cultural concept. However, this does not prevent people from using the adjective "international" in its worldwide meaning. This sometimes causes complications in discussions between East Central and Western Europeans, although a timely clarification of terms can help.[61] Cultural identity covers a much broader area than mere ethnic background. Conversely, the word "ethnic" sometimes refers to a much broader spectrum of origin criteria that are not self-chosen and that also do not apply merely to a person's descent from a certain people. In East Central Europe, the term "nation" still contains within it a great many undertones that ultimately derive from Romantic thought. In Western Europe, the term "nation" is much more strongly informed by elements derived from the Enlightenment.

What is the modern status of the alliance between the republic and the nation, 200 years after the latter's emergence in Europe? Today, both allies have entirely different foundations than they did a few decades ago. First, let us talk about the ally, the republic. This is the term for a certain form of government that is characterized by the democratic participation of its citizens. It is a category within the framework of statehood. The present-day Western European nation-state is being challenged in its order function in two respects: first, globalization takes away its ability to regulate matters that it had previously regulated on its own; second, at the same time, it is relinquishing its competencies to the European Union. To be sure, these two phenomena differ only insofar as globalization displaces previous national regulations, only to abandon them to a frequently unregulated sphere or to a sphere regulated entirely by market mechanisms, which does not apply to the transfer of competencies to the European Union. Furthermore, one can observe a displacement of statehood "downward," below the level of the nation-state, as competencies are delegated to the substructures of nation-states. This is frequently a result of the "subsidiarity principle," according to which public functions are always performed on the lowest level at which they can still be meaningfully performed.[62] These phenomena can also be observed in East Central Europe or are likewise developing with regard to the eastward enlargement of the European Union. At the same time, however, in this part of Europe steps are still being undertaken that to some extent have already occurred earlier in Western Europe. In many places, the alliance between the nation and the republic was forged only in 1989, when democratic forms found their way into existing "national" states. New nation-states are being founded, whereby one cannot ignore a tendency toward harmonizing political and cultural frontiers. Viewed across the entire European region, the other ally, the nation, finds itself in various stages simultaneously with regard not only to its own development but also to its relations to its ally the republic, in the sense of statehood.

If statehood and thus the citizens' "republican" participation show a tendency to expand across the level of the nation-state—and, to some extent, beneath this level—then this leads to a gradual detachment of statehood from the nation, or, conversely, it leads to a gradual detachment of the nation from statehood. The republican idea shatters the vessel of the nation, so to speak, which it had used for 200 years with greater or lesser degrees of success. It pushes upward and downward simply because statehood is in the process of expanding upward and downward. To the extent that the movement spreads "upward," to the supranational level of the European Union, new forms of republican participation must be invented, which is one of the tasks of the convention that has been put into place by the heads of state and government of the European Union. In contrast to the events of more than 200 years ago, however, this "republican act" is no longer emotionally anchored within a national identity, for Europe is not a nation and will not become one, even if the republican act is one day successful and completed. This is not due to the geographical dimensions of the European Union within its future borders; after all, the example of the United States demonstrates emphatically that national identity on such a geographical scale is possible. Rather, the reason is rooted in European history. The national identity of Europeans will continue to remain anchored more or less where it has been before, namely, on the level of the previous nation-states or even in smaller-scale units. The attempt to postulate a kind of Romantic *Heimat* identity on the European scale would be misguided for other reasons to which we will return in the final chapter, where we discuss the relationship between the Enlightenment and Romanticism.[63]

Things are somewhat different with regard to the other movement, namely, the "downward" one. At first it appears somewhat simpler, since a common cultural identity on the levels below the nation-state can certainly be present. Due to its origin, national identity as a cultural phenomenon is community-oriented and small-scale. This means that if the republican idea were to spread downward, it would not need to abandon its alliance with the nation. However, that is precisely the problem. If decentralization efforts are motivated by the desire to help assert the subsidiarity principle, they arise from the republican idea and promote civic identity. If, however, such efforts are motivated by a desire to harmonize political and cultural boundaries, they already contain within themselves the germ of nationalist secessionist efforts and thus oppose civic identity.[64] If this second option is to be avoided, it is also necessary for the downward movement to bid farewell to the alliance between the republic and the nation.

"Secularization" of the Nation?

What these different development situations have in common—no matter how unsimultaneously they occur across the continent and no matter how differently they are perceived—is a slowly progressing separation of state political and cultural identity, whereby the nation is again gradually becoming a purely cultural category, as it had been originally.[65] It is obvious that this process can proceed only where nationalism is not an issue. If, in one's "holy zeal," one attempts to harmonize cultural and political boundaries, this process leads to setbacks. If nationalist excesses assume murderous forms, as was the case in World War II and—although within a quantitatively smaller but no less horrifying framework—in the Balkan Wars, this can later lead to the realization that the process is truly inescapable after all. If the separation of state political and cultural identity proceeds, the process can soon provide protection from nationalist relapses. Once the separation has been established, state political and cultural identity can take different paths. The individual's state political identity is ultimately located on all levels at which he or she is confronted with statehood: in communities, towns, and municipalities with which one's temporary stay is linked through residence, work, or other factors; the "nation" states themselves, in which these municipalities are located, whose citizenship one possesses or in whose territory one temporarily resides without yet possessing citizenship; and finally the European Union. Regardless of the different ways in which republican rights of participation on these levels may be regulated—for example, they might be entirely absent on the municipal level, and on the EU level they have to be defined—on all of these levels, a state political identity that is tantamount to both affiliation and responsibility can develop for the individual. One could also describe this identity as a civic one because it refers to statehood in general. However, for the moment we will avoid this term since, first of all, it is understood to apply only to the nation-state level and, second, it could be confused with citizenship, with which it has nothing directly in common. Within this conception, state political identity is also still linked with the nation-state level, but simply because this level also takes its place within the cascade of different levels listed previously and not because, viewed in the long term, this identity requires any elements from the area of the nation. It would be important to examine to what extent a state political identity on the global level can be added at the top of these levels. However, we shall leave this question open since we are dealing with the development in Europe.

This expansion of state political identity to various levels runs parallel to the corresponding movement of national identity, which is slowly and almost imperceptibly becoming a purely cultural one—or which is perhaps becoming once again a cultural one. These two movements result in a state of affairs whereby cultural identity gradually declines to demand implementation within state political categories. It is also conceivable that this is a two-step process. Nationalism—the most intensive and virulent conjunction of culture and politics—is first broken down into a national identity that seeks neither physical nor ideological conquests abroad and does not attempt to extinguish foreign elements within it. The transformation of national identity into a cultural category would then represent only the second step. Just how slow such developments occur is demonstrated by Western European history. If we proceed from the two-step theory, the first step occurred in the middle of the twentieth century, and the second is going full tilt a half-century later, as can be observed within the framework of the European Union. East Central Europe is now located on precisely this line of development. The membership candidates for the European Union are already being confronted with the second step, but at the same time they are facing the first one, particularly in connection with minority issues, to which we shall return later on. With all its cruelty, Southeastern Europe has grappled with events that have demonstrated, or should have demonstrated, the desperate necessity of the first step in this process. Thus, our work in Bosnia lay precisely in helping people to set aside their ethnic spectacles. This was the first step toward returning nationalist thought to a national identity in the Western European understanding of the term, an identity that would no longer undertake "ethnic cleansing," to use this horrible expression after all, and that no longer seeks to make conquests abroad. But in reality, our work was part of a longer-term line of development—that of the slow separation of state political and cultural identity.

Today I know that it was this originally intuitive perception that caused me to shiver every time I drove past the destroyed National Library in Sarajevo. At first I ascribed my inability to take my eyes off this building to my general feeling of horror over the events of the war. But even later, when the other destroyed buildings no longer particularly impressed me, this building did not cease to terrify me. I sensed that a deeper meaning lay hidden there. Whenever and wherever books are burned and libraries are set on fire, politics and culture combine in the worst way imaginable. The library was made one of the first targets during the siege of Sarajevo, and it was deliberately laid waste because it represented a provocation to the besiegers. But if there is one place in Europe where cultural variety and tolerance can continually withstand state political events, it is Sarajevo, and its National Library remains a symbol of this tradition. As Konrad Paul Liessmann wrote in 1994: "Just as the old Europe of the fin de siècle went down in the gunfire of Sarajevo, the *New Europe* is being born in the shadow of the besieged and shattered Sarajevo. But it must recognize in this conflict that it still bears the old within itself, and it will not know for a long time just what is supposed to be new about it."[66] The "short twentieth century," as Eric J. Hobsbawm has called it, and which lies between these two events, lasted almost 80 years.[67] This is the scale on which such development processes occur. But it is ultimately this slow separation of state political and cultural identity that represents the bracket between East Central Europe and Western Europe. Both parts of Europe are caught up in the same pattern of development, which is not linear—often taking twisted paths—yet again and again points in a general and consistent direction. In both areas of Europe, the individual states have advanced at very different rates, and sometimes they appear to go back a step, although later this might prove to be precisely the beginning of a new step forward. This can be observed just as much in East Central Europe as in the European Union, because it would otherwise be impossible for such developments to make headway.

As slowly and unsimultaneously as it may unfold when viewed on a European scale, this process reveals various perspectives. Once it has reached a certain benchmark, national identity can play a full-fledged role in the cultural sector without leading to fears of an about-face into nationalist endeavors. It will have separated itself so far from the political sector that it no longer demands any political implementation within territorial borders.[68] The nucleus of such a nationalist about-face will always remain in every national identity, and yet the knowledge of history makes it possible to prevent it from turning into a "sleeping giant" that can be "awakened."[69] Another perspective of the developments described here is that of cultural multiple identities, which is particularly interesting with regard to immigration. Just as state political identity touches on all vertical levels of possible statehood, cultural identity on the geographical map simultaneously reveals different horizontal links, whether freely chosen or based on one's origin or life situation. Such cultural identities can exist side by side and in an intensive fashion.[70]

We need to look closely at two other sectors where there are points of contact between state political and cultural identity. There is a portion of culture in the broadest sense that can be ascribed to state political identity, namely, political culture, state culture, and legal culture. These elements should be borne and shared by all those who belong to the same state and thus must assume the corresponding responsibility.[71] Conversely, state political identity must be distinguished from citizenship, through which the "nation" states determine a relationship of special rights and duties to certain persons, which is not to be confused with state political affiliation and responsibility.[72] The regulation of citizenship is one of the few sectors in which, for historical reasons, politics and culture cannot be—or cannot *yet* be—viewed and handled separately. The way in which European nation-states adjudicate citizenship varies greatly, which can be explained only by the growing national identity.[73] Nevertheless, this status of the individual bases its democratic participation on the level of the "nation" state, that is, a very decisive "republican" element. However, this does not prevent the development process from continuing its course by circumventing this island. Today, non- or "not yet" citizens are increasingly being drawn into public life within the framework of the detachment of citizenship from the nation and the expansion of republican participation beneath and above the level of the traditional "nation" state, even if this does not include the formal right to vote for national parliaments.[74] This promotes a development within this sector that is leading—if somewhat more slowly—in the direction of the separation of state political and cultural identity.

If state political and national identity are gradually separating from one another, this is tantamount to a kind of secularization of the nation, whereby the term "secularization" is used figuratively. Secularization refers to the detachment of increasingly comprehensive aspects of life from religion. The European state ultimately developed through secularization, as we have already seen. After religious practices had served from the dawn of human history to guarantee cohesion between individuals, this task was later detached from religion and assumed by the state. In Europe, values that the individual absorbs in the private conflict with his or her religion must be transferred to the level of public conflict, where they are confronted with differing values that may come from the areas of morality and culture or other contexts. This is exactly what happens a few centuries later on with the nation, when state political and national identity go their separate ways. The secularization process now also encompasses national identity, which returns to the cultural dimension where it had developed in the first place. After the completion of this process, national impulses can certainly reach the level of discussion within the framework of the public, state order structure, but they must be translated onto this level. In this way, it is possible to prevent the emergence of a demand to join the relevant impulses as national appeals—or, in a worst case, as nationalistic appeals—just as secularization has stopped people from contributing private religious practice to the public discussion as religious values.[75] Since the nation is following the same path as religion, it is more than justified to call this process secularization.[76] When one considers that nationalism has taken the place of religion and that there are parallels between certain manifestations of religion and the development of nationalist movements, this description is certainly meaningful.

Different Paths to Europe

As already mentioned, the nation today finds itself in various different stages when viewed on a European-wide basis. It entered into new alliances with its traditional partner, the republic, in 1989 and is still entering such alliances in East Central Europe, whereby new nation-states are developing or previously existing nation-states are assuming republican forms. And yet we can now ask the following: for those countries in which the nation has remained a cultural category, is it possible to forego the alliance between republic and nation, pass over the 200-year journey, and, so to speak, take a running jump through history? This matter is not just a question of chronology but also one of content. In East Central Europe, the frontiers of the nations—understood as a cultural category—and those of the states no longer match one another. The fateful nationalist notion that these borders should be harmonized cannot fail but lead to "ethnic cleansings," with all their horrible consequences. In this view, there is no place where it is more important to separate cultural and political identity than in those countries where such nationalist notions can easily break out again. Such emotions can be aroused in connection with the minority question if culturally conceived nations are located in several states, or if states span several culturally understood nations. There are not only differences of chronology between Western Europe and East Central Europe in the relationship between state political and cultural identity, but also differences of content. Although the goal of development is the same, the starting position differs greatly. While the Western European "nation-state" is heading in the direction of a state "beyond the nation," the East Central "state of the nations" is developing into a state "beyond the nations." This leads to a conclusion that might at first sound strange in Western European ears: in the understanding of the nation as a cultural category, East Central Europe may be closer to the goal of this process than Western Europe. However, in its eagerness to harmonize culture and politics, East Central Europe is more distant from the goal than Western Europe. That is why Western Europe will have to take the lead in this regard. And yet, surprisingly enough, Western Europe's path toward this goal is longer than that of East Central Europe, to the extent that East Central Europe does not set off on the 200-year journey of the alliance between the republic and the nation.

But within Western Europe, too, different paths are being taken. When the French Revolution reached for the vessel of the nation to contain its republic, the nation was transformed from a culture nation to a state nation, or, more accurately, a citizen nation. The nation became the bearer and messenger of all the Enlightened and universally valid ideals, whereby school education had an important function: the school was now always the "school of the nation." Through the French language, a general French-national legal and state culture was transmitted. Regional languages vanished and were replaced by the unitary language—whose purity is still safeguarded by the Académie Française—and in this process regional or other small-scale cultural identities were repressed. This was possible only because a culturally understood surrogate identity was offered, namely, one on the national level. In other words, the political identity was culturally charged. Henceforth, the French would view culture as the greatest achievement of this *Grande Nation*, including not only the works of their creative elites, but also the universally valid accomplishments of the Enlightenment, democracy, human rights, and, in more general terms, republicanism as created by the French Revolution. In this combination, the new idea conquered not only Europe but also other parts of the world over the ensuing centuries. It is particularly important to note at this point that French state political identity still includes cultural elements that go beyond political culture, state culture, and legal culture. These three elements can be attributed to legal culture, even in the gradual separation of cultural from state political identity. French film production is indisputably a product of the

Grande Nation, and its defense against Hollywood is an act of republican pride. In France, state political identity and cultural identity continue to be more intense and emotional than in many other Western European states.

As already shown, the process in Germany was almost the exact opposite. Cultural and political identity remained separate for a long period. Jean-Marc Ferry has described the process of the formation of the German nation—in contrast to the formation of the French nation—in the following terms: "In somewhat idealized fashion, one could say that the dogmatic method of the determining movement, with whose help the French state attempts to plant universals (meaning the universally valid achievements of the Enlightenment) into the cultural and political body of the nation via the school, stands opposed to the critical method of reflective movement, with the help of which the German nation in the form of its many states attempts to develop its very own culture toward universals via the universities."[77] The German intellectuals assumed the philosophical notions of the French Revolution without first being able, or even desiring, to place it into a political framework, so that these notions did not come to contradict the more small-scale cultural identities. When the nation-state was finally created, these smaller-scale cultural identities continued to withstand it, and state political and cultural identities remained more separate than in France, where, in a manner of speaking, the state political identity absorbed the cultural identity. Thus, for the general European development of state political and cultural identity, within Western Europe one gradually comes to a realization that is just as astonishing as that which emerged from the comparison of Western and East Central Europe: although they share essentially the same goal, the path to this goal appears somewhat longer with regard to the French state political identity when compared with the German state political identity. This is particularly surprising because the French understanding of the state most clearly realizes those factors—and we shall now once again refer to the subject of this entire chapter, namely, the Western Europe/East Central Europe/United States triangle—that make up European statehood and that are thus diametrically opposed to the equally history-based conditions across the Atlantic. We will take a closer look at this dimension in the following pages, first by comparing the role of the group and that of the individual.

Minorities, Group Rights, and the Individual

In Western Europe, minority problems usually crop up within the existing states due to various methods that were employed during the formation of the nation-states in an attempt to weld together the new nation and perhaps to present a shared myth of origin. If this did not occur with the necessary prudence and caution—especially if minority groups were integrated with force—then this can backfire decades or even centuries later, as already described in the pattern of a sleeping national identity that can be politically "awakened."[78]

East Central Europe is subject to precisely the same mechanisms, and yet its minority situation is more complicated, which in turn goes back to the historical development and the cultural understanding of the nation. If the members of a culturally conceived "nation" live in several states and if the "nation" in question represents a clear majority in one of these states, all the classic factors are present for the development of nationalist dreams of shifting the political boundaries in order to harmonize them with the cultural ones. If this can be avoided, a desire frequently develops to regulate the relations between the adherents of the culturally understood "nation" and the state in which these persons may not themselves reside, but in which members of the same "nation" are in the majority. One can hardly argue with this if we are dealing with persons who possess the citizenship of this state, for citizenship justifies a special bond between the state and the individual, even if the individual does not live in the state of his or her citizenship. If, however, the adherents of the culturally understood "nation" do not possess the citizenship of that other "home" state, then the legally regulated relationship of this state to the "nation" will become problematic. A bond that could be defined in state political terms does not exist in such cases. Instead, the relationship is a purely state political one and thus a matter to be regulated by law, whereas the relationship to the state, which embodies the culturally understood "nation," becomes a purely cultural one.[79] This condition has been more or less attained in Western Europe, even if the separation of state political and cultural identity has not been completed by a long shot, due to this region's earlier formation of the nation-state. Perhaps East Central Europe as a whole is close to achieving this, but some states, particularly those in Southeastern Europe, have a considerable challenge ahead of them.

The following example, which admittedly goes back a couple of years, can serve as an illustration. In post-war Bosnia, the term "Bosnian Serbs and Bosnian Croats" already represented an achievement of sorts, since it replaced the term "Serbs and Croats" that was used by nationalistically oriented persons living in Bosnia. First of all, the latter is an expression of the culturally understood nation, whereby the meaning of the neighboring states of Serbia (that is, the Federal Republic of Yugoslavia) and Croatia resonates strongly, which is why the use of this term could signal that one was in favor of annexing the "liberated" sections of Bosnia to these adjoining states. If, however, one spoke of "Bosnian Serbs" or "Bosnian Croats," this was a signal in the opposite direction. In post-war Bosnia, the term "Serbs and Croats" was deliberately used as a symbol for the blending of political and cultural identity. Thus, it could easily happen that an addressee of a letter bearing my signature would angrily send it back to me with the comment that he or she rejected the use of the expression "Bosnian Serbs and Bosnian Croats," which did not stop me from sticking to this usage and explaining in the next letter to this addressee why I believed this was correct. In this second version, we can already see the cultural and state political element side by side in the way that the adjective "Bosnian" represents the state political component that is identical for both, while the noun reveals the cultural component, which in Bosnia, as in all of East Central Europe, is characterized as national.

In our context, however, it is particularly important to note how group rights and the rights of individuals are dealt with. National identity is more concerned with group rights, whereas state political identity is concerned with individual rights. After leaving the Western Europe/East Central Europe/United States triangle aside for our presentation of the long-term development line within Europe, we will now once again incorporate the total context of this chapter. Two transatlantic differences, which we have already mentioned, provide the starting point. While Europe chose statehood for social integration as a response to individualization, the United States chose "community." At the same time, across the Atlantic politics is largely a struggle over rights, whereas in Europe it is a struggle over laws. Law and politics dovetail differently on both sides of the Atlantic. The group and the individual have differing significance.

After decades under the hated, omnipresent party and state structure, which also included a certain economic stability on a modest level, the people in East Central Europe in 1989 abruptly achieved a freedom that was linked with an equally abrupt surge in individualization and accompanied by the gradual loss of the previous certainty of benefits. Even a hated attachment is, after all, an attachment. If, in the midst of this economically and politically difficult situation, East Central European states adopt the idea of compensating for the abruptly increasing individualization by embracing the notion of communities, then the overall European process of the slow separation of state political and cultural identity will take a step backward. The same thing occurs when politics is understood primarily as a struggle for the rights of various minority groups. These developments cannot be viewed independently of one another. The three-question cluster—namely, how politics should function, what attachments should be used as compensation and what they are to consist of, and finally to what extent state political identity should remain linked with cultural (which in East Central Europe means "national") identity—imperceptibly starts taking its place along the same development line between the group and the individual. In this way, the three-question clusters become so interdependent that they no longer have any independent answers. Stated plainly, if East Central Europeans choose to compensate for individualization by seeking attachment in community, in the American sense of the word—in place of the European understanding of statehood—then this promotes the claims of "national" minorities *as groups* for legal and thus state recognition. And if East Central Europeans understand "politics" on the American pattern as a constant conflict of minority groups whose aim is to prevent a majority consensus, this will lead to a legal struggle over the implementation of the claims of "national" minorities *as groups*. Just how this works can be seen by taking a look across the Atlantic, where ethnically defined minorities are becoming increasingly involved in the fight over their place at the social feeding trough.[80]

Such manifestations can never be prevented entirely. What is certain, however, is that they can be controlled only within the framework of a European-wide state political culture resting on the participation of the individual in his or her capacity as a part of the popular sovereign, and not in a politics of competing minority groups on the American pattern, for this form of "politics" leads inevitably to the formation of ethnic groups, which has disastrous effects on states in which nationalist currents remain present.[81]

Let us now return to the subtle differences in the understanding of the nation within Western Europe. Whenever transatlantic differences appear, France is usually standing in the front lines. It would be easy to assume that this is based on hegemonic claims and on the fact that France is particularly sensitive to the hegemonic claims of the United States. However, this assumption is not correct, for the reason lies much deeper, namely, in an extremely clear state political identity, which we have already mentioned in connection with religious sects. This identity also reveals itself in the minority question. France has always taken the position that it contains no national minorities—a position that is consistent with its historical foundation.[82] The massive exertion of the French Revolution so profoundly shaped the *Grande Nation* that it continues to regard itself as the defender of the Enlightenment ideals upon which it is based. In the nineteenth century, the French forged a national identity through the "school of the nation" and the French language, which became the bearer of those ideals and which replaced the smaller-scale cultural identities. The anchoring in the community and group, which may have molded these earlier identities, was replaced by that of the Enlightenment ideals, and they also found an emotional framework on the national level. The breakthrough to the Enlightenment was identical to the overcoming of smaller-scale cultural identities and the replacement of the community and the group with the individual. That is why for France the notion of the mere existence of minorities represents treason against the republican idea and the French Revolution. Thus, the community order structure, which in the United States provides the individualized person with attachment and ensures the cohesion of society, like the understanding of politics as a struggle for rights by minority groups, represents an even stronger contrast to the state political identity that has developed in France than to the identities that characterize other European states. Thus, state political identity on the French pattern is the purest antithesis of American identity. This is the reason why France is often in the front lines during transatlantic conflicts.

We cannot discuss all facets of the minority question in this chapter, but let us point to an additional aspect in which the cultural and state political dimensions once again lead to different solutions. If we are looking for an opportunity to consider small-scale factors within the framework of a state political dimension, then the federal organization of the nation-state has much to offer. The organization of a state in component states or even smaller units is based not on group rights but on the individual as part of the sovereign people, whereby this individual possesses a multiple-state political identity, which is distributed vertically. If, by contrast, the cultural dimension takes the foreground—in the East Central European understanding, this is the national dimension—then the inevitable result will be that people will think in terms of group rights, which leads to persons with the same cultural background demanding recognition and special treatment as a group. The first approach is thoroughly reconcilable with the overall European development of gradually separating state political and cultural identity from one another. The second approach countervails this development.[83]

Freedom through Shared Sovereignty

In the previous chapter we saw why the American Revolution, in contrast to the French Revolution, did not lead to the founding of a state but, on close analysis, led to the founding only of a nation. There is no doubt that the United States acts as a nation-state on the foreign policy level. And there is no doubt that, in formal terms, the same thing happened in the American Revolution as in the French Revolution, namely, the founding of a nation-state. The differences lie in the area of identities. Identity develops through attachments, which the individualized person accepts. The French Revolution offered the individual freedom in the form of state political identity. The American Revolution, by contrast, offered freedom in the form of national identity. This was not an offer of state political identity, for there was no need for that in America: the individual, liberated by the preceding, individual act of emigration, sought attachment, but not attachment through statehood, for he had already freed himself from the collective attachment through statehood. That is why today Americans still do not have a state political identity. For Europeans, state political identity is the foundation of the freedom of the individual and has been the basis of the peace order since 1945. Both are based on shared sovereignty. Viewed historically, the individual relinquished his or her primal freedom, yielding it to the state, and in return received a freedom that is no longer the "freedom of the stronger," but a freedom to which everyone subject to the state is equally entitled. This freedom also manifests itself in popular sovereignty, which consists of jointly determining the basic state political order. Equality is always an inseparable component of the European understanding of freedom. This represents a fundamental difference from the United States, where although everyone is also entitled to freedom, those who fight for their freedom enjoy more of it. And, along the same lines, on the next higher level the European states are prepared to relinquish some of their sovereignty in exchange for which they receive a peace order that has hitherto proven itself to be stable. It is true that larger states have a greater influence within the European Union than smaller ones, and yet one cannot speak of a blatant "right of the stronger states," for shared sovereignty actually has a more far-reaching impact for the larger states than for the smaller ones, which would have even less of a say in the interaction of states if this shared sovereignty did not exist.

The fundamental difference from the United States with regard to shared sovereignty by states is the same as with shared individual sovereignty. Across the Atlantic, the notion of the freedom of one's own nation-state is linked not to the notion of the equality of all nation-states, but to the notion of the right of the stronger state. In the United States, the right of the strong is not just an argument that is employed depending on the momentary balance of interests when someone can draw benefit from it because one happens to be stronger; rather, it is a fundamental principle that has developed intellectually over the course of centuries. It is one of the few enduring principles in American thought and serves as the basic pattern in the regulation of many areas of life. It would thus be erroneous to attribute the American mentality to its present-day position as the sole surviving superpower. While power interests may well drive the behavior of the United States, the roots of this behavior lie much deeper, and they would remain active even if the country's power position should someday weaken.

Practically all transatlantic differences can be traced back to the existence of a state political identity in Europe and its non-existence in the United States, characterized by the lack of the concept of sovereignty in the US Constitution, the consistently successful attempt to prevent the emergence of a political force presuming to speak in the name of the people, and the negatively evaluated notion of shared individual sovereignty in favor of the state. This fundamentally different attitude toward shared sovereignty has various roots, and we should not forget that one of these roots is of a religious nature. In the American tradition, man is alone with his God, and no one should be able to interfere in this relationship. The previously cited political scientist Otto Kallscheuer describes the background of this loneliness with God as follows:

> One possible interpretation of this "inner abundance" of American loneliness … has to do with the symbolic history of wandering, as in the covenant of the Chosen People, with the crossing of the open frontier. "America," as we have seen, was founded on the emigration to democracy. This wandering continued in the drive to the West and imposed the experience of frontier and loneliness on the wanderers. The Californian philosopher Josia Royce, an idealistic "communitarian" of the turn of the century, described God's presence as the flip side of the desert experience on the great wagon trains on their trek to settle the West of the continent. Whom else could one encounter in the desert aside from God?… On the great migration, the God of the Bible could not speak through institutional deputies, and even the text of the Book of Books had to be lived in personal experience.[84]

The uniqueness of the individual is also experienced in the American tradition through religious identity, whereas in the tradition of the French Revolution it is experienced through state political identity. We will return to this in the next chapter in connection with the Enlightenment and Romanticism. As astonishing as it might at first appear, at this point too we can once again discern the crossroads of 1648.

Another root of Americans' lack of receptiveness to shared sovereignty has already been mentioned. Popular sovereignty tends to include more and more categories of persons, independently of any accession talks or commitments.[85] In other words, in the long term, popular sovereignty always tends toward equality, which is part of the way Europeans (but not Americans) view freedom.

European state political identity is based on existential belonging. European statehood requires no commitment, no joining, no membership. It is the very antithesis of the activity of an association or an economic enterprise. In the end, it is not concerned merely with finding solutions that are acceptable for oneself or for a group to which one belongs. Instead, it is always concerned with finding solutions that, once accepted, do not entirely exclude anyone's interests, even if the acceptance will always be less for some than for others. And this should not be understood as philanthropy or charity, but rather viewed on the basis of the very rational relinquishment of sovereignty that the individual performs in the thoroughly egoistic consideration that he or she will gain more than he or she loses. The great freedom that the individual gains lies in the certainty that the decisions of others, in which one is not directly involved, will at least to some extent take one's own interests into consideration. This was made possible only as a result of a long, painful history. Unrestricted sovereignty led to such a massive and extended use of violence that shared sovereignty was either invented or recalled in later years and transformed into the definitive basis for the social order. European history is the evidence of this process.[86]

Shared sovereignty thus also means replacing violence with law. The individual relinquishment of sovereignty leads to the state legal order, which replaces the law of the jungle among individuals. Shared state sovereignty leads either to order through international law or else—as in Europe—to supranational law, and both replace the rule of force between states.[87] Shared sovereignty has a negative connotation across the Atlantic. In both the foreign policy and domestic spheres, this leads to a certain concept in the management of violence. We have already spoken of the tendency of Americans to accept and even practice more individual violence. The state monopoly on the use of force represents the converse to this. The police exert legal violence in the state, whereas the practice of violence by private persons is illegal and punishable, subject to a few expressly stated exceptions. In the United States, the state monopoly on the use of force is beginning to crumble, both on the "lower" and "upper" ends of the social scale between the poor and rich. There are urban districts where the law of the jungle is back in force and which the police dare not enter. At the other end of the scale we find the previously mentioned gated communities. Surrounded by high walls, they are guarded by private security services, which also guarantee the order within. Such districts no longer need a state police. All they require is an army to defend themselves along with a state security system run by secret services in order to prevent their protected compound from suddenly being wiped off the map. Thus, the residents of such compounds are more in favor of military expenditures than of the strengthening of police security. The use of force is therefore becoming privatized for both very poor and very rich individuals. This is tantamount to the abolition of the state in increments. If the crumbling of the state's monopoly on the use of force is more readily accepted in the United States than in Europe, this is also due to the unfamiliar notion of shared power across the Atlantic and the lack of state political identity. And this is precisely what makes comparable phenomena in Europe unimaginable. And where such phenomena do crop up, Europe must react much more quickly.[88]

But shared sovereignty also touches on the law as such. In the previous chapter, we saw how European law tends to strive for a peace order, whereas American law is concerned with adversary culture. This statement can also be incorporated in a further context, namely, in that of shared sovereignty. Depending on whether law develops upon or outside the foundation of a notion of shared sovereignty, it is logically based on various fundamental elements. State political identity, which brings with it shared sovereignty, makes it possible to establish an objectively valid legal order that establishes a framework of order and a certain legal stability. Seen more closely, state political identity thus becomes a legal and state political identity, for the legal order develops within the framework of a statehood created in this way. If a sharing of sovereignty has not occurred, then law develops on the basis of the subjective rights of the individual, which continually collide, whereby "the law" remains in a permanent state of flux. A legal and state political identity in the European meaning of the term does not develop this way. Instead, a kind of direct legal political identity develops instead of the state. However, it is set up differently from the European model. Lacking shared sovereignty, it essentially leapfrogs the state level and the phase of agreeing on a legal order. The individual jumps right into the struggle for subjective rights. If, under these conditions, the struggle before the courts—rather than the run of business in the parliaments and the government—becomes the arena that ends up assuming the function of what Europeans define as politics, there will be only one logical result. This is one of the basic lines of the American legal understanding, which also manifests itself in America's dealings with international law. This legal understanding cannot be called democratic, as it is based on a different understanding of democracy from that which has developed in Europe. By contrast, the rule of law in the European understanding is based on shared sovereignty.[89] According to Immanuel Kant, "the private legal sovereignty of the individual and the resulting objective lawlessness" describe "the natural state," that is, the period of time before the individual has relinquished sovereignty.[90] Subjective rights certainly exist in this state of nature, but individuals have not yet agreed on what objective law should be, that is, they have not agreed on the legal order. The comparable European process on the state level can be illustrated by a quotation from Jacques Delors, the former president of the European Commission:

This common project, undertaken by protecting the identity of its participants, has become possible thanks to the invention of a new political realm in which the nation-state in no way disappears but in which it agrees to delegate some of its elements of sovereignty when it perceives a demand of power, but also of generosity. This realm, in which sovereignties are limited depending on the situation, compete or cooperate where something emerges that is not a super-nation-state (which would mean creating another center of hegemony), but rather a complex network of responsibilities and rights—and that is the European Union.[91]

At the beginning of this chapter we took a look at the Dayton Agreement, whereby we discussed some of its structural shortcomings. In post-war Bosnia, these shortcomings represented only one side of the problem. The other side was rooted in the practical implementation and in daily work, where the lack of state political identity on the part of the Americans had understandable consequences: what you do not have yourself, you cannot offer to others. This was one of the reasons why civil identities in Bosnia did not become an issue to the extent that would have been needed to normalize the situation. And yet it is a shame that sometimes the Europeans acted as if they also had little or no state political identity. So in connection with popular sovereignty, let us return briefly to the peace agreement, because in this regard too it has proven itself to be very "American." On the occasion of its fifth anniversary, Edin Šarčević analyzed the Bosnian constitution, which was enacted as an annex to this agreement under international law. Among other aspects, he criticized not only the failure of this document to safeguard popular sovereignty but also the fact that popular sovereignty did not even make an appearance. Today, the Bosnians are further away than ever from a constitutional understanding that would accommodate popular sovereignty. Šarčević wrote: "The Dayton constitutional system ethnicizes the Bosnian-Herzegovinian *pouvoir constituant* with the result that the Bosnian people (understood as *demos*) has been replaced by the three 'nations' (understood as *ethnos*). Instead of forming a state, the agreement created three ethnic groups that, on the basis of an international agreement, are in a latent conflict."[92] The United States was concerned with bringing order to Bosnia and did not care how it accomplished this. On the one hand, it relied on pressure from the international community: "Despite opposition from the United States, I stuck to my position that democracy has to develop step by step and cannot be forced on us by the power of a High Representative," Wolfgang Petritsch said at the conclusion of his activity as the High Representative in Bosnia.[93] On the other hand, the architects in Dayton apparently assumed that the conflicts between the ethnic groups would lead to the desired results. For this purpose they invented things such as the "power of veto," which allows each ethnic group in the parliament to block decisions if it feels that its "vital interest" is being violated. For a long time, this instrument led to a general blockade of the legislature, at least in important matters of state. Carsten Stahn points to the fateful consequences of this concept for the Bosnian state and uses the term "ethnic democracy," which, on the basis of this concept, has apparently taken the place of a democracy based on popular sovereignty.[94] In various ways, this pattern is reminiscent of the history of the United States: it is a game between minority interests, based on a constitution that essentially stands above the entire people once it has been enacted. While the Bosnian constitution can be altered, the power of veto makes constitutional changes very difficult, if not impossible.[95]

As far as the Western Europe/East Central Europe/United States triangle is concerned, we can sum up this chapter by saying that the growth of state political identity in East Central Europe is essential. If an identity of community were to develop in the place of state political identity, it would be virtually impossible to integrate the nationalist forces into a whole. In this part of Europe, these forces manifest themselves even more virulently than in Western Europe, where they are still very much alive. The cornerstone of European state political identity is shared sovereignty. This is of such central importance on the individual level for the freedom of the individual and on the state level for the maintenance of peace that state political identity and the associated rule of law represent the foundations of Europe, which this continent has no choice but to defend. The social order of the United States is based on other elements, namely, on a national identity that also has a religious basis and that centuries ago took the place of state political identity on the European model. The United States views shared individual sovereignty as something negative and largely rejects shared sovereignty under international law. In the coming years, it will be necessary for both parts of Europe, which are once again coming together, to be aware of these transatlantic differences with their centuries-old roots that lurk in the intellectual historical field. Europeans must reclaim their European identity in the state political sector and never let it out of their sight.

Notes

1. See Carsten Stahn, "Die verfassungsrechtliche Pflicht zur Gleichstellung der drei ethnischen Volksgruppen in den bosnischen Teilrepubliken—Neue Hoffnung für das Friedensmodell von Dayton? Zugleich eine Anmerkung zur dritten Teilentscheidung des bosnischen Verfassungsgerichtes vom 1. Juli 2000 im Izetbegovic-Fall," *Zeitschrift für ausländisches öffentliches Recht und Völkerrecht* 60 (2000): 672. In May 2002, the high representative in Bosnia appointed the seven judges for the court and thus eliminated this shortcoming of the Dayton Agreement.
2. The preconditions for the acceptance of Bosnia into the Council of Europe, which would have permitted the ratification of the European Convention on Human Rights under international law and recognized the court's authority, were regularly discussed in the responsible organs of this organization. There were good reasons for both an early and a late accession to the Council of Europe on Bosnia's part. When a non-member state intervenes in the Council of Europe, this is in

itself highly out of the ordinary, and such an action is usually not very popular among the various members. If, however, the justification for such an intervention lies in the fact that the court's responsibility for human rights could have an obstructing effect on a state's positive development, then this particularly permits conclusions on the condition of the intervening state. Apparently, Bosnia was viewed in Washington, DC, as the fifty-first state of the United States, which is why it was essential to hold America's protective hand over this state and shield it from international jurisdiction. Bosnia finally acceded to the Council of Europe in April 2002.

3. *Deutsche Aussenpolitik 1995. Auf dem Weg zu einer Friedensregelung für Bosnien und Herzegowina: 53 Telegramme aus Dayton. Eine Dokumentation.* Ed. Auswärtigen Amt (Bonn, 1998), 81f., 98.

4. A brief and concise account of these events can be found in Thumann, "Der unvollendete Triumph des Nationalstaats," 15ff. Thumann also points out that following the failure of the Vance-Owen Plan, "ethnic cleansing" occurred precisely in places where this plan had called for mixed regions.

5. Before this conference in Washington, the later director of the German delegation in the Dayton peace talks stated the opinion that "it is entirely unacceptable for Europe" to hold the planned conference outside of Europe. "It is, after all, a European problem" that needed to be solved in Europe and not in the United States. Europe had to abandon this position in order to ensure the participation of the American armed forces in Bosnia, for only by holding the negotiations at a location in the United States was it possible to move the American government to support this mission. Ischinger, "21 Tage Dayton," 32.

6. Thumann, "Der unvollendete Triumph des Nationalstaats," 20.

7. Lothar Rühl, in a review in the aforementioned publication of the German Foreign Office, *Neue Zürcher Zeitung*, 10 October 1998.

8. *Neue Zürcher Zeitung*, 11 November 1999. The report notes that this was not a matter of diplomatic prestige but concerned the question of whether Bosnia should be westernized on the American or European model. The conclusion of the report, which concerned foreign capital investments in Bosnia—and which thus lies beyond the scope of this book—states: "The most recent evidence and proof of the resistance to progress [in one study] is the fact that not even McDonald's has found its way into Bosnia. After detailed studies, the Americans decided to fry their hamburgers elsewhere. Of course, one can view this as a victory of the Bosnian cevapcic over the workaday beef patty—a bit of Balkan identity was rescued and a European tradition was defended against an American standard."

9. See also chapter 2, note 73.

10. The term "monitoring" is discussed in chapter 2 in the section "Law and Morality," subsection "Human Rights."

11. In fact, the Bosnian state and constitutional order has more to do with international law than with domestic concerns, since it is so strongly subjected to the control of the international community of states. This moved the Bosnian Constitutional Court to interpret the preamble of the Bosnian constitution by falling back on the 1969 Vienna Convention on the Law of Treaties, which is applicable only to treaties under international law. Stahn, "Die verfassungsrechtliche Pflicht zur Gleichstellung," 686.

12. See chapter 2, note 68.
13. The expression "provisional legal status" derives from Immanuel Kant, who used it to describe the phase in which—by way of example—an individual takes possession of an object but cannot yet regard it as his definitive property, since he and other individuals, lacking a state, have not yet agreed upon a common legislative apparatus that provides the property with an objective legal basis. For more on this, see the section "Naturzustand—Eigentum—Staat" in Wolfgang Kersting, *Wohlgeordnete Freiheit: Immanuel Kants Rechts- und Staatsphilosophie* (Berlin, 1984), 205ff. Regarding "willing" coalition partners, see, in this volume, chapter 4, section "The Pivotal Role of 'Law,'" subsection "Legal Order and 'Voluntarism.'"
14. Ladurner's brief article appeared in *Die Zeit*, 24 January 2002, under the title "Verheererde Lektion: Bosnien beugt sich Amerikas Druck und beschädigt den eigenen Rechtsstaat."
15. In addition, this system excludes all those Bosnian citizens from their passive voting rights who declare themselves as neither Bosnian Serbs, Bosnian Croats, or Bosniacs. They represent about 8 percent of the Bosnian population. Edin Šarčević, "Völkerrechtlicher Vertrag als 'Gestaltungsinstrument' der Verfassungsgebung: Das Daytoner Verfassungsexperiment mit Präzedenzwirkung?" *Archiv des Völkerrechts* 39 (2001): 313ff. Stahn has raised the question as to whether this represents a violation of the discrimination ban of the UN's International Covenant on Civil and Political Rights, the European Convention on Human Rights, and other conventions. Stahn, "Die verfassungsrechtliche Pflicht zur Gleichstellung, 696. In a report from 24 October 2001, the previously mentioned Venice Commission made a statement to the effect that this system was particularly problematic because it seeks to link territorial and ethnic elements with one another.
16. In its memorable decision of 1 July 2000, the Constitutional Court of the overall state recognized that the constitutions of the two autonomous republics violated the constitution of the overall state in the way that in the Serbian Republic only the Serbian people are described as "constituent" for the autonomous republic, and in the federation only the Bosniac and Croatian population are described this way. Interestingly enough, the political component of the constitutions stands on such a wobbly foundation that one of the three international judges involved in the decision could not follow its reasoning. The decision had to be supported by the human rights component of the basic organization, which forms a counterweight to the basic structure. Stahn, "Die verfassungsrechtliche Pflicht zur Gleichstellung, 690.
17. The *Neue Zürcher Zeitung*, 9 March 2000, reproduced such a report: "The American Secretary of State Albright continued her European tour in Bosnia on Wednesday. She met with the political heads of the country, particularly with those politicians who are being supported by Washington in the reorganization of Bosnian domestic policy."
18. See note 5.
19. Regarding the term "legal person," see chapter 2, note 64.
20. See note 5.
21. Let us return once more to a formulation by Preuss defining the peculiarities of the 1989 revolutions: "The democratic principle of self-government should not be realized through the influence of concentrated political force on social living

conditions—even if it is legitimized through democratic elections—but rather through the application of the available forces residing within the society for self-guidance. If a utopia exists, then it is the opposite of the utopia of a unity of collective reason and secularized supreme power institutionalized in the state: the idea of the autonomy of civil society and its ability to act on itself through discursive processes and through smart institutions." Preuss, *Revolution, Fortschritt und Verfassung*, 64.

22. Howard notes that it is "this 'American' form of a political revolution whose result is the liberation of society which the revolutions of 1989 sought to imitate," after he formulated the difference as follows: "One can say of American political theory … that it unleashes society and frees self-interest, while the French notion seeks to control and guide both for their own good, a good that is defined as the good of the whole." Howard, *Die Grundlegung*, 18.

23. See chapter 2, note 52.

24. Joas, "Gemeinschaft und Demokratie," 54f.

25. An overview of the communitarian moral theory can be found in Reese-Schäfer, *Grenzgötter der Moral*, 236ff. For the sake of completeness, let me mention that the American term "community" can also include territorial communities, which in their European definition as the lowest units of state structures under public law would scarcely count as communities. This also contains a certain logic, since Americans make no distinction between state and society. Regarding the term "community," see also Joas, "Gemeinschaft und Demokratie," 50ff. Asked in an interview about the low interest that the American public shows toward democratic processes, Ralf Dahrendorf pointed to the great difference existing between interest in local and national politics: "Local elections and participation in civil society characterize American democracy much more distinctly than does political life on the federal or state level." Dahrendorf, *Die Krisen der Demokratie: Ein Gespräch mit Antonio Polito* (Munich, 2002), 59.

26. Ernest Gellner, *Nationalismus: Kultur und Macht* (Berlin, 1999), 17, 123.

27. Regarding the relationship between the state and the family, a comparison of the following two personality portraits is interesting. In an article in *Die Zeit*, 24 June 1999, under the title "For the Albanians, the Family Is Everything—the State, by Contrast—Is Nothing," Norbert Mappes-Niediek described young UÇK fighters. In an article in *Die Zeit*, 19 April 2001, the new American ambassador in Berlin was quoted as saying "A strong state destroys the family and the community."

28. Thumann writes briefly and to the point: "The modern Bosnian conflict was thus not of an ethnic or religious nature. It was unleashed by an alliance of unscrupulous politicians, radical intellectuals, unrestrained military personnel, and ordinary gangsters who viewed themselves as a national avant-garde for the creation of their own state." Thumann, "Der unvollendete Triumph des Nationalstaats," 19. This says it all.

29. Altermatt points out that the Bosnian war led to a ghettoization of the Bosniacs by discrediting mixed marriages and more strongly imposing clothing regulations and customs. Altermatt, *Das Fanal von Sarajevo*, 124. It should be noted that such phenomena have been especially promoted by missions of Islamist fundamentalism from states outside of Europe and that so far Bosnian society, due to its traditions, has not been very receptive to such influences.

30. This translation achievement is also mentioned by Joas in an article in *Die Zeit*, 7 February 2002, in which he discusses the term "post-secular" as used by Jürgen Habermas in his speech on the occasion of his being awarded the 2001 Peace Prize of the German Book Trade, whereby there is no consistently clear distinction between private religious practice and religion as a public order structure.

31. Regarding the participation of non- or "not yet" citizens, see note 74.

32. In an essay on the topic, "the status and significance of religion in a 'civil society,'" Ernst-Wolfgang Böckenförde describes the relationship as follows: "Religion ... can ... certainly achieve social and political significance; it has not been driven back to the private sphere and thus does not lack a potentially public character. But even if it achieves such importance, it nevertheless lacks participation in that which makes up the practical and institutionally necessary and general aspects of political order. This is no longer determined by a particular religion, but by the secular purposes of the political commonwealth. Religion ... has no institutionally authentic share. It has genuine significance, but not the status of legal-normative binding character within the polity." Böckenförde, *Staat, Gesellschaft, Freiheit: Studien zur Staatstheorie und zum Verfassungsrecht* (Frankfurt am Main, 1976), 260.

33. Casanova, "Chancen und Gefahren öffentlicher Religionen," 202f.

34. In a biographical work that provides an example from the Islamic cultural sphere, Moroccan sociologist Fatima Mernissi describes her happy, adventurous childhood, which she spent in a harem in the city of Fez. Alongside the external restrictions of female life, her depiction shows the transmission of values based on values of consideration and responsibility that retain their validity far beyond the Islamic cultural sphere. Mernissi, *Der Harem in uns: Die Furcht vor dem anderen und die Sehnsucht der Frauen* (Freiburg, 1994).

35. Martin Riesebrodt describes how and why secularization and the return of religion do not exclude one another but actually correspond to each other, although he does not making a consistent distinction between private religious practice and public order structures. Riesebrodt, *Die Rückkehr der Religionen: Fundamentalismus und der "Kampf der Kulturen"* (Munich, 2000), 48ff.

36. Hagen Schulze describes this shift as follows: "The idea of the nation has a religious echo; since the nation is not an immediately visible reality, it must be believed; nationalization is the secular religion of the industrial era. The new state no longer received its justification from God, but from the nation." Schulze, *Staat und Nation in der europäischen Geschichte* (Munich, 1995), 172.

37. Altermatt, *Das Fanal von Sarajevo*, 110. Altermatt goes on to describe the exchangeability of religion and nationalism using the following example: "Nationalism is apparently in the position to replace religion because it satisfies religious needs of meaning and community. To the extent that human beings distanced themselves from the established Christian religion and its everyday religious practice, they began to search for substitutes. The decisive turning point in nearly all countries was industrialization, which promoted religious indifference and loosened the relationship to the churches. This resulted in a spiritual vacuum that in Europe was filled with nationalist faith tenets."

38. Gellner, *Nationalismus*, 24. Regarding the national "awakening," Gellner states more precisely later on (25): "The 'slumbering state' of nationalism is one of the very central teachings of nationalism, even if this term is seldom used. And that is truly

no accident. Without this doctrine, nationalism would be lost. Without it, it would be impossible to reconcile the natural, exalted, and universal status that is attributed to the nationalistic principle (and which the nationalist emphasizes with passion) with the fact that it is frequently disregarded in history. (The proponents of the slumbering nation only grudgingly and bitterly admit to this, quickly pointing out that this is a superficial truth that is regrettable and must be corrected as quickly as possible.)"

39. Kallscheuer states that the fundamental principle of American religion lies in the "personal experience of God instead of a credo based on fixed dogmas," and points out that this method is quasi mass-produced: "The commotion of the heart, which America's first great theologian, the colonial Puritan Jonathan Edwards, viewed as evidence of genuine religiosity, has become a reproducible pattern in the American modern spirit, all the way to the present-day electronic Pentecostal fire of Jimmy and Donny Swaggart, as well as countless other television preachers and shamans. This is particularly true of America's evangelist Billy Graham, whose 'sermon of rebirth' even managed to transform all of Eastern Europe into a camp meeting." Kallscheuer, *Gottes Wort und Volkes Stimme*, 136f.

40. Casanova, "Chancen und Gefahren öffentlicher Religionen," 207f.

41. In an essay on the developmental processes of identity, André Berten explains that identity is generally a multiple identity, as long as ideological or other influences do not hamper this multiple identity. Thus, one could feel oneself to be part of "a certain nuclear or extended family, a certain line of descent, a family organization, a class, a region, a religion, a race, a certain country, a certain sex or a certain sexual minority, an ethnic group, a certain fan group, a certain company etc., without one of these identities becoming comprehensive and excluding the others." Berten, "Europäische Identität—Einzahl oder Mehrzahl? Überlegungen zu den Entstehungsprozessen von Identität," in *Projekt Europa. Postnationale Identität: Grundlage für eine europäische Demokratie?* ed. Nicole Dewandre and Jacques Lenoble (Berlin, 1994), 58. Berten does not neglect to point out that monolithic identities have led to unspeakable disasters throughout history. The essay is derived from a talk at a colloquium on the subject "Identity and Difference in Democratic Europe," which was held in Brussels in May 1991, before the outbreak of the Balkan Wars. Otherwise, the historical references would have been expanded with references to the present.

42. Richard Münch points out that nowhere else on earth do immigrants show a greater willingness to assume the identity of the target country, and nowhere else on earth does the populace show a greater willingness to "adopt the impulses from a variety of identities from all across the world for the purpose of renewal. In general, we see here the predominance of an optimism that selection through competition and the attractiveness of the American way of life will in any case make all those who set their foot in this country into success-obsessed Americans." Münch, *Das Projekt Europa: Zwischen Nationalstaat, regionaler Autonomie und Weltgesellschaft* (Frankfurt am Main, 1993), 92.

43. The phenomenon has been studied in Germany, too, particularly with regard to Russian-German *Aussiedler* and Turkish immigrants, as reported by Regina Römhild in *Die Zeit*, 14 March 2002. Altermatt describes persons with such multiple identities as "hyphenated citizens." Altermatt, *Das Fanal von Sarajevo*, 245.

In theoretical terms, Jürgen Habermas has made a distinction concerning the cultural life form of origin, which immigrants should be allowed to retain as long as they agree to accept the political culture of their new homelands, since "the identity of the political commonwealth, which must not be infringed upon through immigration, primarily depends on the legal principles anchored in the political culture and not on a specific ethnic-cultural life form as a whole." Habermas, "Staatsbürgerschaft und nationale Identität: Überlegungen zur europäischen Zukunft," in Dewandre and Lenoble, *Projekt Europa*, 27.

44. In an article titled "Vom Schmelztiegel zum Salatschüssel," in *Neue Zürcher Zeitung*, 21–22 October 2000, Sieglinde Geisel has demonstrated the transformation of multicultural identity in the United States.

45. Münch speaks of a "subculture of violence," which has now become a standard object of investigation in the United States and which he connects to the drug trade as well as to gang criminality of various kinds. "The struggle of ethnic groups over their social position is linked to the American idea of success in competition with others, even if it undermines the idea of *individual* access to equal civil rights independent of one's group affiliation." Münch, *Das Projekt Europa*, 94.

46. Klaus Lubbers describes how the temporal basis of the national identity of the United States, which was anchored in the religious realm, was later superseded by a spatial one. "In contrast to the temporal imaginative access, starting around 1800 a spatial one emerged that anticipated, accompanied, and justified the actual transcontinental expansionism. This soon began inspiring imaginations more than the temporal access. Among other things, the spatial access allowed people to imagine the actual appropriation of greater and greater territories in the West. I doubt that the teleological rounding off of the American identity model would have been such a smashing success if the future orientation rooted in Puritan covenant theology had not been turned around into the spatial dimension and thus made visible and tangible, i.e., manifest." Lubbers, "Modelle nationaler Identität in amerikanischer Literatur und Kunst 1776–1893," in Berding, *Nationales Bewusstsein und kollektive Identität*, 95.

47. A direct—if tragic—line leads from the American phenomenon back to the genuine "chosen people of God" of the Old Testament, who after long wanderings finally reached the "promised land" and whose "chosenness" Americans merely imitated. The conquest of the land through individual settlements, linked with the willingness to defend oneself, was also undertaken in modern Israel. This apparently became a conscious strategy at a time when the previously rare immigration from the United States increased. Be this as it may, these states share two elements: on the one hand, the individual willingness of settlers, historical or contemporary, to defend themselves, and, on the other, a national identity that also has religious roots. The special affinity between these two states is usually attributed to the great influence of the Jewish community in the United States. This is doubtless correct, and yet the intellectual parallels should not be underestimated.

48. Various authors emphasize that Europe's identity can be understood only on the basis of the fractures and divisions that have continually reoccurred over this continent's long history. A summary can be found in Konrad Paul Liessmann, *Der Aufgang des Abendlandes: Eine Rekonstruktion Europas* (Vienna, 1994).

49. Gellner, *Nationalismus*, 109.

50. In seventeenth-century Europe, the term apparently meant one's country of origin, so that the town of Mannheim guaranteed immigrants various privileges "with no respect to nations." See "Das Mannheimer Experiment: Einwanderung, Zuwanderung, Multikulti in Deutschland? Die Stadt zwischen Rhein und Neckar hat im 17. Jahrhundert gezeigt, dass das geht," *Die Zeit*, 31 January 2002.
51. Gellner, *Nationalismus*, 114.
52. The quotation can be found in Böckenförde, *Staat, Nation, Europa: Studien zur Staatslehre, Verfassungstheorie und zum Verfassungsrecht* (Frankfurt am Main, 1999), 48.
53. Gellner, *Bedingungen der Freiheit*, 119f.
54. Eisenstadt describes this unity of state and king as follows: "In many of the continental regimes, the state was attributed with an exclusive, secularly defined sovereignty, even if the absolutist kings claimed a form of divine legitimacy, 'kingship by the grace of God.' In the sovereign—the king or the state (*l'état c'est moi*)—they saw, although this was never entirely unchallenged, what was later called the *volonté générale* and embodied the common good. A further innovation, the idea of popular sovereignty, led ... to the Great Revolutions." Eisenstadt, *Die Vielfalt der Moderne*, 41.
55. In an article on the minority question in Europe, Jean De Munck describes this historical situation as follows: "Over the course of the bourgeois revolutions, the democratic ideal gradually assumed a national form, ultimately merging with it entirely. The new regime took possession of the central state as a legacy of the kings it overthrew in order to advance its development." He goes on to say: "Thus, one of the fundamental traits of our historical dynamic is an alliance that nevertheless bears within itself the germ of profound contradictions." De Munck, "Europa und die Minderheitenfrage—eine sich wandelnde Problemstellung," in Dewandre and Lenoble, *Projekt Europa*, 88f.
56. Habermas describes this transformation as follows: "The meaning of 'nation' had thus transformed itself from a pre-political quantity into a characteristic that is constitutive for the political identity of the citizen of a democratic commonwealth.... The citizen's nation discovers its identity not in ethnic-cultural commonalities but rather in the praxis of citizens who actively exercise their democratic rights of participation and communication. Here the republican component of citizenship separated itself completely from affiliation with a pre-political community integrated entirely by origin, shared traditions, and a shared language. Viewed from this perspective, the initial blending of national identity with republican sentiments had a merely catalytic function." Habermas, "Staatsbürgerschaft und nationale Identität," 13.
57. A summary description of these transformations can be found in Böckenförde, *Staat, Nation, Europa*, 48ff.; a comprehensive description can be found in Schulze, *Staat und Nation*.
58. Schulze, *Staat und Nation*, 171f.
59. Kallscheuer and Leggewie explain that the German nation too ultimately rests on the will to form a nation: "The German political code of community formation of/to the nation is ... no less 'voluntaristic' *in statu nascendi* than the 'daily plebiscite' of Ernest Renan. But the subjective will to the nation is first a cultural will whose statehood shows up in a utopian and showy fashion and nevertheless

remains precarious." Kallscheuer and Leggewie, "Deutsche Kulturnation versus französische Staatsnation?" 160.

60. This example is derived from Altermatt's book, in which he points out that this particular constellation is not necessarily advantageous for the affected parties. Altermatt, *Das Fanal von Sarajevo*, 36.

61. A more complete description of developments in Central and Southeastern Europe can be found in Altermatt, *Das Fanal von Sarajevo*, 53ff., and in Gellner, *Nationalismus*, 68ff.

62. In this context, De Munck also points to the abolition of the equation "nation-state = law": "In Strasbourg and Luxembourg, European judges dispense supranational law. This is a new updating of the universality potential of liberal law: the dimension we have shown within the framework of the nation-state, which has freed itself from its first matrix, is now facing a new destiny." De Munck, "Europa und die Minderheitenfrage," 94. Theo Sommer discusses this movement "upward" and "downward" in connection with the sovereignty rights of the states in *Die Zeit*, 22 October 1998.

63. In an article titled "Europa braucht keine gemeinsame Identität," Richard Herzinger summarized some of these reasons in *Die Zeit*, 6 August 1998. In one respect, this point of departure is different: Herzinger rejects a European identity because it is aimed at separation, namely, from the United States. Within the framework of a Romantically conceived European identity, this would indeed be detrimental, particularly for Europe. State political identity, by contrast, entails a transatlantic separation, which will intensify even more when this identity also unfolds on the European level.

64. Dahrendorf uses strong language to describe the situation: "The phenomenon we are currently observing is not localism in a narrow sense but rather regionalism, which I emphatically reject because it threatens the values of the liberal order in a particularly insidious fashion. If it were merely a matter of self-determination for towns and municipalities, then the issue would be less explosive. But here we see the emergence of alleged advocates of regional autonomy or—in extreme cases—proponents of ethnic cleansing.… Today we are observing on the one hand the departure of political decisions from the nation-states to the outside, to frequently unknown and distant authorities, and on the other hand a simultaneous displacement of political decisions inward, toward political units that often are not democratic. I am referring not only to the aggressiveness of people like Bossi and Haider, but also to a diffuse regionalist Romanticism that is anything but liberal. This applies to Scottish and Welsh nationalism as well." Dahrendorf, *Die Krisen der Demokratie*, 28f.

65. The idea of separating political and cultural identity within the framework of the European Union is hardly new. At a colloquium on the topic, "Identity and Difference in Democratic Europe," which was held in May 1991 in Brussels, a number of talks were aimed in this direction. For example, Jean-Marc Ferry asserted: "The European Community could perhaps defuse the identity-related, national or regional particularistic demands by making a clear distinction between the legal realm of the political community and the cultural realm of national identity." Ferry, "Die Relevanz des Postnationalen," in Dewandre and Lenoble, *Projekt Europa*, 33. Schulze has the following to say about the future of the nation:

"Europe does not have to overcome the idea of the nation, but rather the fiction of the fateful, objective, and inescapable unity of people, nation, history, language, and state." Schulze, *Staat und Nation*, 337. A similar consideration in a somewhat different context can be found in Ulrich Steinvorth: "As long as the dominant social form was the tribe or caste, the individual belonged to it, and was scarcely able not to give priority to its values. For [this form] Herder's nationalism was the appropriate attitude; it allowed for collective guilt and collective achievement. Industrial society, which created the modern state and its nation, supersedes this segment-dependent social cohesion and demands that individuals communicate directly with one another. It excludes the possibility that nations will be held together by the same emotional bonds as tribes and castes. It does not transform its individuals into *national* or *people's comrades* [*Volksgenossen*], but rather into *legal comrades* [*Rechtsgenossen*]. To demand nationalism means to transform a nation into a tribe." Steinvorth, "Brauchen wir einen Nationalismus?" in *Aktuelle Fragen der Rechtsphilosophie*, ed. Kurt Seelmann (Frankfurt am Main, 2000), 82 (emphasis added).

66. Liessmann, *Der Aufgang des Abendlandes*, 126.
67. See chapter 1, note 2.
68. Along with various other elements, Gellner mentions "deterritorialization" as an appropriate development to avoid nationalism. Gellner, *Nationalismus*, 177.
69. Regarding the "slumbering state" and "awakening," see note 38.
70. In *Die Zeit*, 14 March 2003, Regina Römhild points to the "Frankfurt Turks" as an example of co-existing cultural identities.
71. Regarding this and the issue of multiple cultural identities, see note 43.
72. In this context, Ferry speaks of a "differentiation between citizenship and citizen status." Ferry, "Die Relevanz des Postnationalen," 33.
73. While every child born in France possesses French citizenship, high formal demands are placed on the acquisition of German citizenship. However, both concepts are being challenged, and it cannot be ruled out that in the long term a convergence will take place, so that the pure *jus soli* in France will be expanded by new conditions and, conversely, the demands of *jus sanguinis* in Germany will be softened.
74. The inclusion of non- or "not yet" citizens in public life largely occurs via civic activities. See the comments in chapter 4, section "The Role of Statehood," subsection "'Civil Society.'"
75. Cf. in this chapter with the section "Community and Statehood," subsection "The Return of Religion."
76. The idea that the separation of statehood from the nation can be seen within the framework of the secularization process is hardly new. Under the heading "Die Entstehung des Staates als Vorgang der Säkularisation," Böckenförde in 1976 had already written the following: "The process of secularization was at once a great process of emancipation, the emancipation of the secular order from conventional religious authorities and ties. It experienced its culmination in the Universal Declaration of Human Rights. Now the individual relied on himself and his freedom. However, in fundamental terms, this could only lead to the problem of new integration: the emancipated individuals had to find their way to a new commonality and homogeneity if the state were not to succumb to inner dissolution, which would then lead to a total control from the outside. This problem remained hidden

at first, since in the nineteenth century a new unifying force took the place of the old: the idea of the nation. The unity of the nation followed the unity of religion and founded a new if more exterior political-oriented homogeneity, within which people continued to base their lives on the tradition of Christian morality. This national homogeneity sought and found its expression in the nation-state. Since then, the idea of the nation has lost this shaping power, and not just in many European states." Böckenförde, *Staat, Gesellschaft, Freiheit*, 59f. Later publications by the same author indicate that he is again emphatically giving the nation an important role in the cohesion of society. Böckenförde, *Staat, Nation, Europa*, 58.

77. Ferry, "Die Relevanz des Postnationalen," 36. Regarding the French nation, the author has the following to say in the same text: "Universalism did not burn itself into the flesh of the [French] people, if one can say this, through an autonomous movement of the regional cultures which form the nation, but rather through the acculturation of individuals torn from their origin. This could only occur through the dogmatic process of a 'determining' and not 'reflecting' movement in the Kantian sense, whose direction ran from top to bottom, from the state to the society, from politics to culture. For this reason, an identity tacked together in this way could permit only monoculturalism in which the nationalistic principle is inherently present."

78. Regarding the "slumbering state" and "awakening," see note 38.

79. One example of this is the Hungarian law on the material support of the Magyar minorities beyond the border, which was passed in October 2001. The Hungarian minister president of the time justified it by saying that the intention was to "vault" the political frontiers, "and thus ... reunite portions of the Hungarian nation" without intending to alter the political frontiers. *Neue Zürcher Zeitung*, 30 October 2001.

80. See note 45.

81. Thus, the Council of Europe's Framework Convention for the Protection of National Minorities expressly states that this protection is granted to persons who belong to minorities, and that these persons can exercise their rights individually or else together with other persons. This also entails a rejection of the concept of group rights.

82. The other state that has taken this position in the European discussion on minorities—particularly within the framework of the Council of Europe—is Turkey. This is largely due to the Kurdish question, since the Turkish government has not been prepared to grant this ethnic group minority status.

83. Altermatt—using terms tailored to East Central Europe—has succinctly formulated it as follows: "One can be federalist without being multinational. But if the state is multinational, then it must be federalist." Altermatt, *Das Fanal von Sarajevo*, 244.

84. Kallscheuer, *Gottes Wort und Volkes Stimme*, 134.

85. Nor is the criterion of citizenship ultimately decisive. Cf. in this chapter the section "The Future of the Nation in Europe," subsection "'Secularization' of the Nation?"

86. Edgar Morin points out that in connection with such experiences, one must also pose the question of guilt: "Europe has taken a few concepts to the extreme and spread them across the world: the breathtaking and insane quest for salvation, religious intolerance, capitalism, totalitarianism, industrialism, technocracy, the unbridled pursuit of profit, the frenetic myth of growth, the destruction of human

cultures and the environment. Europe has spread disaster across the entire world, going back to an exaggerated simplification, one-sidedness, and the extreme magnification of all its developments and historical realizations. We have ourselves suffered the damage we have inflicted and have had to experience the tragedy of nationalisms and totalitarianisms all the way to the bitter end. We are only now slowly starting to come up with antidotes to the evils we have ourselves caused, and we can gradually begin to help the world to dispose of the disaster that we have inflicted upon it." But he also points out that this can lead to perspectives for the future: "If it would renounce the role of the privileged center of the world once and for all, Europe can become for all times a center of reflection and innovation destined to help people on their path to peace, create hospitality (again), and civilize our home soil." Morin, *Europa denken* (Frankfurt am Main, 1991), 220f.

87. In an article marking the 350th anniversary of the Peace of Westphalia, Heinz Schilling wrote: "The secularization of politics lastingly informed the continent's historical-political culture—all the way to the present day. Every European is profoundly shocked when a war of religion flares up, whether in Northern Ireland or in the Balkans, and when elsewhere religious fundamentalism calls for it. The Peace of Westphalia represented a model with which future conflicts could at least be reined in and brought to a solution. This meant the release of a visionary dynamic of the quest for peace that could no longer be suppressed. Viewed this way, both Kant's great blueprint 'On Eternal Peace' of 1796 and the confidence-building measures and conferences on the renunciation of violence in the late twentieth century are founded on the achievement of the Congress of Munster and Osnabrück." *Neue Zürcher Zeitung*, 24–25 October 1998.

88. "The state's monopoly on violence is being annulled from above and below, and can be maintained more or less only within a shrinking middle range," Erhard Eppler explains, estimating that each German policeman is matched by an employee of private security services, while in the United States the ratio is already at 1:3 and 1:4 in California. Eppler, *Vom Gewaltmonopol zum Gewaltmarkt? Die Privatisierung und Kommerzialisierung der Gewalt* (Frankfurt am Main, 2002), 28, 80.

89. "Americans are more loyal to the Constitution than to democracy. They speak of democracy, but that is an abstraction. The Constitution has proved itself for more than 200 years. This has nurtured confidence. Even though people don't exactly know what's in it, they believe in it." Fritz Stern in an interview in *Die Zeit*, 16 November 2000. During a democracy forum in Prague in June 2000, France refused to sign the so-called Warsaw Declaration, which contains the official result of the conference. The report on this occasion provides the corresponding standpoints as follows: "American Secretary of State Albright as the chairperson of a podium discussion of 29 foreign ministers demanded among other things that the democratic states should form an interest group in the UN and other international organizations in order to assert their worldview and to represent the cause of democracy more efficiently. France, however, argued that the conference should not be understood as a starting signal for an 'action program.' An official statement said that the creation of adequate conditions for the promotion of the idea of democracy was a complex matter that allowed no generalizations. Foreign Minister Védrine stated at a press briefing that the West sometimes shows a tendency to view democracy as a sort of faith to which one must merely be converted. Instead,

it is an evolutionary process for which no one has a magic formula." *Neue Zürcher Zeitung*, 28 June 2000.

90. Kersting, *Wohlgeordnete Freiheit*, 205. When examined closely, the term "objective lawlessness"—although the author likely did not intend it this way—accurately describes American legal understanding from the dogmatic perspective of a strict continental European legal tradition. But here again we should note that the transatlantic differences in the legal understanding have very little to do with the differences between the continental European and the Anglo-American legal circle. The only historical connection lies in the fact that the majority of emigrants to the New World came from the English legal system. Precisely the considerations on the conditionality of the legal understanding through the previous or not previous relinquishment of sovereignty make clear the extent to which British legal thought is ultimately European: not only is British state political identity almost axiomatic, but moreover the British are among the inventors of shared solidarity. It was from their stance on this—and not so much from that of the prevailing French aristocracy and royalty—that the immigrants to the New World consciously distanced themselves. See chapter 2, section "Law and Morality," subsection "Legislation and Jurisdiction."

91. Dewandre and Lenoble, *Projekt Europa*, 6.

92. Šarčević, *Die Schlussphase der Verfassungsgebung*, 334.

93. *Neue Zürcher Zeitung*, 27 May 2002.

94. Stahn has called this instrument the "power of veto," holding it responsible not only for blocking the legislature but also for fundamentally promoting the nationalistic point of view: "In connection with the already weak competencies of the total state, the concept of 'ethnic democracy' results less in the integration than the separation of the various population groups in Bosnia-Herzegovina; even worse, it almost looks as if it has contributed to the legitimacy of the ethnic nationalism practices on the level of the member states." Stahn, "Die verfassungsrechtliche Pflicht," 677f.

95. In a statement on the accession of Bosnia-Herzegovina to the Council of Europe, which preceded its membership in April 2002, the Parliamentary Assembly emphasized that the institutions of the total state must be strengthened, whereby it expressly considered a revision of the constitution.

Chapter 4

Western Europe

For more than half a century, Western Europe has enjoyed the great privilege of having been able to build upon a peace order that the East Central European countries could not even consider joining until 1989. This involves a great responsibility on the part of Western Europe, with the farsightedness that experience has brought it, to stand up for the identity of this continent, which is finally growing back together. At the same time, Western Europe would be ill advised to underestimate the political—and peace-affecting—dynamite that East Central Europe could bring into the great European marriage if this part of the continent were to adopt American intellectual traditions. Because of its history in the second half of the twentieth century, Eastern Europe is more receptive to such traditions than Western Europe. But in Western Europe too, and thus across the entire continent, one can discern an Americanization that affects both the economic sector and lifestyles. Europe has a long tradition of dealing with the "other" and the "foreign," and it knows how to take good advantage of the great enrichment that this new situation brings. On the surface, neither economics nor lifestyles have any connection with state political identity. Such a connection emerges when economics and lifestyles demand other state political parameters than those that the European tradition has allowed so far. An evaluation of this development is possible only on the basis of an unprejudiced debate over the differences that have existed between Europe and the United States from the beginning. Fortunately, efforts are being made at better understanding these differences in both Western and East Central Europe.

Notes for this chapter begin on page 155.

Understanding the differences does not mean passing judgment in favor of one or the other shore of the Atlantic. This is not a question of moral appraisal. It is simply a matter of understanding how and to what extent Europe is different from the United States or—viewed chronologically—why the United States is different from Europe. And based on this, Europeans are particularly concerned with recognizing to what extent the foundations of European identity in the state political sector can be shaken over decisive questions. The American self-conception goes back to a centuries-old demarcation of the New World from the Old. This does not mean that no one in the United States is acquainted with European ideas. Particularly in the wake of the September 11 terrorist attacks, many voices have made themselves heard in public, since this event has been interpreted so differently on both sides of the Atlantic. However, in this book we are concerned not so much with differences between individual persons but rather with the social backing in which these differences manifest themselves. To the extent that European identity deviates from American identity, its core affects statehood and law. We shall now examine these two areas more closely.

The Role of Statehood

When Europeans discuss state functions, they are usually concerned with economic questions, such as how much of a welfare state is appropriate today and whether the market economy in Europe should or can continue to be a social one. It would be an illusion to assume that these discussions are solely about economic concerns. If Europe were to start adopting the American social welfare model, this would entail a rapprochement with the American understanding of law and the way that the country deals with violence. Such an outcome would not be primarily a direct effect of a revamped social policy on these other two areas. Instead, such a rapprochement would weaken the European notion of shared sovereignty upon which these two areas are based. Without a doubt, the economic and non-economic roles of the state are directly dependent on each other, and without a doubt an effective welfare state also contributes to state political identity in general. However, state political identity can by no means be solely attributed to economic factors. The opposite is more frequently the case: the invention of the social market economy in Europe was derived from the philosophy of an existential affiliation, which is based on shared sovereignty. This philosophy may well resonate in current economic discussions, but it is rarely mentioned by name since politicians who are acquainted with economics speak relatively rarely about legal and state philosophy, which does not mean that they are not interested in such things. The European philosophy of existential affiliation has had a profound influence on economics, and yet its foundation and its effects go far beyond economics. And when economic and non-economic motives lead to different actions, non-economic motives can easily gain the upper hand. The wars in the Balkans have again reminded us of the tremendous irrationality with which non-economic motives can sweep away economic ones: monolithic ethnic identity fundamentally excludes European state political identity, even among economically privileged people. Nationalism, racism, and xenophobia have long since ceased being only a consequence of economic deprivation, even if one can show that economic insecurity promotes these phenomena.[1]

If in the following—as we have already seen in previous discussions—we speak of statehood, and only in exceptional cases of the state, this is intended to illustrate how state political identity in Europe is beginning to expand both upward and downward. My comments on this issue are aimed at these (to some extent) new levels, just as they are aimed at the traditional "nation" state, so that my choice of words is pointed more at the future than at the past. At the same time, they express how state political identity today can be observed as becoming increasingly separated from national identity, even if this separation process in Europe is in some cases further and in others less advanced, or is even just at the beginning stages, which, however, should not exclude a future-oriented mode of expression.

Denationalization as an Ideology

Today, with the search on for new forms of cooperation between state and non-state authorities and institutions, state activity is undergoing a transformation. Even if such changes are occasionally discussed under the category of "privatization," one cannot really say anything against them, since within a well-conceived interaction, effective results can be achieved that can just as easily accommodate the increasing individualization as the earlier, purely state solutions. The basic condition for such solutions is still ultimate control by the state, particularly the state's guarantee of equal treatment.[2] The boundaries for the acceptance of this transformation lie at the point where this notion transforms itself entirely into an ideology of denationalization or "destatification." Ideologies are thought constructs that cannot be logically explained, only believed. The quest for new and meaningful forms of interaction between the public sector and private actors, which can efficiently ensure the implementation of the European philosophy of an existential affiliation, is not ideological in itself. However, some privatization efforts are undertaken solely for the sake of privatization itself, ending up as a sort of "ideology of denationalization." In East Central Europe, where there was a certain need for privatization in light of the previous state-run economies, it is not easy to recognize the boundary along which this shift from rational reforms to pure ideology is taking place. In Western Europe, consultancy firms, whose headquarters are often located in the United States, are now hard at work. Their employees, infused with a self-assurance that betrays an ideological background, take the idea of privatization straight to the public administrations. The consequences of denationalization in the economic sector are ascertainable and are discussed in numerical terms. In the non-state sector, however, denationalization is largely hidden, which brings with it the danger of a gradual displacement of the European philosophy of existential affiliation and its substitution with American affiliation, which, as we have seen, has to be fought for. This process of displacement would become problematic for Europe as soon as shared sovereignty is encroached upon, although people probably would not notice it much at first since Europeans are not particularly aware of this centuries-old background. Over time, such a growing refusal to share sovereignty would manifest itself directly in an increasing, ideologically motivated rejection of statehood. Indirectly, it would show up in a gradual rejection of the European integration process, since individual shared sovereignty is inextricably linked with the state's shared sovereignty, which forms the basis of this integration process. In other words, to the extent that Europe is being Americanized, and to the extent that this is adding up to an ideology of denationalization, in the long term this will have an impact not only on the European understanding of freedom but also on the European peace order.

As an ideology, denationalization has further consequences in the non-economic sector in the way that it weakens statehood as a public order structure—an order structure that has so far ensured Europe's social cohesion. Every society needs and possesses a public order structure. If this order is not based on statehood, then something else takes its place. Since the ideology of denationalization has an American background, one can surmise what elements are waiting in the wings to serve as a public order structure—namely, the community, based on religious elements, which we described in the preceding chapter. We can look to the axiomatic term "clash of civilizations" for an example. The American political scientist Samuel Huntington uses this term to describe a confrontation caused by the collision of cultures that are characterized by different religions. Huntington casually deposits Europe into a camp in which this old continent does not actually fit with regard to its understanding of the state, the nation, and religion—namely, the camp of the American-dominated West. Now there is no question that Europe sees itself as part of the West, but within this West there are fundamental differences that directly influence dealings with other cultural groups and religions. "Huntington's paradigm of cultural conflict ... practically throws us directly back into the age of the wars of religion and refutes the entire European tradition of rational peace policies," Wolfgang Kersting notes.[3] Many contemporary developments in the transatlantic tug-of-war can be understood only when we look back at the year 1648. Today it is simply not true that denationalization is resulting in infinite freedom, no matter what the protagonists of the ideology of denationalization may understand by freedom. Something else is taking the place of statehood, and that something is religion.[4] It manifests itself directly in either religious or moral categories that demand adherence without a protective filter in the form of legislation.

An individual freed of statehood seeks attachment. When state political identity fades, then another attachment must step up to fill its place. After all, every person needs a balanced relationship between freedom and attachment, whether or not he or she is aware of it. Thus, denationalization is concerned not so much with more or less freedom, but rather with the question of how freedom is defined. Lacking a state political identity, Americans to some extent need to commit themselves to "voluntary communities" in order to balance freedom and attachment. National identity, reinforced by religious elements, ensures social cohesion. In Europe, this cohesion is guaranteed by state political identity; conversely, Europeans have the possibility of designing their lives free of commitments and free of attachments to communities, leaving national identity behind. Denationalization therefore involves two movements: on the one hand, shifting freedom from one area to another and, on the other, shifting attachment from one area to another.

In concrete terms, denationalization might mean that the value of individual shared sovereignty could be transformed from something positive into something negative. In Europe, denationalization is turning the clock backwards, all the way to the crossroads of 1648, only to turn the relationship between the state and religion on its head. As if that were not enough, the fact that nationalism replaced religion in Europe is a historical phenomenon that nothing can reverse. That is why not only statehood has been able to take the place of religion, but nationalism, too.

A third factor exists in all societies, whenever and wherever these societies are or were located on this planet. This third factor goes beyond purely horizontal relationships between individuals. It provides society with cohesion and allows the individual to develop a social identity that reaches beyond these horizontal relationships. At the dawn of humanity, this third factor was religion. Later, the third aspect was generally a mixture of religion and the state. In the Middle Ages the state and religion began competing more and more, as both claimed to embody this third factor. In 1648, the state won in Europe, and religion won across the Atlantic. When Romanticism later invented the nation, this served on both sides of the Atlantic as a cloak for the respective third factor: the United States dressed religion in the cloak of the nation, whereas Europe dressed the state in the mantle of the nation. In today's Europe, the third factor—that is, statehood—is gradually starting to take off the mantle of the nation. Some of the bloodstains on this mantle are fresh, others are faded, and the cloak is threadbare. Only now are people becoming aware that the third factor really is not the same on both sides of the Atlantic. In fact, it has not ever been the same: the two cloaks in which the third factor has been dressed on both sides look very similar.

And thus it is no accident that people across the Atlantic are looking with irritation at what is emerging from the cloak that Europe is slowly dropping from its shoulders, namely, Europe's statehood and the state political identity of Europeans. People in the United States thought that they had left what is now coming to light definitively behind them. Religion, which makes up the third factor across the Atlantic, will not take off the cloak of the nation in the coming decades, because in the United States people cannot conceive of religion without the mantle of the nation. Statehood and the nation have fit together quite well in Europe over the past 200 years. However, the wheel of history has kept turning, and suddenly we are realizing that the shedding of the cloak has been in the works for a long time. Every society—including European society—needs a third factor. In Europe and the United States, this third factor is either statehood or religion. It is never both at once, and it is always one or the other. It cannot be the nation alone, because the nation is only the cloak. If one takes away a people's third factor, then another third factor is immediately created as a replacement for what has been taken away. In Europe, statehood is a very valuable, intellectual historical asset.

"Civil Society"

Language often reveals much more than one would assume. First, let us take a look at the change in meaning that the words "civil" and "civilian" have recently undergone. Until a few years ago, "civil" was an antonym of "military." It was also used in the sense of "civilized" and referred to the non-violent resolution of conflicts. In humanitarian international law, the "civilian population" referred to non-military persons in general. If there was no need to distinguish military matters, then people spoke simply of "the population." Today, this use of "population" has practically vanished from the media's vocabulary. Hurricane X threatens the "civilian population," and such natural disasters make no distinction between military and non-military facilities. It is true that "civilian" is still used as an antonym of "military" or in the sense of "civilized," but the word also seems to have become an antonym in other spheres as well. In the discussion over sanctions against Zimbabwe and also Iraq, we heard how sanctions should be permitted to affect only the government of these states, not the civilian population. The word "civil" seems to be gradually moving toward the "for/against governments" axis—that is, toward "non-governmental"—and thus into the vicinity of the various efforts surrounding the value of statehood.

The word "society" has experienced a similar fate. It is also rarely heard in today's usage. "In recent decades, a new ideal was born or reborn: civil society. Previously, one could assume that a person who was interested in the concept of civil society was an intellectual historian studying Locke or Hegel. But the expression itself remained without any contemporary resonance and evocative power; in fact, it seemed dreadfully outmoded. Now it has been suddenly lifted up, thoroughly dusted off, and has become a radiant symbol." That is how Ernest Gellner begins his book on civil society, and this quotation can be found under the title "A Catch Phrase is Born."[5] There is scarcely another term that is used in so many different meanings as "civil society," whereby some of these interpretations are diametrically opposed to and mutually exclude one another.[6]

In Germany, the term *Bürgergesellschaft* (citizen's society) has asserted itself as a translation for the English term "civil society." "This refers to the civic identity that is contained within society, i.e., the political culture and the various underlying organizations and institutions that lie outside of the direct state power apparatus, i.e., the associations and self-administering bodies, the notability structures, moral courage etc."[7] This understanding of civil society is concerned with the various associations and organizations in which the individual can form an opinion and perform activities for the sake of activity or in order to exert influence on political events. This social association not only is reconcilable with the European understanding of state political identity but actually strengthens it, even if new forms of interaction between state and non-state authorities are being pursued. It may be that a strengthening of this identity will lead to new forms of this kind to the extent that the previously mentioned parameters of equal treatment and democratic control are not affected.

At the same time, however, there is also an understanding of civil society through which attempts are made to repress state political identity and replace it with a community-oriented identity, which, as we have seen in the preceding chapter, is an American-influenced notion. One striking example of this is the American publication *To Empower People: From State to Civil Society*, which first appeared in 1979 and was republished with new commentaries in 1996.[8] Its stirring prose informs us of the "resurrection of civil society," which is preparing to square off against statehood through a "mediation structure project." "No longer understood to be the instrument of high national purpose, the federal government comes to be seen instead as a distant, alienating, bureaucratic monstrosity. In the wake of this development, it was inevitable that the American people would return to the idea of community that finds expression in small participatory groups such as family, neighborhood, and ethnic and voluntary associations—an idea far more natural and easier to sustain."[9] And in response to the title question, "What is the role of civil society?" we are given an impressively clear answer:

The term for all these non-statist forms of social life—those rooted in social human nature, under the sway of reason—is *civil society*. That term includes natural associations such as the family, as well as the churches, and private associations of many sorts: fraternal, ethnic, and patriotic societies; voluntary organizations such as the Boy Scouts, the Red Cross, and Save the Whales; and committees for the arts, the sciences, sports, and education. Human associations come in a multitude of forms. Civil society is normally 'thick' with many types of civic association. In free and complex societies such as those of Western Europe and the United States, a single individual is likely to belong to many different associations at once. Some are natural (the family), some are voluntary but endure across generations, and still others are founded for limited purposes and are quite transitory. In a sense, therefore, the 'mediation structures project' is simultaneously a project in the strengthening of civil society, as defined against the state.

Finally, the author of these lines goes on to put forward a vision for the twenty-first century: "The logic of the past 60 years led to an overpromising, under-achieving state. A correction, of course, is both essential and healthy. If the twentieth century unfolded under the sign of the state, pictured as a beneficent mother sheltering her children at her bosom, the twenty-first century is likelier to see a rebirth of the idea of freedom, in communities of men and women eager to practice self-government both in their private and in their public lives."[10] This publication represents the starting point for the core concept of "compassionate conservatism," which reaches far beyond the party of the current president and has found followers in the camp of the Democratic Party. Its adherents no longer wish to administer welfare through state agencies but increasingly through church organizations, not least in the declared intention of using such benefits to exert a spiritual influence on the needy.[11]

Among all the different meanings attributed to the term "civil society," we can make a fundamental distinction between a "denationalizing" concept of civil society that has its roots across the Atlantic, and one that is suitable to supporting and promoting state political identity on the European pattern. These two concepts mutually exclude one another.[12] Against the background of an American understanding of the state, it makes sense to put civil society in place of state institutions. However, this presupposes that the public order structure is derived from other coordinates, namely, communal, religious, and national ones. This is in contrast to the European notion of civil society, which thrives only within the framework of state political identity. If the basic state political structure is lacking, then all efforts are in vain. For years I observed how in Bosnia countless representatives of non-state organizations, both individuals and those coming from international or national projects, crisscrossed the country with the good intention of calling civil society to life, while what the country truly and desperately needed was state political identity, and what its inhabitants needed was civic identity in order to overcome the monolithic ethnic identity. A civil society in the European understanding of the term cannot be brought to bear without the state political identity of its members. And civil society in the American understanding makes no sense in Europe.[13]

In Europe, the term *Bürgergesellschaft* is a happier choice than civil society, even though it too can be interpreted in different ways. When using both terms, it is essential to state exactly what one means. If the term is used in both the European and American understanding, this can give rise to some unforeseen situations. The activity of international development helpers from all over the world in crisis regions, where they are involved in the reconstructions of state structures, can result in highly contradictory signals being sent to the inhabitants of their respective countries, which in turn can lead to confusion in the public discussion. And this can trigger activities that mutually neutralize one another. It is hardly surprising that the American "destatifying" concept of civil society is being hawked on the East Central European marketplace, since this is a result of the revolutions of 1989, as we have described them in the preceding chapter. It is much more surprising that this concept is also showing up on the Western European marketplace. One reason for this could be the relatively brief period of time that has passed since 1989. The transatlantic differences—particularly those of an intellectual historical nature—have just recently emerged from the shadow of the Cold War and are only now being noticed.

The Pivotal Role of Law

For those who wish to compare the European and American understandings of law, there is a somewhat abbreviated formula that can be applied both to legal relations between private persons and to those between states: Europe requires the "strength of the law," while the United States is satisfied with the "law of the stronger."[14] Only if certain conditions are fulfilled can Europe use the concrete scope of action that is present in the sector of law. First of all, Europe's legal political identity must be clearly and directly established, including its background and objectives, particularly in those areas where it differs from the American identity. Second, this identity must be made clear in a consistent fashion. And, third, it must be represented with absolute consistency on the international stage. If this does not occur, a vicious circle ensues. If the "strength of the law" and the "law of the stronger" concepts face off against each other, this does not mean that justice and injustice are facing off, but simply that they are different concepts. Thus, it makes no sense for the proponent of the "strength of the law" to tell the protagonist of the "law of the stronger" that he is standing up for *the strength of the law*, because the protagonist of this opposing position immediately announces his agreement, since he understands law as the "law of the stronger," which the other person certainly did not mean. The conflict really gets underway when the use of the term "law" is challenged, and the legal and state political identity behind each legal understanding is named. And since every protagonist of the concept of the "law of the stronger" will talk only to a negotiating partner considered strong enough, the proponent of the "strength of the law" needs a dual strategy: he has to use his opponent's method to get his point across, for otherwise he will achieve nothing.

Europe in particular will achieve nothing if it criticizes the United States for its behavior on moral grounds, first, because this interests very few people across the Atlantic, and, second, because no one will understand it anyway, since the moral premises on the two shores are simply too different. Only one language is understood across the Atlantic—that of clear and consistent political behavior that is adhered to without fail.[15] Europe's best chance lies in stating clearly what it intends to do, citing what principles it bases these intentions on, and keeping strictly to those principles.

To try to frame the confrontation between both concepts as a moral issue makes least sense of all. Each shore of the Atlantic simply has its own centuries-old intellectual history. Today, both concepts are colliding more and more often—and more and more intensively—because the world has become so small. In the spring of 2000, in an article titled "A Protectorate Becomes Independent," Egon Bahr described Europe's future as follows: "The relinquishment of violence represents the contractual implementation of a realization: the right of the stronger is the right that is also binding for the stronger. Europe will have discovered a silver bullet if it turns its weakness into a strength by using treaties, controllable attachments, cooperation, and preventive diplomacy to create a stability in which the preponderance of the military is reduced."[16] He later continued this idea, suggesting a possible "division of labor" between the United States and Europe: "If America develops its military backdrop, then Europe should develop its political sector so that the military may remain unused to the greatest extent possible. This would be a division of labor that would not take away any of America's strength and would perhaps even avoid a war, and it would also give the weaker, i.e., most countries, the opportunity to demand the strength of law."[17]

The intriguing thing about this division of labor—going back to the metaphor of the backdrop—is the way that two stages can be installed in two different sections of the same theater. The stage in front of the military backdrop will always resound to the music of the "law of the stronger," with its powerful kettledrums. That fits the backdrop. But on the other stage, in front of the non-military backdrop, the melody of the "strength of law" can be played as long as enough orchestra members can be found who know how to play the music. And because of the separation of the two stage areas, this melody can be clearly heard in the other part of the theater, undisturbed by the powerful drumbeats from across the way. Since the terrorist attacks of September 11, no one can close their eyes to the fact that differences have arisen between Europe and the United States, all of which range along the axis of the "strength of law" and the "law of the stronger." They particularly touch on the future international legal order, whether one sees this as classic international law or as a preliminary stage in the development of a future "world law." The stocktaking is simple: "The US is no longer prepared to accept international accountability. Just as it continually rejects agreements that would impose equal obligations on the superpower like those placed on other countries, it also wants to keep international law away from its borders," analyzes Christian Schmidt-Häuer.[18] In pure power political terms, we cannot now pursue whether Europe will be granted a role in the conflict between the United States and the "rest of the world," and, if so, what that role might be. Instead, we should merely ask about Europe's role in the intellectual historical aspect of this conflict. Like no other continent, Europe is in a position to analyze the intellectual historical roots of the current discord over the emergence or non-emergence of an international legal order and to derive behavioral perspectives from this analysis. In these matters of identity, which underlie the resistance of the United States to the growth of an international legal order, the New World across the Atlantic has always been developing as the antithesis of Europe.

In the following—and these are examples, not a systematic analysis—I would like to focus on a couple of topics in which we can see the early symptoms of an Americanization of European legal thought. If Europe wishes to perform its role in the intellectual historical analysis of the transatlantic differences, it will need to show great sensitivity in this regard. These examples are restricted to the area of human rights and international law.[19] Europe is hardly influenced by the American legal tradition. Nevertheless, for the sake of completeness I would like to mention that transatlantic differences in legal thought are occasionally discussed in the United States too, and not only in an anti-European sense. On the contrary, the interest that Americans show in the European legal tradition is frequently rooted in their own search for alternatives.[20]

Legal Order and "Voluntarism"

In Europe the relinquishment and sharing of individual sovereignty has led to the formation of statehood, within whose framework the citizens, in a democratic process, decide on a shared legal order to which they all equally submit themselves. Within this legal order there are areas in which all those who submit to the law have to act the same—namely, "obligatorily"—and other areas in which action is "voluntary." School attendance for children is obligatory, street traffic rules are obligatory, security measures are generally obligatory since they would not work otherwise, just to name a few examples. Everything that is not obligatory is regarded as voluntary. However, this area is also subject to the shared legal order, which goes back to the sharing of individual sovereignty.[21] Defined differently and meaning the same as "non-state," the American understanding of "voluntarism" is actually the opposite of the sharing of individual sovereignty, which has a negative connotation across the Atlantic. But since the European conception of the legal order requires the sharing of individual sovereignty, the American notion of voluntarism can also be used as an antonym for the European understanding of the legal order. Of course, there is an aspect of voluntarism that applies to both sides of the Atlantic in the definition stated above. This is the idea that a certain behavior should not be prescribed or forbidden by law. Instead, the hope that private persons will behave appropriately of their own volition—that is, that they will do or will not do something voluntarily—also makes sense in European usage. To the extent that "voluntary" is an antonym for a legally binding regulation, this term has the same meaning on both sides of the Atlantic. One example of the implementation of this kind of voluntarism is the creation of certain labels. Manufacturers are allowed to furnish their products with these labels as long as specific guidelines are maintained. Ecological concerns, for example, are implemented in this way by using market mechanisms, and this sometimes works more quickly than legal regulations. This is also an example of the search for new forms of cooperation by state and non-state authorities and institutions.

On the "non-voluntary" end of the scale—which on this side of the Atlantic runs from "voluntary" to "obligatory" and across the Atlantic runs from "voluntary" to "state"—we find similar regulations, for example, the rule of driving on the right or left side of the road. However, only this end of the scale is identical. At the other end, the paths go their separate ways because these antonyms are not genuine opposites. One example of this transatlantic difference is so-called volunteer work, which Americans call all those activities that proceed from the network of the countless "voluntary associations" and that take the place of the state. When the United Nations proclaimed an International Year of Volunteers, this basically made sense for Europe, too, and that year discussions began in many European states on the relationship between paid and unpaid work, on activities during "leisure time" alongside one's profession, on how people view their main profession vis-à-vis part-time work, on activities aimed mainly at the common good, and on the concept of "honorary positions" and other terms. Above all, people discussed the anchoring of this kind of activity in a supportive environment. What makes no sense for Europe, however, is calling these kinds of activities "volunteer work," which is linguistically meaningless. This term lacks any foundation in Europe because "voluntary" does not mean "non-state" but rather "non-obligatory." When the term is nevertheless used in Europe, it ends up bringing a denationalizing element into usage, which hardly anyone notices but which for that reason is all the more problematic.

The fact that the concept of voluntarism cannot be applied to Europe in the American sense is also demonstrated by the transference of this term to the area of international law, as was recently undertaken by the US Department of Defense. In a retrospective analysis of the war in Afghanistan and a look into the future, the department characterized the strategy of the United States as follows: in the twenty-first century, wars would be waged by "coalitions of the willing" under American leadership. It emphasized that the United States itself had taken command of military actions in the Afghan war, but deliberately refused to give the coalition partners a voice in the war's objectives.[22] This concept of a "coalition of the willing" represents the elevation of a kind of volunteer ideology up to the level of international law. Here we can discover a complete analogy to shared sovereignty. Just as the American interpretation of voluntarism in the individual sphere means that the individual does not want to submit to any legal regulations that would thus be applicable to everyone since Americans are not willing to relinquish their sovereign, fundamental freedom for the sake of a shared legal order, at the same time the United States apparently does not want to enter into any consultations with its allies because it demands unrestricted and absolute sovereignty at all times and is not willing to consider even the slightest relinquishment of this sovereignty. The concept of the "coalition of the willing" undermines the comprehensive involvement of the international community and serves to weaken the international legal order. Voluntarism on the American pattern is the opposite of the relinquishment of international sovereignty, just as the American notion of voluntarism in the sense of the "coalition of the willing" is the opposite of the relinquishment of state sovereignty. As intended by its creators, this neologism is promoting the process by which the "law of the stronger" is taking the place of the "strength of the law."

It is thus essential to undertake a cautious demarcation between the level of existing state legislation and the international level. In the inner-state sector, voluntarism can be meaningful within an atmosphere of good cooperation with legal regulations. To the extent that this is the case on the inner-state level, there is nothing to be said against a parallel approach on the international level. If, however, such an effort is aimed at creating a future international legal order, whether one views it as classic international law or as the preliminary stage of a future world law, the call for voluntarism practically amounts to the replacement of the "strength of law" by the "law of the stronger." One of the most blatant examples of what from the European point of view must appear as a negative implementation of voluntarism is the matter of human rights. It would be gratifying if internationally active corporations would commit themselves to maintaining at least minimal human rights guarantees. If, however, they ensure that the states upon which they exert influence do not recognize international human rights conventions and particularly individual complaints, then this can have fateful consequences—the privatization of human rights. The officials responsible for internationally active corporations are even open about how they recognize privately negotiated human rights guarantees with the intention of avoiding state norms.[23]

For all of these reasons, Europe should be cautious with the concept of voluntarism. As with "civil society," one can always find a more precise term for what one is really trying to say. Substitutes for "voluntarism" can be such previously mentioned terms as "paid and unpaid labor," "honorary positions," "community work," or others that remain to be defined. The fact that in Germany, for example, a survey committee has been set up "for the future of civil involvement," and that this term is now used as the generic term for the entire range of issues, reveals an awareness of the problem. But once again, we must take note that Europeans have only begun developing their own sensitivity to such matters for just over a decade. So much for the current treatment of voluntarism on the individual level.

As far as the state level and the voluntary participation of states in future "coalitions of the willing" are concerned, this issue is understandably explosive for Europe, and perhaps another image of the two stages in the single theater can help. The military aspect is presented on the stage in front of the military backdrop in a building where the rhythm of powerful drumbeats can be heard, and it may be that some European states will still want to play their individual roles there for a while. However, the issue has an international law dimension, which is presented on the stage in front of the non-military backdrop. Since the melody of the "strength of law" can be played here without being rocked by the powerful drumbeats of the other stage, it appears that we cannot entirely exclude the possibility that at least on this stage a common European position may be formed. No doubt it is still too early to dream that the two stages could be placed under a single director, since the intriguing aspect of this image lies in the fact that the two stages are currently kept separate, so that the "strength of law" can take shape without being hindered by the "law of the stronger."

Human Rights and International Criminal Law

The statute of the International Criminal Court went into effect just four years after its promulgation in Rome when 60 states ratified this treaty under international law. This represents great progress. We have already seen why the United States fought against this criminal court, and there is no need to return to this issue. I will, however, point to a different aspect, which I would like to illustrate by relating an experience I had. While I was working in Bosnia, whenever I mentioned the function I was performing, both in the country itself and at conferences in Western or East Central Europe or in other discussions, probably 9 out of 10 people spontaneously assumed that I was collecting material in Bosnia for the indictments before the International Tribunal in The Hague. Even after I briefly explained the tasks of my institution—namely, receiving complaints about human rights violations—many of my discussion partners were eager to know whether I passed information to the prosecution authorities whenever I happened upon such material. I experienced countless discussions of this kind, and it became obvious that there was a broad public conception that measures to protect human rights were largely focused on the prosecution of persons who had taken part in human rights violations as offenders. This public impression has continued to grow in recent years. Before I present the problems this view entails, let me state again that the establishment of the International Criminal Court, as it was created with the Rome Statute on 17 July 1998, is a great achievement of human history.

In its legal classification, this achievement is only marginally concerned with the classic protection of human rights. Criminal law regulates the violation of protected legal assets committed by *individuals*, and inner-state criminal law has formulated an extensive catalogue of crimes, whereas international criminal law is currently restricted to genocide, crimes against humanity, and war crimes. By contrast, human rights can be violated only by *states*, and these states act through authorities as well as individuals in state functions, or in any case through individuals presuming to fulfill state functions. This brief and cruel but crystal-clear example can illustrate the difference. When one person brutally murders another, then that is a murder that is prosecuted and punished by the state. Life is a legal asset protected by the state, and anyone who violates such a legal asset will be held legally accountable. However, this case does not represent a violation of human rights. But if one person brutally kills another and a policeman stands alongside and does nothing, then this is both a murder *and* a violation of human rights: the murder was committed by the assailant, but the human rights violation was committed by the policeman, who could have acted in the name of the state and applied the state's monopoly on force, but who did not fulfill his state protective function. We exhaustively examined the post-war situation in Bosnia in chapter 1. It is evident that in this "lawless and stateless" society, situations like the one described here stood at the very center of our work, even if, fortunately, they eventually diminished in frequency. The constellation underlying the comparison presented above was so central because many authorities and the police had slipped into a mono-lithic ethnic identity, even if they were not among the nationalistic hard-liners. However, acting in the name of an ethnic group is not the same thing as acting in the name of the state, so that the notions of "private" and "public" became blurred. Private persons turned into defenders of public order, which was thus denationalized, that is, privatized.

If we wish to preserve human rights—certainly the greatest human achieve-ment of the past century—we need to make a consistently clear distinction between, on the one hand, state-protected legal assets that are violated by private persons, and on the other, human rights assets that are violated by states. Even if these legal assets are the same—life, physical integrity, or prop-erty—the two situations are entirely different. In the first situation, exclusively private persons are involved in the violation, as victims and perpetrators. The state arrives on the scene as a prosecutor and judge in the subsequent criminal procedure, possibly ruling on the victim's compensation demands toward the perpetrator, and the state will at most be active on the basis of victim assistance legislation.[24] Individuals have always been called to account on criminal charges. In the human rights sector, however, the breakthrough to codification do not occur until after World War II, when it became pos-sible to call states to account, namely, in suits dealing with classic protection of human rights before the international bodies of the international commu-nity. The basic pattern for this procedure derives from Anglo-Saxon law. It has asserted itself worldwide in human rights issues and has seen its greatest implementation so far in Europe.

Since the beginnings of the international codification of human rights, there has always been an inner connection between these rights and criminal law in the way that the rights of criminals, particularly those of imprisoned persons, have been specified: prison conditions, protection from torture, the rights of the accused on trial. By contrast, the discussion of the victims of crimes in connection with human rights is a relatively recent phenomenon, and the discussion surrounding it should be conducted with great conceptual clarity. The introduction of international criminal law—and this is the issue in the proceedings before the International Criminal Court—also serves to protect human rights, but this is the sole point that international criminal law and the classic protection of human rights have in common. The totality of the protection of human rights consists of three categories: the classic protection of human rights, humanitarian international law, and international criminal law. The classic protection of human rights represents the main axis along which the idea of human rights has developed continually since 1948. It is suitable for peacetime and also retains certain functions in emergencies—that is, in times of human rights "relapses." Humanitarian international law, by contrast, and international criminal law are applied only in emergency situations where there have already been massive and particularly grievous human rights violations. The main axis of the classic protection of human rights also retains an important function during these emergency situations, because it defines which human rights are to be respected.[25] In emergency situations, however, humanitarian international law and international criminal law come to the rescue. It is only in exceptional circumstances that international criminal law becomes a kind of "extended arm" of the general protection of human rights.[26]

If—as increasingly appears to be the case—international criminal law is viewed as the main axis in the protection of human rights, then this represents an enormous weakening of the idea of human rights, since the perspective is narrowed to crisis situations. It would be equivalent to declaring that general international law is not so important because, after all, humanitarian international law is always there for emergencies. Furthermore, it narrows the perspective to individuals and distracts attention from the responsibility of states. It creates an "individualization" in public opinion regarding the responsibility for human rights violations, and this is one point where an Americanization of the European understanding of law could occur. In order to explain this, we have to return to the difference in the transatlantic understanding of law and the state, which appears again in the different understanding of human rights and displays itself clearly in the historical development since World War II. The Universal Declaration of Human Rights first began in the private apartment of Eleanor Roosevelt, then the chair of the UN Commission on Human Rights and the widow of the president of the United States. In February 1947, she had invited like-minded women and men to her home, an act that changed the world and whose importance cannot be overestimated.[27] It was intended that such a declaration would strengthen awareness of human rights throughout the world. This action thus represented the implementation of a moral appeal. At practically the same time, a Briton reached for his pen and drafted the European Convention on Human Rights, which includes enforcement mechanisms and the Court of Justice, so that this convention could be passed just two years after the Universal Declaration. This can be attributed to Europe's singular dismay over the events of World War II.

However, a further reason lies in the fact that if Europe wishes to remain true to its intellectual historical tradition, it must transform moral notions into law. And because in Europe the state represents a third factor reaching beyond the purely horizontal social contract, the transference of active responsibility for the implementation of human rights to this state—and holding it accountable to the community of states—is seen as a necessity, for otherwise, according to the European understanding of the state, not all actors would have been included. For the legal understanding across the Atlantic, a pure declaration was completely sufficient, since moral principles flow directly into the society and into the conduct of cases before the court. In Europe, by contrast, there is a need to include basic human rights norms in legal regulations.[28] Thus, already in 1948, Europe and the United States viewed the concept of human rights in different ways, both in line with their centuries-old conditioning. It is therefore no accident that Europe immediately went one step further. But it is also no accident that the United States has continually rejected and opposed binding and actionable norms, and it is ultimately no accident that the worldwide community of states moves between these two goalposts within the framework of the United Nations, but always toward the goalpost that seeks the imposition of law.

With the establishment of the International Criminal Court, a discussion has emerged along the same lines, and it is anything but coincidental. An argument has been raised that international criminal law represents the highest level of the guarantee of human rights since the sanction opportunities it opens up provide human rights guarantees with the most intensive form of legal protection on the international level. European lawyers immediately challenged this idea, among other things with the previous definition of the role of international criminal law and its relationship to the classic protection of human rights: "With its deterrent effects, international criminal law contributes to the creation of the peace conditions that are required for the very existence of state structures, within which the implementation of universal values can be guaranteed. Ultimately, *states* bear classic responsibility for human rights protection norms."[29]

The thesis according to which international criminal law is the highest and most effective defense of human rights rests on the American understanding of law and the state, which not only makes no sense for Europe but can also weaken Europe's human rights culture, particularly because it promotes a denationalization of human rights by individualizing them. The fact that ever since the arrest of General Pinochet in Great Britain—in itself a purely criminal law matter—dictators can no longer travel the world at will is an extremely positive development. But it can remain positive only if it is not classified incorrectly. It would be disastrous to personalize the human rights violations in Chile to such a degree that the matter can be viewed as at an end the moment that the dictator dies. Whoever tortured others in Chile must still be called to account after the dictator's death. In human rights terms, the state is and always remains responsible, and the individual perpetrator always bears criminal responsibility. This has been the standpoint of the United Nations.

International Law and Morality

When classic international law was established by the Peace of Westphalia in 1648, the European states agreed never again to wage war against each other for moral reasons.[30] At that time, state sovereignty was put into law and linked with an absolute ban on intervention into the internal affairs of the individual states. In 1948, exactly 300 years after the first step, the world agreed on the Universal Declaration of Human Rights. Since 1648, it has been understood that military intervention is the wrong means to impose morality, and that instead moral concerns should influence the regulations of international law. Since 1948, it has been understood how human dignity should be protected, namely, through international law, through the individual as the subject of international law, and through actionable human rights. This three-century-old process is now in danger of being reversed by the apparent acceptance of the idea of intervening in other states "in the name of human rights." To the extent that European states participate in such actions, Europe is being forced to accept certain aspects of the American concept of human rights. As we have seen in chapter 2, the understanding of human rights that prevails across the Atlantic distinguishes itself from the European concept by the fact that it has a political rather than a legal basis. A military intervention that invokes the preservation of human rights sweeps the legal foundation of human rights off the table with one stroke of the pen and replaces it with a political objective. In two respects, military intervention "in the name of human rights" represents a reversion into the era before 1648: first, it derails the principle of state sovereignty, which has formed the foundation for the entire international legal order since 1648;[31] second, morality comes marching back into law. In the wake of the terrorist attacks of September 11, it became apparent just how easily moral categories can override human rights. "Good" and "evil"—moral categories par excellence—dominate the public debate in the United States so strongly that even the ban on torture has been seriously challenged with regard to the interrogation of suspected terrorists.[32]

Human rights can be maintained only when law and morality are kept separate: not only the virtuous person possesses these rights, but also the unvirtuous—and he needs them most of all—regardless of what one understands by "unvirtuous." Today there is a tendency that originated in the United States and is bent on "remoralizing" human rights.[33] Europe is heavily affected as well. The NATO war against the Federal Republic of Yugoslavia was an attempt to "relativize the *legality* of the existing international legal order by appealing to the *legitimacy* of a universal morality," Preuss writes.[34] Collective punishments that do not affect the guilty can be justified only morally—if at all—and not by law. Many people in Yugoslavia paid with their lives for the fact that they were residing in a state that had been morally disqualified. Although this aspect is only one among many that must be looked at when evaluating the situation, it is a much more important factor in connection with human rights, in whose name NATO's war took place to begin with. Morality naturally has a meaning for human rights, for the motivation that brought humanity to codify these rights in 1948 and to implement them within international law is a moral one. However, this implementation into positive law separates law and morality. The reversion to the era before 1948 and certainly to the era before 1648 leads to a kind of "human rights fundamentalism," which ultimately works against human rights.[35]

In recent years there have been increasing demands that such interventions, if they must occur at all, should involve only international peace forces. This means an increased emphasis on the "strength of law," since military operations always tend to be disproportional and overturn the law, while police operations—even if they deploy massive means—must remain embedded in civil, that is, non-military, law.[36] This position has also been introduced and argued by European states, which, by taking small steps, can often contribute to the strengthening of the international legal order.[37] This is all the more important because they themselves have experienced American pragmatism through their cooperation with the United States over recent years. The Gulf War was still covered by a UN mandate. In the war against the Federal Republic of Yugoslavia, the United States decided that a UN mandate was no longer necessary, and focused on NATO. But already in the Afghan war, the United States viewed its NATO partners as an unacceptable restraint on its sovereignty, at least as far as military action was concerned. While the NATO states proclaimed their solidarity on the political level, when it came to military action, the Great Power itself invented the new concept of the "coalition of the willing." This development has been downright breathtaking. The whole drama has been acted out on the stage in front of the military backdrop where the United States sets the tone.

The European states have a better chance of contributing their own ideas on the other stage, before the non-military backdrop of international law—in the UN, in NATO, or in the decision as to whether or not they want to participate in a "coalition of the willing." Europe can define its own values within the framework of universally valid international law. The European states are free to come to their own agreements on how they want to deal with human rights. They can demand the provision of police forces, or they can contribute to the "strength of law" by agreeing that they will deploy these forces only with partners who have given clear evidence that they provide the greatest possible protection for human rights. This evidence can take the form of ratifying all international treaties and their protective mechanisms. The European states can also agree with one another to participate in such actions only when all participants are subject to the jurisdiction of the International Criminal Court. Agreeing to such an arrangement does not represent a moral sermon to the world public; rather, it represents a public declaration of the criteria according to which one intends to act. The sole consequence of such a stance is that one becomes a calculable, dependable, and principled partner for those who respect such qualities in a partner. In itself, such an approach, even if it is not noticed or adopted by potential partners, represents a contribution to the "strength of the law."

The French Revolution Continues

This last chapter is titled "Western Europe," and in the introduction I pointed to the greater responsibility on the part of Western Europe, with the farsightedness of this privileged sector, to stand up for the identity of this continent, which is finally growing back together. This special responsibility does not mean going it alone. As far as the Western Europe/East Central Europe/United States triangle is concerned, both parts of Europe have different options, and in particular they proceed from different historical preconditions, which we have already seen in the previous chapter. Europe will be able to find and name its identity in the dialogue between the two halves of the continent, for Europe genuinely is a single continent and not two or more. That was always the case, but during the Cold War, Western Europe viewed itself as "Europe par excellence." "Eastern Europe was never as European as it was in those days when it was so far from Europe," writes Imre Kertész. Drago Jančar explains: "Central Europe has experienced the co-existence of different cultures and people, immense creativity and tolerance, along with national and social hatred, base intolerance, and violence. Living with such an experience, with both experiences, diving into this experience, means understanding many things; it also means steeling oneself for the beautiful and evil surprises that await us within the pan-European context."[38] And yet there is one area in which the starting point for Western and East Central Europe is so different that we should pick up on it again with regard to Western Europe. It concerns the separation of cultural from state political identity, as we have outlined it in the previous chapter.

Enlightenment and Romanticism

We have already seen how the Enlightenment brought forth the "republic" and how Romanticism brought forth the "nation," and how the two allied themselves in the French Revolution, just as we have already discussed the historically rooted difference between the state political identities of France and Germany. We will now examine this difference in connection with the separation of this identity from cultural identity. Both patterns of state political identity partially help and partially hinder this separation process, but in different ways. State political identity on the French pattern most clearly represents the Enlightened, European-republican idea and is therefore the best-suited starting point for this process of separation. The only hindering aspect of the French pattern on this process is that the state political identity is almost inseparably embedded in the cultural identity of the French nation and is more intensively and emotionally linked with it than in many other Western European states, which still shows today that the alliance between "republic" and "nation" was sealed in France. The fact that the final stage of this process is the separation of precisely these two identities shows that this hindrance is quite enormous, even though France's state political identity would actually appear to be the ideal starting point. Precisely at this point, the German pattern of state political identity seems more propitious, since in Germany state political and cultural identity have always remained more separate than in France. Furthermore, for historical reasons Germany has preserved a certain restraint in the formulation of national identity: the emotional foundation of the state political identity is less national and more the product of historical insight—at least among the middle and older generations.[39] For a younger generation, the emotional foundation of their state political identity may even diminish over time. This in turn would not be an ideal precondition for this process, for the gradual separation of state political from cultural identity is not intended to make the former disappear. On the contrary, the point of this separation lies in bringing the state political identity to bear via different vertical levels of statehood and to strengthen it by gradually separating it from the direct relationship to the Western European understanding of the nation—and also from the often highly burdensome relationship to the East Central European understanding of the nation in a cultural sense. Since the process runs very differently for the different regions of Europe, we are using this chapter to look at Western Europe alone. Let us emphasize once more that the process of separating state political from cultural identity in its entirety could become highly significant for the cohesion of Western and East Central Europe. It could help Europe grow together precisely because although there are various starting points, the line of development leads in the same direction.

The elements of state political identity that can demand its separation from cultural identity are present in both the French and German patterns; however, they are in entirely different areas and are always linked with an obstructive counterpart. In the French pattern, European-republican statehood is still so well anchored in the nation that it is almost impossible to separate the two. In the German pattern, it is possible to separate statehood and the nation, but the very fact that they are separate in this way could weaken state political identity in the long term. This comparison of state political identity in Germany and France and the apparent hopelessness of the question recalls the paradox once formulated by Ernst-Wolfgang Böckenförde: "The liberal, secularized state lives from conditions that it cannot determine by itself."[40] If this is the case on the level of the traditional nation-state, how much more extreme must the same problem be with regard to a state political identity that is beginning to expand across different levels? This expansion across different levels also points to a different dimension: 200 years ago, the republic, which was a child of the Enlightenment, was forced to ally itself with an element of Romanticism if it was to be effective. It would appear that the Enlightenment is most sustainable when it incorporates Romantic elements. And it may be that when, in an orgy of Enlightened zealousness, Romanticism is chased out of the house and the door is slammed behind it, it will soon return through the back door in a form that causes even more disorder in the Enlightened house than would have been the case if it had not been chased our but rather provided with measured support in the first place.

What does this Romantic element with its underpinnings of Enlightened reason look like? The national idea no longer fits the bill. As we have already seen, Romanticism in the form of the nation cannot lead the way to state political identity. It could take us along a downward path, but it should not do so, and for reasons we have also already discussed. The Enlightenment philosopher par excellence, Immanuel Kant, once said: "Two things fill the mind with ever increasing wonder and awe the more often and the more intensely the mind of thought is drawn to them: the starry heavens above me and the moral law within me."[41] When I let these words sink into my mind, I begin to hear a thoroughly Romantic echo—Enlightened reason supported by Romantic elements. So the question should be, is there a clear boundary between the kind of Romanticism that destroys the Enlightenment and the kind that helps bring it to fruition? The question must remain open. But as far as state political identity is concerned, I will attempt an answer, in short form first and then on a more sophisticated level. The short formula goes like this: inclusive Romanticism can support Enlightened reason, while exclusive Romanticism destroys Enlightened reason. On a more sophisticated level, this formula—always restricted to the field of state political identity—can be explained as follows: nationalistic notions of community are founded on exclusive Romanticism. They rest on the exclusion of the "other": we are good, the "others" are less good, if not downright evil; we want to keep to ourselves; the "others" should be "ethnically cleansed"; evil must be exterminated. This form of Romanticism involves identity through exclusion and affiliation only with one's own separate group. The antipode of this is the universal view, which I am calling inclusive Romanticism. While the "other" is included, in this view it is neither good nor bad—it is simply different and is allowed to remain different. I am not required to adapt this "other" to my own life situation, nor does it demand anything from me. I am permitted to remain foreign if I want, and the "others" are permitted to remain foreign if they want, and all of this is based on the unalterable universal principle that every person is of equal value—identity through affiliation with the whole. The idea of human rights represents a concrete implementation of this principle.

But the decisive point lies in the fact that the universal principle is simultaneously an individualistic one. It emphasizes the unmistakable uniqueness of each individual person and thus resists the quest for identity through the community, particularly opposing compulsory group formation.[42] The universal principle considers it downright undignified for a person to be placed against his will on borders where he has to decide whether or not he belongs to a certain group: the individual human being is so unique that this should not be asked of him. For this reason, the universal principle leads to an existential affiliation requiring no commitments. I will never forget a conversation I had at a foreign congress a few months after starting my work in Bosnia. The intellectual I spoke to had fled Bosnia at the beginning of the war. When I asked if he intended to return, he answered that in the current situation he was not in a position to do so. It hurt him too much to be continually asked by people whether he was a Bosnian Serb, a Bosnian Croat, or a Bosniac, because he was a human being with his own individual human value. This person had not been directly traumatized by the war, but he perceived the compulsion to pose such questions as an affront to his human dignity.

Romantic feelings rest on emotional intimacy, on a feeling for what is "special."[43] This special quality can be found in the uniqueness of an individual person with whom one develops an emotional bond. In this view, universality is no longer "abstract" and "cold," as Gellner has described it, but is the starting point for the Romantic invention of the nation. Perhaps this is because today's world has become so small, and we can see images of people far away. In any case, in the present day, it is both conceivable and possible to develop an emotional connection with people living across the globe while perceiving a Romantic echo of devotion and sympathy. Perhaps it is this idea of a bond with an individual that still resonates in Kant's quotation from more than 200 years ago. Returning now to the comparison of the German and French patterns of state political identity and the question of what the two patterns can contribute to the process of the separation of state political and cultural identity, the Romantic element that the state political identity reached for in its manifestation as the *République* 200 years ago in order to become operative called and still calls itself the "nation." But from the Napoleonic Wars to the present, this nation has practically never been the bearer of elements that we have termed "exclusively Romantic." From the very beginning, the French nation was always profoundly influenced by universal and individualistic principles, which we have identified as inclusive. Whenever post-revolutionary France came into conflict with other European states or colonized regions, this was due to the striving for world power and not to a glorification of the nation in the sense of ethnic-Romantic community.

The fact that both "nation" and "state" ultimately have different identities is borne out by a comparison of France and the United States. The French expression *état* is always backed up by the state political identity, which also stands behind the expression "nation." Furthermore, the *Grande Nation* is backed up by the proud French state political identity, which promotes the universal principle and not, for example, the nation as a Romantic notion of community. Or, stated differently, the *Grande Nation* refers to the content and not the vessel that was selected for this content 200 years ago. When Americans say "nation," they mean *their* nation. When they say "country," they also mean their nation.

And when they say "America," they mean their nation more emphatically, based on religious components and community thinking. As surprising as it may seem, since Americans ultimately have no understanding of a state political identity, but merely a national one, to them the word "state" is backed by a national identity and not a state political one.[44] With regard to content, we can see a still unclear but approximate line for the Western European process of the separation of state political from cultural identity: state political identity, which can also be a European one, has strong roots in the French tradition.

After the euro was introduced, Helmut Schmidt stated the following: "When General de Gaulle was still alive, I understood that the unification of the European states would be possible only when and if France embraced this unification as its own concern. I still believe today, after the end of the Cold War, that as far as the first decades of the twenty-first century are concerned the key still lies in France."[45] As far as the introduction of the unified currency is concerned, I am prepared to believe one of its architects. I am convinced that this statement is also valid with regard to state political identity. France discovered more than 200 years ago which Romantic elements Enlightened reason must employ to provide sustainable potency to the universal principle of human dignity and existential affiliation through state political affiliation. The growth of state political identity is essentially a continuation of the French Revolution. However, the French pattern of state political identity has one peculiarity that is hardly applicable to Europe as a whole—that is, its distinctive centralism. In the preceding chapter, we saw why this centralism had to develop in the alliance between the republic and the nation 200 years ago if the Enlightenment was to incorporate the Romantic element that had also been more small-scale in France. France's state political identity will likely continue to have a harder time with the "path downward" than other states. On the "way up," however, it will have to dispose of the centralist element to some extent, since as a thought pattern it stands in the way of the general trend of the process through which it is expanding across various vertical levels of statehood.

It is within this context that the German pattern of state political identity is being brought to bear. From the very beginning it has entailed a multistage structure in the sense of an inner differentiation. Precisely this multistage quality of state political identity can assist the French pattern on its path upward to take off its surplus of centralist elements without—and this is decisive—abandoning the sustainable amalgam between Enlightenment and Romanticism that lies at its core. The German pattern of state political identity can do so for a very simple reason: the organization of a European state into component states, or even smaller units, does not rest on the kind of group or community thinking that we have described here as "exclusively Romantic." Instead, as we saw at the end of the preceding chapter, it rests on the individual as part of the sovereign people, whereby this individual possesses a multiple state political identity that is vertically arranged. That is why this pattern of the separation of state political from cultural identity should be emphatically promoted in

Western Europe. Similar considerations are conceivable for many patterns of state political identity in other Western European or—seen from a long-term perspective—Eastern European states, since they all contain unique elements that can contribute to this general European process. I am restricting my observations here to the French and German patterns for two reasons. First, a reconciliation between the Enlightenment and Romanticism could be undertaken on the basis of these two patterns. Second, the relationship between these two states has been the core of the European peace order.

European state political identity encompasses further elements that cannot be listed here. Instead, I have been concerned with showing to what extent universalism and the dignity of the individual determine one another. The ideology of community and group identity is confronted with a state political identity based on universalism and the dignity of the individual. These differences are of fundamental importance in any comparison between Europe and the United States. They also reflect those areas in which attachment is accepted on both sides of the Atlantic and how differently freedom is understood.

Eurocentrism?

Is it possible to speak of European values in a global sense—that is, not so-called Western values but those of Europe, which are not identical to those of the United States? Or does this smack of a centuries-long colonialism that this continent has burdened itself with? In the human rights issue, for instance, a certain restraint is called for. While these rights are universally valid—and their equal validity for all persons is what makes them so crucial—they have been consciously formulated abstractly since they are intended to be accessible to different interpretations within an absolute framework that can take cultural factors into consideration.[46] In its dealings with those continents that are not included in the West, Europe with its colonial past is indeed well-advised to show a certain restraint. Because of its legal and state culture, Europe is accustomed to incorporating moral notions into law and, on the international stage, to exerting its influence through the creation and strengthening of a future global legal order to which the continent itself is bound. Such restraint is not appropriate in Europe's relationship to the United States, for it in turn exerts global influence on the basis of its intellectual historical background—not on the basis of the "strength of law" but of the "law of the stronger"—and through the direct assertion of its own moral values.

Some states across the world plainly follow one of these patterns; some states follow the other. There are also states that know how to follow both patterns, depending on the situation. And there are probably additional states that would like to employ the right of the stronger but which—because they are weak—nevertheless make use of the alternative. The choice of pattern is often determined on the basis of intellectual history or of experience, at least with regard to Europe and the United States. There is a clear, worldwide conflict of interest between these two values and a fundamental disagreement deriving from them. This is certainly the case for the two protagonists, Europe and the United States. Europe must make sure it is counted in the chorus of states that wish to promote the "strength of law" across the world. It would be nonsensical to withdraw from this role by saying that it could be perceived as "Eurocentric."[47]

One problem that can be tackled only from a specifically European perspective is the increasingly obvious crisis of democracy, which manifests itself in entirely different phenomena. It has become the fashion in certain circles to demonize politics as such. It is particularly popular to attack the function of the parliaments and thus to weaken them, usually by appealing to the "people," which, however, is not viewed as the sovereign. Instead, such critics take the existence of the opinion of a homogeneous population group for granted, namely, in a pre-ordained thought direction set from above.[48] This "people" is always just one part of the sovereign, and those who do not share the prescribed opinion are excluded because they no longer belong to the people, or else apparently belong to another people. Furthermore, Western Europeans also fall back on the notion of homogeneous, ethnocultural national communities in the attempt to replace state political identity with cultural identity. I would also like to mention a phenomenon whereby people come to view a state as a private company, so that the citizen involuntarily sees him- or herself depicted as an "employee," which is irreconcilable with the European pattern of state political identity.[49] Regarding the phenomenon of radical right-wing violence, it is said that the young people who commit such violence are not unenlightened; rather, they aggressively reject the Enlightenment. In fact, the identity of right-wing violence and the previously mentioned new or resurrected notions of the "people" contain precisely those "exclusively Romantic" notions—"we" and the "others"—that destroy Europe's state political identity and its foundation, namely, existential affiliation.

Europe needs to respond to these phenomena with specifically European answers, and it would be mistaken to describe these answers as Eurocentric. The knowledge of transatlantic differences also plays a certain role, for in the United States such phenomena must be countered with entirely different forms. As presented in chapter 2, Europeans and Americans do not understand democracy in entirely the same way. In Europe, democracy is a political event that rests on the political cultural of conflict between various ideas in public, which occurs most distinctively in the parliaments where the individual participates in his or her function as a citizen. In the United States, these mechanisms have been at least to some extent replaced—or rather, conceived and developed differently—by an adversary culture in the legal realm that is conducted by individuals or groups and where the individual participates as a legal person.[50] Since all these phenomena weaken state political identity, Europe is more quickly and painfully affected by them than is a society based on the American pattern, where state political identity is practically non-existent. Modern-day Europe is faced with a difficult task: "How can [liberal society] accept an absolute declaration of enmity without betraying its own premise—that there is fundamentally no non-integrable 'other' in society? In doing so, how can it avoid the mysticism of an 'absolute evil' that is to be permanently excluded from society? In addition, the danger that an open society could undermine its own rule of law in a defensive struggle against its antipodes and cross over the boundaries of thought control in its use of the state monopoly on violence must not be underestimated."[51]

Finally, we need to mention yet another aspect pointing to the benefit of promoting state political identity on the European pattern across the European continent. The European notion of state political identity entails at least a minimal regard for interests that are not loudly proclaimed but that must be evident to everyone who seeks solutions for pending issues. First, this affects persons who do not have the means, financial or otherwise, to assert their own interests and who have no powerful advocate. If one transfers a state political identity on the European pattern, particularly the aspect of existential affiliation, to the global level—which is certainly possible, even if no genuine supra-national structures exist on this level—then this identity can lead to a situation wherein the living conditions and needs of these people will be paid a certain degree of consideration. Second, there is a need to incorporate other non-articulated interests, namely, those of future generations. In both areas, the consideration of these non-articulated interests occurs on the European pattern because of the highly practical historical experience that a locally limited and/or short-term thought structure can easily lead to disaster. It is no longer enough to include the *geographically* distant "other"; also considered must be the *chronologically* distant "other," which will eventually be confronted with the consequences of present-day actions. It is likely that, as sustainability increases in importance, this most fundamental of transatlantic differences will manifest itself with growing frequency over the coming years.

The different positions of Europe and the United States on climate protection thus represent only a starting point in a story that has been going on for a long time. The debate over the question of whether or not articulated interests should be included is by no means new. As Jörg Paul Müller writes: "Eckhart's bold observation that he who loves God more than the most distant and impoverished among men does not love God completely has not been used in all its explosive potential by Christianity against fundamentalism. In his bull of 27 March 1329, Pope John XXII condemned the Dominican's statement as heretical. Are we today more prepared to transcend the narrowness of our own worldview and to see our categorical duty not outside of our fellow man, but rather in him and through him?"[52] If we are to give this question a positive interest for the benefit of future generations, the European offer of state political identity should not be devalued and rejected by casting it as Eurocentrism. It is essential to link this European intellectual offering with other related points of view from different continents that are also based on the existential affiliation of all people—and, depending on their perspective, of nature itself.

Intellectual Offerings, Sense of Mission, and National Interest

I have just described the introduction of the European view into the global discussion as an intellectual offering. Europe has such a long and guilt-ridden history—not only within the continent itself but also in the colonized regions of other countries—that, definitively following World War II, it had to start afresh and give up its claim to evangelize others for its own convictions. And when Europeans take part in development projects, there is something else that holds them back from regarding a single approach to be possible and correct—the experience of inner-European diversity. This is not the case with Americans, who have a pronounced sense of mission that has been engrained in them from childhood. This sense of mission can be understood only against the backdrop of American religious identity, whereby today the religious categories are primarily expressed in moral ones.[53] "The impact of religious notions toward the state is … particularly evident in the foreign policy of the US. Because the Americans are profoundly convinced of the correctness and soundness of their ideology, and because they understand their value concept as a normative idea of universal validity, they are simultaneously convinced that this concept must be realized globally," writes Klaus Stüwe.[54] The general American public does not perceive its own belief as one among other global possibilities, but rather assumes its absolute truth: "*Everyone* should share in *this* 'complete' truth. The moralization of political options in the US reveals this dimension of a divine justification of one's own path."[55] During one of the many public discussions on the political dimensions of the September 11 terrorist attacks and the related conflicts between Europe and the United States, a European voiced his suspicion that many Americans assume that God is an American citizen. He was apparently trying to draw a picture of the religious roots of the American national spirit. This relatively one-sided self-referential perception—which is applicable to the general American public and not to informed persons and professionals—can be traced to the fact that media interest in foreign events is much lower than interest in domestic affairs. This leads to a focus on domestic issues that would be inconceivable in Europe.[56]

The difference between European intellectual offers and the American sense of mission also goes back to the transatlantic crossroads of 1648. Because the Americans decided *for* religion and *against* the state, and because the nation serves as the vessel for religion, the American nation has supreme importance. There is almost no aspect of American foreign policy that cannot be justified with the domestic political argument that it serves the interests of the nation. This proposition appears to be utterly self-evident to the vast majority of the population. Conversely, foreign policy actions that do not fulfill this most important of criteria can scarcely be made acceptable at home. The argument that something lies in the national interest is always the most fool-proof "killer argument."[57] If the United States first signed the statute of the International Criminal Court because it wanted to be involved in the development of the detailed regulations to weaken the new mechanism as much as possible, then it did so in the national interest. If it later withdraws its signature, this also occurs in the national interest. And if it prepares a law according to which smaller states will lose American military support as soon as they ratify the statute, then this too is done in the national interest. To European observers, this process appears unprincipled or even immoral. However, Europeans would be making a great mistake if they applied such judgments.

In fact, this is not a question of morality but rather a rational insight. The American national interest is not comparable with the French or German national interest, nor is it comparable with the British national interest, because the very term "national interest" means something entirely different in the United States—not only quantitatively but also qualitatively—from what European states understand by it. Whenever the American national interest is brought into a debate, it is always implicitly clear that this nation is the "chosen people of God." This is the only way to understand the indissoluble link between national consciousness and a sense of mission that cannot tolerate the emergence of other intellectual historical points of view. The American national interest is a continually renewed confirmation of the covenant with God. It cannot be measured by European moral yardsticks because it represents a moral yardstick in its own right that is simply not negotiable. This yardstick has come down from a higher authority and stands by itself. It is essential for outsiders to recognize this yardstick, to understand it, and to classify it rationally. Those who fail to do so may succumb to a helpless anti-Americanism, which may be understandable as a reaction to the absolutism of the American sense of mission, but which does nothing for secularized Europe. Based on this insight, such knowledge is particularly important for outsiders in the boundary area where the different moral concepts collide. Words whose definitions are entirely dependent on the respective concept of morality, such as "pragmatic," come into play. The previously mentioned meanings of this concept according to the American view are directly linked to the national interest. Those who support America's approach to the statute of the International Criminal Court would probably call it "pragmatic."[58]

The effects of these different points of departure were very evident in Bosnia. A social worker of Asian origin, who had been working in the country for a long time, reported that unlike all the other social workers, those from the United States always began every new contact by proclaiming "We liberated you," after which they got down to work. In fact, many members of the American armed forces cannot imagine that they will not be joyfully greeted as helpers in all parts of the world because they have grown up and been educated under the shadow of this conviction. One can also note tangible cultural imports from across the Atlantic. For example, in Bosnia one encounters policemen and policewomen wearing practically the same uniforms with the same octagonal caps as the New York City Police Department, which gained tragic fame after September 11, 2001, and which are otherwise rarely seen elsewhere in Europe—doubtless a generous gift from across the Atlantic. In view of these different understandings of statehood, whether it is really so infinitely wise to dress in American uniforms those persons who mostly clearly represent statehood and its monopoly on force is certainly open to question. But when cultural imports start turning into cultural imperialism, the Bosnian authorities also seem to be showing resistance, for example, when an American organization tried to force the Education Ministry to introduce a particular educational program in the schools.[59]

One image in particular illustrates this qualitative difference in the national self-conception, and thus also the qualitative difference in the national interest. Those who take their place in the long line in front of the Berlin Reichstag, who visit the Parliament in London, or who tour the Assemblée nationale in Paris or the seat of the French Senate may not necessarily share the same emotional experience, but they do have one thing in common: they are all visiting places where individuals whom one has chosen in common are expected to organize public life rationally, and one hopes that they will do so responsibly. One has the same experience when viewing the great buildings of the new Europe in Strasbourg and Brussels, although a few worried questions might arise regarding whether and how it will be possible to build this Europe. Ultimately, these are all buildings where leaders think, negotiate, act, and sometimes also scheme. But they are definitively not buildings of religious faith. Even the monumental structures through which the *République* proudly stages itself are clearly not houses of religious faith. Of course, it is certainly possible to experience uplifting feelings when visiting the various cities of Europe, depending on the visitor's personality and his or her personal history. Differences may arise between the generations born either before or after World War II, as between persons of different ethnicities or nationalities. But in all of these buildings, one can feel the spirit of the Enlightenment, for after all its historical flights into unreason, Europe has become a matter of reason.

The situation in the United States is entirely different, as we can see from this quotation from Klaus Stüwe:

In keeping with [the] religious analogies, the American nation has also created its own sacral sites and shrines. Particularly the federal capital, Washington DC ... has been furnished with so many monuments over the course of time that one can easily describe it as a place of pilgrimage for America's civil religion. Every American who can afford it will travel to Washington at least once in his lifetime to see the sites of national greatness, which he knows from television, in person. Every day in the summertime, sightseeing buses transport thousands of visitors through the District of Columbia to the most important altars of American civil religion: to the Washington Monument in the center of the federal capital, a stone obelisk of colossal height. Nearby, a Greek temple was erected for Abraham Lincoln, where he looks down upon the astonished visitors as a larger than life marble statue. On the banks of the Potomac stands the domed shrine for Thomas Jefferson, copied on the Pantheon in Rome. Unlike the original, it was not consecrated to all the gods, but rather to the author of the Declaration of Independence. The National Archives, whose interior resembles a cathedral, houses the shrine for the Declaration of Independence and the Constitution of the US on an altar protected by bullet-proof glass, to which thousands of visitors pay their respects each day. The site where the Constitution is preserved is the place where the Americans' religious constitutional culture becomes tangible. The visitor reverentially takes his place in line and speaks in hushed tones.[60]

America is apparently a matter of faith.

In the country that we sometimes jokingly referred to as the fifty-first state, pilgrimages to the United States were also once very popular. However, they were restricted to high Bosnian politicians who were invited to Washington at regular intervals. Internationals trying to iron out problems with Bosnian officials sometimes complained that it was hard to reach these people because they were always on a junket to the United States. When I think back to those days and remember the structure of the Dayton Agreement, as analyzed in the preceding chapter, it almost appears to me as if we built the Bosnians an ethnic cage. Or it might be more accurate to say that we gilded the bars of the ethnic cage that the Bosnians themselves had built over the years, and we then told them indirectly that the liberation from this hopeless situation could have only one name ("America") and one solution ("If you become like us, you will be better off"). Comparing this situation with ancient Rome, Peter Bender has said: "[If] Madeleine Albright ... almost everywhere she goes, publicly exhorts, warns, censors, advises, and informs that disobedience will have consequences, both she and many other American politicians are acting in the spirit of the ancient imperial power.... Americans behave in the unshakable conviction that their country has a mission in the world—what is good for America is also good for the world."[61]

Instructions of this kind were the order of the day in Bosnia. Whenever it was announced that so many millions in funds would start to flow only if the people behaved themselves in the elections and did not vote for nationalistic candidates, I always felt resentment and seriously asked myself if I as a Bosnian Serb in the Bosnian Serb Republic might not react to such instructions by voting for the nationalists after all, because proud Bosnians—and Bosnians are proud people—could not help but take this as an insult. I felt ashamed for the concept of democracy being expressed here, since I was after all a member of the international community that put out slogans like this. Today I would no longer be resentful over this American behavior. When viewed against its intellectual historical background, this behavior is absolutely consistent and logical. The thing that really surprised me was how many internationals of European origin working in Bosnia adapted their thinking to the American behavior patterns. I can explain this only from an intellectual historical perspective: we are still strongly rooted in the thought patterns of the Cold War. Intellectual history does not develop over months or years, but over decades.

Notes

1. Schulze states this clearly: "Even one of the most widespread Western assumptions thus seems to have been refuted: the idea that the urgent need for Western capital and Western investments will exert sufficient pressure on the Eastern European states to weaken nationalistic ambitions and make them approach Western democracy models in a peaceful fashion. The Western European 'prosperity materialists' must realize that national sentiments can be stronger than economic interests." Schulze, *Staat und Nation*, 333.

2. Gunther Teubner provides an overview of the corresponding developments, particularly in Germany. Teubner, "Polykorporatismus: Der Staat als 'Netzwerk' öffentlicher und privater Kollektivakteure," in Brunkhorst and Niesen, *Das Recht der Republik*. Eppler states: "A European democracy is not necessarily harmed by a neo-liberal wave as long as it encounters enough headwind early on. It will always be possible to deregulate something that perhaps had a meaning once upon a time but which has outlived its original function by decades. In addition, Western European states—I am thinking of France—are so present in the minds of their citizens that they will not be collapsing any time soon. They lose part of their ability to act—and their taxes—only when they have to start competing for international capital as one location among many." Eppler, *Vom Gewaltmonopol zum Gewaltmarkt?* 83.

3. Referring to Jean Bodin, Thomas Hobbes, and Hugo Grotius, whose writings he calls "threshold documents in which the transition from the theological-confessional age to the era of rational natural law is reflected," Wolfgang Kersting goes on to note that through the Peace of Westphalia, this revolution of legal thought became a political, constitutional reality. Kersting, "Globaler Rechtsfrieden und kulturelle Differenz: Huntington und die politische Philosophie der internationalen Beziehungen," in *Politisches Denken: Jahrbuch 2000*, ed. Karl Graf Ballestrem, Volker Gerhardt, Henning Ottmann, and Martyn P. Thompson (Stuttgart, 2000), 64. Eppler makes the same historical connection regarding Africa and Asia: "The warlords of Africa and Asia, like those at the end of the Thirty Years' War, are businessmen and commanders at the same time." Eppler, *Vom Gewaltmonopol zum Gewaltmarkt?* 52.

4. Jörg Lau used the subtitle "Rückzug des Staates, Vormarsch der Religion" in an article on "compassionate conservatism" in a section explaining the current attempt to transfer American welfare activities from government agencies to church-run or "faith-based" organizations. *Die Zeit*, 20 December 2000.

5. Gellner, *Bedingungen der Freiheit*, 10.

6. Interpretations range from "civil society as a temporal, secular political order" (Böckenförde, *Staat, Gesellschaft, Freiheit*, 259) to a description of it as a "separate identity outside of the political realm" (Reese-Schäfer, *Grenzgötter der Moral*, 287), or one describing the "actors ... in the pre- and non-state space, i.e., in an intermediate area between the individual and the state" (Hans-Jürgen Puhle, "Demokratisierungsprobleme in Europa und Amerika," in Brunkhorst and Niesen, *Das Recht der Republik*, 326). Altermatt again attributes civil society with the cultivation of cultural tolerance for which the state merely provides the political framework (Puhle, "Demokratisierungsprobleme in Europa und Amerika," 326), and Müller describes the "global public" as "civil society" (Jörg Paul Müller, *Der*

politische Mensch—menschliche Politik: Demokratie und Menschenrechte im staat-lichen und globalen Kontext [Basel, 1999], 192). There are occasionally even dis-cussions on whether or not the economy is part of "civil society." Teubner explains the historical roots of the broad range of interpretations with the way Montes-quieu and Locke drafted various models of civil society even before the French Revolution. Montesquieu viewed civil society as the core of political society, and Locke outlined a model of it as a pre-political society outside of political reality. Teubner, "Polykorporatismus," 347f. These two basic models have variously influ-enced conditions on both sides of the Atlantic.

7. Reese-Schäfer, *Grenzgötter der Moral*, 285. The author prefers the term *Bürger-gesellschaft*—which goes back to Dahrendorf—to "civil society," since it grants the military a civil role.

8. Peter L. Berger, Richard J. Neuhaus, and Michael Novak, eds., *To Empower People: From State to Civil Society*, 2nd ed. (Washington, DC, 1996).

9. Michael S. Joyce and William A. Schambra, "A New Civic Life," in Berger, Neu-haus, and Novak, *To Empower People*, 25f.

10. Michael Novak, "Seven Tangled Questions," in Berger, Neuhaus, and Novak, *To Empower People*, 138, 141. The term "civic association" refers to associations aimed at the common good, also in a European sense, but which also appear as a component of civil society.

11. On "compassionate conservatism," see "Das Land der gerechten Sünder" in *Die Zeit*, 20 December 2000, as well as the *Neue Zürcher Zeitung* of 5–6 August 2000, which points out that under Governor George W. Bush, the state of Texas rechan-neled a portion of its welfare budget to church organizations. The demand for greater involvement by the churches in social policy is by no means restricted to the party of the current president. It also met with a considerable response in the campaign of his opponent, Al Gore.

12. Birger P. Priddat refers to the ongoing discussions over new forms of coopera-tion between state and non-state authorities and institutions and describes the transatlantic difference over the meaning of the term "civil society" as follows: "'Civil society' is the name for the delegation of responsibility to society. For us Europeans, this entails the risk that the state will be expected to yield up familiar domains. In the American tradition of communities distinct from the state, civil society has a different meaning: what responsibility do citizens attribute to the state? A European copy of this mentality appears questionable. Our traditions refer to a tension between the propertied classes and the state (of the aristocracy); this was an issue of power sharing, not power delegation. The state stands above society or else faces it." Priddat "Gerechtigkeit oder Fairness," 1028. The notion of the third factor is expressed here once more.

13. Daniel Thürer formulates this thought—in connection with the interaction between the legal order, the international community, and the state—as follows: "How can a legal and democratic culture thrive outside of the rich 'thicket' and 'forest' or the soaring branches of political traditions and values that are often linked with the state? In any case, the 'wide field' of markets or 'civil society' alone is ultimately incapable of creating and guaranteeing justice and democracy. I believe that it is a postulate of present-day lawmaking to recast novel concentra-tions of economic power according to the models of constitutional law.... In the

multifarious manifestations of European integration, promising forms of novel order systems have been developed." Thürer, "Recht der internationalen Gemeinschaft und Wandel der Staatlichkeit," in *Verfassungsrecht der Schweiz*, ed. Daniel Thürer, Jean-François Aubert, and Jörg Paul Müller (Zurich, 2001), 55f. Eppler provides the following clear analysis of the situation in Africa: "Europeans who recommend the strengthening of civil society as a remedy usually receive a sober response in Africa: where states collapse, civil society—if there are any signs of it at all—is not something that can serve as an alternative to the state, that could replace it." Eppler, *Vom Gewaltmonopol zum Gewaltmarkt?* 56.

14. This formula has existed for years, if not for centuries. I took conscious note of it during one of the semi-annual meetings of the foreign ministers of the Council of Europe. German Foreign Minister Klaus Kinkel described in a speech the objective of his organization as that of replacing the right of the stronger by the "strength of law."

15. An article in *Die Zeit*, 2 February 2000, quotes the German ambassador to Washington, Jürgen Chroborg: "'Only strong partners are taken seriously,' he never tires of hammering into his visitors from Germany. 'Only here in America,' he adds, 'have I really come to understand how important the European integration process is. We have no choice but to reflect on our own power in Europe.' And then comes the chorus: 'Only strong partners are taken seriously.'" .

16. *Die Zeit*, 31 May 2000.

17. Egon Bahr, Dresden speech of 10 March 2002. The author graciously supplied me with his text, entitled "Die Vergangenheit darf die Zukunft nicht behindern." Cf. Gunter Hofmann in *Die Zeit*, 27 March 2002.

18. *Die Zeit*, 7 February 2002.

19. Even outside these areas, various signs of an Americanization of European legal culture are visible. For example, Wolfgang Wiegand has the following to say about private law: "If we want to prevent American models from gradually displacing the concepts of the European legal tradition and thus also the socio-political solutions of European culture, then a standardization of the legal foundations of European private law is of supreme importance. One reason is because this would fulfill an essential condition for the smooth functioning of the European domestic market, whose efficiency will authoritatively determine Europe's future influence in world markets and thus also influence the old continent's geopolitical positioning. In addition, this is probably the only way to create a legal system that is up to the transformed regional and global socio-economic parameters and that will be in a position to offer adequate solutions and thus maintain itself within the framework of the conceptual global competition." Wiegand, "Europäisierung—Globalisierung—Amerikanisierung," in *Vernetzte Welt—globales Recht: Jahrbuch Junger Zivilrechtswissenschaftler*, ed. Martin Immenhauser and Jürg Wichermann (Stuttgart, 1998), 17.

20. Harvard professor Mary Ann Glendon has made critical comments on the American tradition of deriving legal claims from political demands. Glendon, *Rights Talk: The Impoverishment of Political Discourse* (New York, 1991). Michael Ignatieff—also a professor at Harvard—criticizes the way that human rights are used as trump cards in political conflicts. Ignatieff, *Die Politik der Menschenrechte* (Hamburg, 2002), 46.

21. In continental Europe, a distinction is made between public law, which tends to regulate matters in a compulsory fashion, and private law, which regulates matters that can be freely decided.
22. *Neue Zürcher Zeitung*, 1 February 2002.
23. In a section titled "Globalisierung—Notwendigkeit eines neuen 'ius gentium,'" Daniel Thürer pursues the issue of integrating multinational communities into the international protection of human rights. He views the "codes of conduct" for the ethical behavior of the business community as fundamentally new development possibilities, noting at the end: "In the long run, the self-regulation of business behavior and non-binding behavioral standards, whether of a private or public nature, are not sufficient to keep the dynamic processes of a globalized economy in firm channels." Thürer, "Modernes Völkerrecht: Ein System im Wandel und Wachstum—Gerechtigkeitsgedanke als Kraft der Veränderung?" *Zeitschrift für ausländisches öffentliches Recht und Völkerrecht* 60 (2000): 588.
24. Of course, the state can also be a victim, for example, in crimes of property, but in that case it is affected in the same way that a private person would be affected.
25. "Emergency-proof" liberties include the right to life; the ban on torture, slavery, and forced labor; the ban on retroactive laws; the ban on debt imprisonment; as well as the freedom of thought, conscience, and religion.
26. This is how Carsten Stahn and Sven-R. Eiffler describe international criminal law. Stahn and Eiffler, "Über das Verhältnis von Internationalem Menschenrechtsschutz und Völkerstrafrecht anhand des Statuts von Rom," *Kritische Vierteljahresschrift für Gesetzgebung und Rechtswissenschaft* 82 (1999): 269.
27. The history of the Universal Declaration of Human Rights is presented in Ignatieff, *Die Politik der Menschenrechte*.
28. The legal practice of the European Court of Human Rights particularly influences the legal orders of the member states. The laws of one state must often be adapted as the result of a judgment, whereas the financial compensation of plaintiffs sometimes has a symbolic character.
29. Stahn and Eiffler, "Über das Verhältnis," 254 (emphasis added). The view that a functioning state system provides the best guarantee for the protection of individual human rights can also be found in American publications, e.g., in Ignatieff, *Die Politik der Menschenrechte*, 48.
30. The distinction between just and unjust wars, which was customary in the Middle Ages, has since been overcome and replaced by international law. Sybille Tönnies explains: "There is a certain irony in the fact that through the development that led to a general proscription of war, it was not so much the unjust war but rather the just war that was proscribed. However, this development is plausible: historical experience had shown that the moral view did not decrease but rather increased discord. Particularly, the moral appeal to neutral parties to take sides had shown a propensity to escalate conflict. Following the Thirty Years' War, in which morality, encased in religion, played such a fateful role, people no longer wanted to pretend as if the question of war and peace were not really decided by *raison d'état*. Thus, in this question the maintenance of strict value neutrality was agree upon." Tönnies, "Weltfrieden und Völkerrecht: Made in the USA oder Aufgabe der UNO?" *Blätter für deutsche und internationale Politik* 46 (2001): 831.

31. The slow development of the concept of sovereignty after 1648 is described in Roland Meister, "Souveränität und Menschenrechte," *Blätter für deutsche und internationale Politik* 47 (2002): 326ff.

32. According to press reports, a number of al-Qaeda fighters have been "transferred to countries with whose secret services the CIA maintains good connections and where torture is permitted" on the request of the United States. *The Guardian*, 12 March 2002, reprinted in *Le Monde Diplomatique*, German-language edition, May 2002, 3.

33. In an article entitled "Der hohe Preis der Moral," Kurt Imhof describes the entrance of morality into politics and business. He uses the terms *Empörungskommunikation* (outrage communication) and *Empörungsbewirtschaftung* (outrage management), and points out that this development is also a consequence of deregulation. *Neue Zürcher Zeitung*, 7 June 2002. Deregulation means a weakening of the legal order. It may also be possible to make a parallel connection to human rights: here, too, remoralization goes hand in hand with deregulation. Eppler points to one interesting aspect in connection with the expression "failed state," which has become customary as a description of collapsing statehood: "The English word 'fail,' like its German counterpart 'fehlen,' has a strong moral aftertaste. 'I have had many failures' was a standard confession of sin in the nineteenth century. 'Fail' can be translated with *scheitern* or *versagen*. Both translations, the former more than the latter, contain a moral component: someone has not lived up to his tasks.... The term 'failed state' contains within it the entire *contempt for the state and its functions*, which has become fashionable in recent decades." Eppler, *Vom Gewaltmonopol zum Gewaltmarkt?* 83f. (emphasis added).

34. Ulrich K. Preuss, "Der Kosovo-Krieg, das Völkerrecht und die Moral," in *Der Kosovo-Krieg und das Völkerrecht*, ed. Reinhard Merkel (Frankfurt am Main, 2000), 136.

35. Klaus Günther warns against a "human rights fundamentalism" as a response to a fundamentalism that manifests itself in massive human rights violations. Günther, "Kampf gegen das Böse? Zehn Thesen wider die ethische Aufrüstung der Kriminalpolitik," *Kritische Justiz* 27 (1994): 142ff. Hauke Brunkhorst has this to say regarding the same term: "While human rights fundamentalism towers over democratic solidarity in its elitist and expertocratic aspects, the culture of human rights stands at the same level as democracy. The legitimacy of human rights is rooted in democratic principles and not in an anthropologically prescribed human dignity.... That is why in 1795 Kant linked a peace based on human rights to the republic. Those who do not desire the republic, as Kant might have said, will not find peace." Brunkhorst, "Paradigmenwechsel im Völkerrecht? Lehren aus Bosnien," in Lutz-Bachmann and Bohman, *Frieden durch Recht*, 259f.

36. Brunkhorst distinguishes the two types of mission by stating that a military mission bases hard power on soft law, whereas police missions, by contrast, are based on hard law and exercise soft power. Brunkhorst, "Paradigmenwechsel im Völkerrecht?" 269.

37. Hauke Brunkhorst cites one example in connection with the NATO mission against the Federal Republic of Yugoslavia. "If international emergency law is misused, then perhaps, in the Federal Republic of Germany, a court can provide retroactive legitimacy; however, this would scarcely be possible in the case of

China or the US. That is why it was a stroke of luck, due to the decisive action of several continental European governments, that NATO's military action was indirectly legitimized by a retroactive resolution by the Security Council on 10 June. Without this result, which was pushed through politically by converting the G7 economic organization into a G8 organization for crisis management, irreparable damage to the UN security system could not have been prevented." Brunkhorst, "Menschenrechte und Intervention," in *Der Kosovo-Krieg: Rechtliche und rechtstheoretische Aspekte*, ed. Dieter S. Lutz (Baden Baden, 2000), 208.

38. Jančar, "Understanding the World as a Contradiction," *Neue Zürcher Zeitung*, 19–20 May 2001. Kertész's essay is entitled "Zeit der Entscheidung: Wird es auferstehen?!—Europa, von Osten aus betrachtet," *Neue Zürcher Zeitung*, 20–21 January 2001.

39. This kind of insight is also described as *Verfassungspatriotismus* (constitutional patriotism). A collection of various related concepts can be found in Frankenberg, *Die Verfassung der Republik*, 146f.

40. Böckenförde, *Staat, Gesellschaft, Freiheit*, 60.

41. *Kants gesammelte Schriften ab 1902, Akademie-Textausgabe* (Berlin, 1968), *Kritik der praktischen Vernunft*, Bd. V, 161. The biographical background to this sentence can be found in Carola Meier-Seethaler, *Befühl und Urteilskraft: Ein Plädoyer für die emotionale Vernunft* (Munich, 1997), 52ff.

42. On the topic of Europe, for the sake of completeness, it is important to mention that the UN Charter is based on precisely the same values, namely, the concept that universal principles supersede particular ones. The touchy and almost unmentionable question of how this principle came to be used during the Cold War, and why today it is threatened with oblivion, is explained by Tönnies, "Weltfrieden und Völkerrecht."

43. In this book, see the quoted text from Gellner, *Nationalismus*, in chapter 3, referenced in note 51 of that chapter.

44. The US State Department is responsible only for foreign policy. Foreign relations rely on the worldwide formalities of the traditional nation-state.

45. The article in *Die Zeit*, 15 November 2001, reproduces the speech that Schmidt gave in Lausanne on 9 November 2001 on the occasion of his acceptance of a medal presented by the Fondation Jean Monnet pour l'Europe, which was simultaneously awarded to the former French president, Valéry Giscard d'Estaing.

46. For example, the protection of life and bodily integrity are indisputably among its absolute, core components. Conversely, Otfried Höffe cites situations in which the consideration of cultural traditions can lead to judgments other than those that would otherwise be undertaken in the West: "In places where community awareness is as strong as in Africa, something which would be considered legally and morally legitimate in the West, namely, isolating a prisoner for years behind bars, could be viewed as a violation of human rights. Or in places where the extended family is sacred, persons who stick their aged parents in a nursing home would be violating human rights. In the same way, human rights are violated when a colonial government forces the institution of the chieftain onto acephalic [chiefless] tribes." Höffe, "Kein Geschenk, sondern Gabe: Identität im Verschiedenen—Menschenrechte im interkulturellen Diskurs," *Frankfurter Rundschau*, 1 October 1996. We have already seen a different cultural-state political fact in Europe in its relationship to the United States: civil rights and liberties, particularly the freedom of

religion, encounter boundaries in Europe when the maintenance of public order is affected, a restriction that—if at all—is dealt with in a much more restrained fashion in the United States.

47. With regard to European unification, Eppler states at the end of his book: "We need it urgently, and so does the rest of the world. Once we have accustomed ourselves to something like European domestic policy, world domestic policy will no longer give us trouble." Eppler, *Vom Gewaltmonopol zum Gewaltmarkt?* 154. In this volume, see also chapter 3, note 86.

48. "Renewal can come only from the people, understood as a primal and pure force.... The people *is* only a unit; otherwise, it is nothing. In this way, all democratic participation rights are extinguished in favor of an imaginary 'we.' Because, as an imaginary entity, it can only be created 'from above,' it ultimately serves to legitimize an authoritarian government." From an essay by Christian Schlüter, *Die Zeit*, 5 October 2000.

49. The term "employee" (*Betriebsangehöriger*) is used by Thomas Assheuer, *Die Zeit*, 4 April 2002.

50. Regarding the term "legal person," see chapter 2, note 64.

51. Richard Herzinger, "Der Haß zum Tode: Liberale Diskursgesellschaft und rechte Gewalt," *Die Zeit*, 10 August 2000. The comment on the aggressive rejection of the Enlightenment in the previous paragraph also comes from this article.

52. Müller, *Der politische Mensch*, viii.

53. In an article published in 1988, Gustav H. Blanke describes the religious foundations of the American sense of mission over the centuries. Referring to Henry Kissinger, he assumes that this tendency is likely to weaken, so that he quotes from one of his own publications as referring to the past: "The McCarthyists began their moral crusade against 'world communism'; they accused the Soviet Union of an international conspiracy against the 'children of light.' Under the influence of this rhetoric with its simplistic opposition of good and evil, lies and truth, light and dark, freedom and slavery, American world affairs gained the contours of a morality play written for the 'world theater.'" The author had no way of knowing at the time that he was describing a future that would soon become apparent. Blanke, "Das amerikanische Sendungsbewusstsein," 203.

54. Stüwe, "Eine Zivilreligion als Integrationsideologie?" 469.

55. Kodalle, *Gott und Politik in den USA*, 21.

56. Looking ahead to the twenty-first century, Ulrich Schmid describes this situation in the following terms: "It is, however, unlikely that the United States will dominate the coming century to the same degree that it dominated the one that is now coming to an end. Countries like China and India, perhaps even a united Europe, and, somewhat later, Russia too could noticeably shift the global power relationship in their favor. This would probably also help make America become more aware of the rest of the world. One of the most astonishing phenomena of the late twentieth century is the fact that, in the midst of globalization and internationalism, in the midst of the cult of the computer-guided 'new communication,' life in America is determined by the avoidance of the outside world. What Europe or Asia do or think is secondary; America is all that counts. The US will probably awaken from this cultural introspection only when the rest of the world again speaks up in a more assertive fashion." *Neue Zürcher Zeitung*, 24–25 July 1999.

57. Against this background, the "statement of interest" by the president of the United States mentioned in chapter 2, in which he requested that the country's courts end open claims against German companies for the compensation of forced laborers and to allow no new claims because this would be "in the interest of US foreign policy," is particularly interesting. See also chapter 2, note 59.

58. The term "pragmatic" is usually used in a positive context. In an essay titled "Beneš and the 'Czech Dilemma,'" in which he contrasts the terms "pragmatic" and "moral," Czech president Václav Havel uses "pragmatic" in a disparaging sense: "I have always tended toward a critical opinion on [Beneš's] decisions in these fateful moments. After all, these decisions had something in common: he chose the pragmatic solution over the moral solution. However, what interests me much more today than the constant criticism of Beneš for capitulating to evil is the origin of this evil, its development and the social mechanisms of its toleration." *Neue Zürcher Zeitung*, 19 April 2002.

59. The situation is mentioned in the report to the Parliamentary Assembly of the Council of Europe on the accession of Bosnia-Herzegovina, which preceded its membership in April 2002 (report of the Commission des questions juridiques et des droits de l'homme, 5 December 2001).

60. Stüwe, "Eine Zivilreligion als Integrationsideologie?" 465. The United States is such a matter of faith that even one of the few evaluations of the consequences of the terrorist attacks by "dissident" American congressional representatives was formulated in the form of a prayer: "Let us pray that our country will end this war. We never agreed to an endless war, nor did we authorize an attack on Iraq, Iran, or North Korea, nor did we vote to bomb Afghan civilians. We never voted for a permanent war economy, for military tribunals, for the restriction of our constitution. Let us pray for an America without weapons of mass destruction, that does not hunt an 'axis of evil,' that does not break international treaties, but which will form an axis of hope." *The Nation*, 1 March 2002, reprinted in *Le Monde diplomatique*, German-language edition, May 2002, 3.

61. Peter Bender, "Das Amerikanische und das Römische Imperium: Ein Vergleich," *Europa oder Amerika? Zur Zukunft des Westens*, special ed., *Merkur* 9/10 (2000): 896.

Afterword

In 1990, long before the outbreak of the Balkan Wars, Hagen Schulze wrote the following: "If Europe is to have a future, it has no choice but to pick up on the Europe of the past; in this time of upheaval, it is the task of the historians to name Europe's identity, and it is the task of the politicians, and therefore of us all, to distinguish that which is worth preserving from that which is dangerous and self-destructive."[1]

The recent Balkan Wars have again demonstrated in the most vicious way how important it is to distinguish that which is worth preserving from that which is dangerous and self-destructive. I began my research for this book after the completion of my work in Bosnia in order to find answers to the questions that surfaced in the Balkans. My on-site observations and the suspicions they awakened in me were not enough. Even today, many questions have still not found adequate answers. Nevertheless, I thought it was right to set my discoveries down in book form. The task itself—namely, separating that which is worth preserving from that which is dangerous and self-destructive—can be fulfilled only within the framework of a broad, intra-European debate in which knowledge is exchanged, ideas are formulated and rejected, and conclusions are sought and, after long discussion and deliberation, replaced by others that appear even better in the eyes of those who are involved. On this note, I hope that my comments will be not only accepted but also refuted, with analyses and arguments that provide better answers to the questions that I believe must find answers. But on a last point it will be hard to change my mind—that in the transatlantic relationship there are questions that cannot tolerate any postponement.

I could not have written this book without the support of many friends, acquaintances, experts, and practitioners from various fields. I would like first to thank all those who, through their willingness to talk with me, enabled me to continue my work in Bosnia almost to the end of my term.[2] I could not even begin to mention them all here. I would like to thank Danielle Coin

---

Notes for this section are located on page 166.

and Christos Giacoumopoulos, who worked on Bosnia within the framework of the Council of Europe and who provided me with countless valuable insights on this book's topic, as well as Victor Ruffy, a long-term member of the National Council, its president, and a member of the Parliamentary Assembly of the Council of Europe, for his support during these years. A discussion in Sarajevo with the historian Urs Altermatt enabled me early on to place Bosnia into a broader Central European context. Our enormously helpful exchange of opinions became the starting point for this book.

Nor can I mention all of the many people who helped me with information following my return from Bosnia. I would like to thank the Arab studies expert Hartmut Fähndrich for the information he provided me on Islam. I thank the philosopher Carola Meier-Seethaler and the sociologist Judith Jànoska, whose support went far beyond mere factual information. I would like to thank Professor Helmut Steinberger, a member of the Venice Commission of the Council of Europe, for arranging a brief stay at the Max Planck Institute for Foreign and International Criminal Law in Heidelberg. Discussions with the staff of this institute were very helpful as an introduction to the legal portion of this study. I gained valuable information on international law, private international law, and legal understanding from Professors Nicolas Michel, director for international law in the Department of Foreign Affairs; Daniel Thürer in Zurich; Franz Werro in Fribourg; Sabine von Schorlemer in Geneva; Ivo Schwander and Jens Drolshammer in St. Gallen; Thomas Cottier and his assistant Krista Nadakavukaren Schefer in Bern; as well as my former classmates and the Zurich lawyer Georg von Segesser. I would particularly like to thank Jörg Paul Müller, professor for national and international law and the philosophy of law at the University of Bern, for his tireless suggestion that I finally write down everything that I had gathered so far. My thanks include his former assistant, Caroline Klein, who facilitated my access to the library and its operations. Although the information provided by these experts was extremely helpful for my study, this of course does not mean that they would all agree with my conclusions.

The discussions with my Bosnian colleagues meant a great deal to me. My thanks go to all of them for their support and for the many things they told me. Through them I gained in bits and pieces an idea of what it means not to abandon one's dignity in threatening situations. I have always tried to judge the professional competence of my Bosnian colleagues and to treat them accordingly. Over time I recognized that an early and broad reliance on this competence was an important building block in the reconstruction effort, and I noticed that the recognition of this professional competence represented an important element in the dignity of the Bosnians and thus in the dignity of their country. Here I would particularly like to thank Valerija Šaula, professor of international law at the University of Banja Luka, who was, in the second half of my term, my first deputy, along with Biljana Kokeza, who for an extended part of my term was responsible for the administration of the institution. I also thank them for arranging various contacts during a trip in late May 2002, when I visited Sarajevo and Banja Luka again for the first time after the completion of my work.

Over the last two years, a number of friends have encouraged me to continue my work on this book and bring it to completion. I owe all of them great thanks and would particularly like to thank Madlen and Willi Schmidt-Schmidt as well as the author Laure Wyss. They stand for many others. I would like to thank Robert Antretter, a long-term member of the German Bundestag, for his support over the years, as well as for making the contact to the Aufbau Verlag. Finally, I would like to thank Maria Matschuk for her professional and painstaking editorial work.

During the course of my work on this book, it has become clear to me that it affects my personal freedom. This perception had begun in Bosnia on an intuitive level before I could even begin to formulate what it meant to challenge this freedom. The vague and yet distinct feeling was not directly related to my concrete activity, for one should assume such a task only after one has already accepted that, as a mere cog in a giant machine, one will largely be controlled from the outside. Nor was this due to the Bosnian multinational environment, for which I had prepared myself well and whose normalization represented the centerpiece of my work. Instead, it was the international environment in Bosnia that began to have an impact upon me as a person. I felt that something deep within me, something I did not want to give up, was being challenged. Looking back, I recognized that I had experienced the international environment in Bosnia in a highly sectarian fashion: the Bible was the Dayton Agreement; Jerusalem was located in Washington, DC; and the role of fire-and-brimstone preachers was filled by those devout Americans who had not—as diplomats—learned that the world cannot be understood in its entirety through blind faith, particularly not the blind faith of one's own nation. Probably the comparison to religious cults in the left hemisphere of my brain began to take shape when the term "deprogramming" arose from the mists in the right hemisphere. This term describes the therapy through which persons are enabled to live a normal life again after having belonged to a cult.

I felt as if I were going through a deprogramming session myself when, as I wrote this book, I suddenly realized that there are things I do not want to give up, above all, the freedom of rational thought, which informs the political discussion beyond categories of faith and confession. This realization finally made me see the method by which the intellectual historical Americanization of Europe—to the extent that there is such a thing—functions. This method has a sectarian quality, which is shown by the fact that nobody wants to talk about it. Whoever in Europe speaks of transatlantic differences in the intellectual historical field is immediately "Americanized," that is, transported from the "world of reason" to the "world of faith," where a different morality rules that in itself is beyond debate. Why is the issue of transatlantic differences less taboo or even sought after in the economic sector? Could it be because one of the few bits of common ground between ultra-liberals and strict Marxists lies in their mutual tendency to reduce politics to economics?

Following the terrorist attacks of September 11, 2001, many people wondered whether—and, if so, why—American foreign policy could be seen as being insulting to the Islamic world. In these discussions, three dimensions usually took center stage: religion; consumption and lifestyle; and global economics. As far as Europe is concerned, this discussion should also include the intellectual historical dimension, which reaches beyond the three dimensions cited here and also affects the state political level. The self-confidence with which government representatives and non-governmental actors of American foreign policy assume that their understanding of the state, the nation, and religion will triumph globally is insulting—not only to those of different cultural backgrounds, but also to state politically convinced citizens of European states and to state politically convinced Europeans. It provokes aggression at first, followed by helplessness. But both evaporate once one understands why the United States as a nation—as opposed to individual Americans—simply cannot act differently, due to its intellectual historical development. As soon as one realizes this, negative emotions are replaced by the simple desire that Europe find the correct answers in this time of turmoil.

European identity has always developed in turbulent times. This continent has never attempted to live without history. It has never sought to suppress the past in order to make a radical new beginning. Particularly in periods of upheaval, Europe has repeatedly understood that it must react correctly, free from confessions of faith, with a cool head—cautiously, mindful of its history, and in the spirit of reason.

June 2002   Gret Haller

Notes

1. Hagen Schulze, *Die Wiederkehr Europas* (Berlin, 1990), 57.
2. My resignation during my final year in office was intended to help secure a successor and, in addition, to ensure a new legal basis for the institution following the first five-year term.

Bibliography

Adams, Willi Paul. "Verfassungstheorie und Verfassungspraxis der amerikanischen Gründergeneration: Von der konstitutionellen Monarchie Grossbritanniens zum republikanischen Bundesstaat." In Münkler, *Bürgerreligion und Bürgertugend*, 1996.

Altermatt, Urs. *Das Fanal von Sarajevo: Ethnonationalismus in Europa.* Zurich, 1996.

Arendt, Hanna. *Über die Revolution.* Munich, 1974.

Ballestrem, Karl Graf, Volker Gerhardt, Henning Ottmann, and Martyn P. Thompson, eds. *Politisches Denken: Jahrbuch 2000.* Stuttgart, 2000.

Baynes, Kenneth. "Kommunitaristische und kosmopolitische Kritik an Kants Konzept des Weltfriedens." In Lutz-Bachmann and Bohman, *Frieden durch Recht*, 1996.

Bellah, Robert N. "Zivilreligion in Amerika." In Kleger and Müller, *Religion des Bürgers*, 1986.

_____. *The Broken Covenant: America's Civil Religion in a Time of Trial.* Chicago, 1992.

Bender, Peter. "Das Amerikanische und das Römische Imperium: Ein Vergleich." *Europa oder Amerika? Zur Zukunft des Westens*, special ed., *Merkur* 9/10 (2000): 890–900.

Berding, Helmut, ed. *Nationales Bewusstsein und kollektive Identität: Studien zur Entwicklung des kollektiven Bewusstseins in der Neuzeit.* Frankfurt am Main, 1994.

Berger, Peter L., Richard J. Neuhaus, and Michael Novak, eds. *To Empower People: From State to Civil Society.* 2nd ed. Washington, DC, 1996.

Berten, André. "Europäische Identität—Einzahl oder Mehrzahl? Überlegungen zu den Entstehungsprozessen von Identität." In Dewandre and Lenoble, *Projekt Europa*, 1994.

Blanke, Gustav H. "Das amerikanische Sendungsbewusstsein: Zur Kontinuität rhetorischer Grundmuster im öffentlichen Leben der USA." In Kodalle, *Gott und Politik in den USA*, 1988.

Böckenförde, Ernst-Wolfgang. *Staat, Gesellschaft, Freiheit: Studien zur Staatstheorie und zum Verfassungsrecht.* Frankfurt am Main, 1976.

_____. *Staat, Nation, Europa: Studien zur Staatslehre, Verfassungstheorie und zum Verfassungsrecht.* Frankfurt am Main, 1999.

Brugger, Winfried. *Einführung in das öffentliche Recht der USA.* Munich, 1993.

Brunkhorst, Hauke. "Paradigmenwechsel im Völkerrecht? Lehren aus Bosnien." In Lutz-Bachmann and Bohman, *Frieden durch Recht*, 1996.

_____. "Menschenrechte und Intervention." In *Der Kosovo-Krieg: Rechtliche und rechtstheoretische Aspekte*, ed. Dieter S. Lutz. Baden Baden, 2000.

Brunkhorst, Hauke, and Peter Niesen, eds. *Das Recht der Republik.* Frankfurt am Main, 1999.

Bydlinski, Franz. "Rechtsgesinnung als Aufgabe." In *Festschrift für Karl Larenz zum 80. Geburtstag*, ed. Claus-Wilhelm Canaris. Munich, 1983.

Casanova, José. "Chancen und Gefahren öffentlicher Religionen: Ost- und Westeuropa im Vergleich." In Kallscheuer, *Das Europa der Religionen*, 1996.

Dahrendorf, Ralf. "Weltmarkt und Sozialökonomie." *Kapitalismus als Schicksal? Zur Politik der Entgrenzung*, special ed., *Merkur* 9/10 (1997): 821–828.

———. *Die Krisen der Demokratie: Ein Gespräch mit Antonio Polito*. Munich, 2002.

De Munck, Jean. "Europa und die Minderheitenfrage—eine sich wandelnde Problemstellung." In Dewandre and Lenoble, *Projekt Europa*, 1994.

Deutsche Aussenpolitik 1995. Auf dem Weg zu einer Friedensregelung für Bosnien und Herzegowina: 53 Telegramme aus Dayton. Eine Dokumentation. Ed. Auswärtigen Amt. Bonn, 1998.

Dewandre, Nicole, and Jacques Lenoble, eds. *Projekt Europa. Postnationale Identität: Grundlage für eine europäische Demokratie?* Berlin, 1994.

Eisenstadt, Schmuel N. *Die Vielfalt der Moderne*. Weilerswist, 2000.

Eppler, Erhard. *Vom Gewaltmonopol zum Gewaltmarkt? Die Privatisierung und Kommerzialisierung der Gewalt.* Frankfurt am Main, 2002.

Fikentscher, Wolfgang. *Methoden des Rechts in vergleichender Darstellung, Anglo-amerikanischer Rechtskreis.* Vol. 2. Tübingen, 1975.

———. "Staat vs. Government—eine Beobachtung zum Thema Kulturpersönlichkeit." In *Staatsphilosophie und Rechtspolitik: Festschrift für Martin Kriele zum 65. Geburtstag,* ed. Ziemske, Burghardt, Theo Langheid, Heinrich Wilms, and Görg Haverkate. Munich, 1997.

Fleiner-Gerstner, Thomas. "Multikulturelle Gesellschaft und verfassunggebende Gewalt: Staatslegitimation und Minderheitenschutz." In *Die multikulturelle und multi-ethnische Gesellschaft: Eine neue Herausforderung an die Europäische Verfassung,* ed. Thomas Fleiner-Gerstner. Fribourg, 1995.

Frankenberg, Günter. *Die Verfassung der Republik: Autorität und Solidarität in der Zivilgesellschaft.* Frankfurt am Main, 1997.

Geldbach, Erich. "Religion und Politik: Religious Liberty." In Kodalle, *Gott und Politik in den USA,* 1988.

Gellner, Ernest. *Postmodernism, Reason and Religion.* London, 1992.

———. *Bedingungen der Freiheit: Die Zivilgesellschaft und ihre Rivalen.* Stuttgart, 1995.

———. *Nationalismus: Kultur und Macht.* Berlin, 1999.

Glendon, Mary Ann. *Rights Talk: The Impoverishment of Political Discourse.* New York, 1991.

Günther, Klaus. "Kampf gegen das Böse? Zehn Thesen wider die ethische Aufrüstung der Kriminalpolitik." *Kritische Justiz* 27 (1994): 135–157.

———. "Welchen Personenbegriff braucht die Diskurstheorie des Rechts? Überlegungen zum internen Zusammenhang zwischen deliberativer Person, Staatsbürger und Rechtsperson." In Brunkhorst and Niesen, *Das Recht der Republik,* 1999.

Habermas, Jürgen. "Staatsbürgerschaft und nationale Identität: Überlegungen zur europäischen Zukunft." In Dewandre and Lenoble, *Projekt Europa,* 1994.

Hamilton, Alexander, James Madison, and John Jay. *Die Federalist Papers.* Trans. Barbara Zehnpfennig. Darmstadt, 1993.

Hobsbawm, Eric J. *The Age of Extremes: A History of the World, 1914–1991.* New York, 1994.

Howard, Dick. "Demokratische Republik oder republikanische Demokratie? Die Bedeutung der amerikanischen und der Französischen Revolution nach 1989." In Brunkhorst and Niesen, *Das Recht der Republik,* 1999.

———. *Die Grundlegung der amerikanischen Demokratie.* Frankfurt am Main, 2001.

Ignatieff, Michael. *Die Politik der Menschenrechte.* Hamburg, 2002.

Ischinger, Wolfgang. "21 Tage Dayton." In *Deutsche Aussenpolitik 1995,* 1998.

Joas, Hans. "Gemeinschaft und Demokratie in den USA: Die vergessene Vorgeschichte der Kommunitarismus-Diskussion." In *Gemeinschaft und Gerechtigkeit*, ed. Micha Brumlik and Hauke Brunkhorst. Frankfurt am Main, 1993.

Joyce, Michael S., and William A. Schambra. "A New Civic Life." In Berger, Neuhaus, and Novak, *To Empower People*, 1996.

Kalberg, Stephen. "Strukturierte Missverständnisse: Unterschiede der politischen Kultur in Amerika und Deutschland." *Europa oder Amerika? Zur Zukunft des Westens,* special ed., *Merkur* 9/10 (2000): 948–957.

Kallscheuer, Otto. *Gottes Wort und Volkes Stimme: Glaube, Macht, Politik.* Frankfurt am Main, 1994.

―――, ed. *Das Europa der Religionen: Ein Kontinent zwischen Säkularisierung und Fundamentalismus.* Frankfurt am Main, 1996.

Kallscheuer, Otto, and Claus Leggewie. "Deutsche Kulturnation versus französische Staatsnation? Eine ideengeschichtliche Stichprobe." In Berding, *Nationales Bewusstsein und kollektive Identität*, 1994.

Kersting, Wolfgang. *Wohlgeordnete Freiheit: Immanuel Kants Rechts- und Staatsphilosophie.* Berlin, 1984.

―――. "Globaler Rechtsfrieden und kulturelle Differenz: Huntington und die politische Philosophie der internationalen Beziehungen." In *Politisches Denken: Jahrbuch 2000,* ed. Karl Graf Ballestrem, Volker Gerhardt, Henning Ottmann, and Martyn P. Thompson. Stuttgart, 2000.

Kleger, Heinz, and Alois Müller, eds. *Religion des Bürgers: Zivilreligion in Amerika und Europa.* Munich, 1986.

Kodalle, Klaus-M., ed. *Gott und Politik in den USA: Über den Einfluss des Religiösen. Eine Bestandsaufnahme.* Frankfurt am Main, 1988.

―――. "Zivilreligion in Amerika: Zwischen Rechtfertigung und Kritik." In Kodalle, *Gott und Politik in den USA*, 1988.

Leggewie, Claus. *Amerikas Welt: Die USA in unseren Köpfen.* Hamburg, 2000.

Liessmann, Konrad Paul. *Der Aufgang des Abendlandes: Eine Rekonstruktion Europas.* Vienna, 1994.

Lubbers, Klaus. "Modelle nationaler Identität in amerikanischer Literatur und Kunst 1776–1893." In Berding, *Nationales Bewusstsein und kollektive Identität*, 1994.

Lutz-Bachmann, Matthias, and James Bohman, eds. *Frieden durch Recht: Kants Friedensidee und das Problem einer neuen Weltordnung.* Frankfurt am Main, 1996.

Martin, David. "Europa und Amerika: Säkularisierung oder Vervielfältigung der Christenheit―Zwei Ausnahmen und keine Regel." In Kallscheuer, *Das Europa der Religionen*, 1996.

Meier-Seethaler, Carola. *Befühl und Urteilskraft: Ein Plädoyer für die emotionale Vernunft.* Munich, 1997.

Meister, Roland. "Souveränität und Menschenrechte." *Blätter für deutsche und internationale Politik* 47 (2002): 325–333.

Mernissi, Fatima. *Der Harem in uns: Die Furcht vor dem anderen und die Sehnsucht der Frauen.* Freiburg, 1994.

Morin, Edgar. *Europa denken.* Frankfurt am Main, 1991.

Müller, Jörg Paul. *Der politische Mensch―menschliche Politik: Demokratie und Menschenrechte im staatlichen und globalen Kontext.* Basel, 1999.

Münch, Richard. *Das Projekt Europa: Zwischen Nationalstaat, regionaler Autonomie und Weltgesellschaft.* Frankfurt am Main, 1993.

Münkler, Herfried, ed. *Bürgerreligion und Bürgertugend: Debatten über die vorpolitischen Grundlagen politischer Ordnung.* Baden Baden, 1996.

_____. "Bleiben die Staaten die Herren des Krieges?" In Ballestrem et al., *Politisches Denken*, 2000.

Novak, Michael. "Seven Tangled Questions." In Berger, Neuhaus, and Novak, *To Empower People*, 1996.

Petritsch, Wolfgang. *Bosnien und Herzegowina fünf Jahre nach Dayton: Hat der Friede eine Chance?* Klagenfurt, 2001.

Preuss, Ulrich K. *Revolution, Fortschritt und Verfassung: Zu einem neuen Verfassungsverständnis.* Berlin, 1990.

_____. "Der Begriff der Verfassung und ihre Beziehung zur Politik." In *Zum Begriff der Verfassung: Die Ordnung des Politischen*, ed. Ulrich K. Preuss. Frankfurt am Main, 1994.

_____. "Der Kosovo-Krieg, das Völkerrecht und die Moral." In *Der Kosovo-Krieg und das Völkerrecht*, ed. Reinhard Merkel. Frankfurt am Main, 2000.

Priddat, Birger P. "Gerechtigkeit oder Fairness: Der Staat in der Zivilgesellschaft." *Europa oder Amerika? Zur Zukunft des Westens*, special ed., *Merkur* 9/10 (2000): 1026–1031.

Puhle, Hans-Jürgen. "Demokratisierungsprobleme in Europa und Amerika." In Brunkhorst and Niesen, *Das Recht der Republik*, 1999.

Reese-Schäfer, Walter. *Grenzgötter der Moral: Der neuere europäisch-amerikanische Diskurs zur politischen Ethik.* Frankfurt am Main, 1997.

Riesebrodt, Martin. *Die Rückkehr der Religionen: Fundamentalismus und der "Kampf der Kulturen."* Munich, 2000.

Šarčević, Edin. *Die Schlussphase der Verfassungsgebung in Bosnien und Herzegowina.* Leipzig, 1996.

_____. "Völkerrechtlicher Vertrag als 'Gestaltungsinstrument' der Verfassungsgebung: Das Daytoner Verfassungsexperiment mit Präzedenzwirkung?" *Archiv des Völkerrechts* 39 (2001): 297–339.

Schambeck, Herbert. *Ethik und Staat.* Berlin, 1986.

Schulze, Hagen. *Die Wiederkehr Europas.* Berlin, 1990.

_____. *Staat und Nation in der europäischen Geschichte.* Munich, 1995.

Sennett, Richard. *Verfall und Ende des öffentlichen Lebens: Die Tyrannei der Intimität.* Frankfurt am Main, 1983.

Spillmann, Kurt R. *Amerikas Ideologie des Friedens: Ursprünge, Formwandlungen und geschichtliche Auswirkungen des amerikanischen Glaubens an den Mythos von einer friedlichen Weltordnung.* Bern, 1984.

Stahn, Carsten. "Die verfassungsrechtliche Pflicht zur Gleichstellung der drei ethnischen Volksgruppen in den bosnischen Teilrepubliken—Neue Hoffnung für das Friedensmodell von Dayton? Zugleich eine Anmerkung zur dritten Teilentscheidung des bosnischen Verfassungsgerichtes vom 1. Juli 2000 im Izetbegovic-Fall." *Zeitschrift für ausländisches öffentliches Recht und Völkerrecht* 60 (2000): 663–713.

_____. "Gute Nachbarschaft um jeden Preis? Einige Anmerkungen zur Anbindung der USA an das Statut des Internationalen Strafgerichtshofs." *Zeitschrift für ausländisches öffentliches Recht und Völkerrecht* 60 (2000): 631–658.

Stahn, Carsten, and Sven-R. Eiffler. "Über das Verhältnis von Internationalem Menschenrechtsschutz und Völkerstrafrecht anhand des Statuts von Rom." *Kritische Vierteljahresschrift für Gesetzgebung und Rechtswissenschaft* 82 (1999): 253–277.

Steinvorth, Ulrich. "Brauchen wir einen Nationalismus?" In *Aktuelle Fragen der Rechtsphilosophie*, ed. Kurt Seelmann. Frankfurt am Main, 2000.

Stüwe, Klaus. "Eine Zivilreligion als Integrationsideologie? Das amerikanische Beispiel." *Stimmen der Zeit* 57 (1997): 457–472.

Teubner, Gunther. "Polykorporatismus: Der Staat als 'Netzwerk' öffentlicher und privater Kollektivakteure." In Brunkhorst and Niesen, *Das Recht der Republik*, 1999.

Thumann, Michael. "Der unvollendete Triumph des Nationalstaats—Bosniens Weg zum Abkommen von Dayton." In *Deutsche Aussenpolitik 1995*, 1998.

Thürer, Daniel. "Modernes Völkerrecht: Ein System im Wandel und Wachstum—Gerechtigkeitsgedanke als Kraft der Veränderung?" *Zeitschrift für ausländisches öffentliches Recht und Völkerrecht* 60 (2000): 557–604.

———. "Recht der internationalen Gemeinschaft und Wandel der Staatlichkeit." In *Verfassungsrecht der Schweiz*, ed. Daniel Thürer, Jean-François Aubert, and Jörg Paul Müller. Zurich, 2001.

Tönnies, Sybille. "Weltfrieden und Völkerrecht: Made in the USA oder Aufgabe der UNO?" *Blätter für deutsche und internationale Politik* 46 (2001): 829–836.

Vollrath, Ernst. "Die Trennung von Staat und Kirche im Verfassungsverständnis der USA." In Kodalle, *Gott und Politik in den USA*, 1988.

Weber, Max. "Die protestantischen Sekten und der Geist des Kapitalismus." In *Die protestantische Ethik I: Eine Aufsatzsammlung*, ed. Johannes Winckelmann, 8th ed. Gütersloh, 1991.

Wiegand, Wolfgang. "Europäisierung—Globalisierung—Amerikanisierung." In *Vernetzte Welt—globales Recht: Jahrbuch Junger Zivilrechtswissenschaftler*, ed. Martin Immenhauser and Jürg Wichermann. Stuttgart, 1998.

Zehnpfennig, Barbara. "Die Federalists zwischen Gemeinwohl und Partikularinteresse." In Münkler, *Bürgerreligion und Bürgertugend*, 1996.

Index

absolutism, 152
affiliation, 27, 28, 29, 30, 31, 34, 36, 37, 38,
    39, 45, 46, 87, 90, 117n45, 118n56,
    127, 145
    ethnic, 5, 9
    existential, 37, 38, 90, 125, 126, 127,
        146, 147, 149, 150
    religious, 5
    social, 27, 29, 30, 31, 38
    state political, 30, 93, 97, 99, 147
Afghan war, 135, 142
Albright, Madeline, 113n17, 122n89, 154
al-Qaeda, 42, 50, 62, 76, 159n32
American Declaration of Independence,
    35, 59n26, 154. See also Bellah,
    Robert N.
American Revolution, 24, 25, 33, 34, 40, 59,
    62, 63n47, 80, 106
"American way of life," 20, 29, 38, 87, 116n42.
    See also Eisenstadt, Schmuel N.
Americanization, 62, 124, 127, 134, 149,
    157, 165
"awakening," 86, 115n38, 120n69, 121n78.
    See also Gellner, Ernest; "slumbering
    state"

Balkan Wars, 5, 20, 38, 83, 91, 93, 97, 116, 163
Banja Luka, 5, 14, 164, 165
Bellah, Robert N., 19, 35, 57, 61, 63. See
    also American Declaration of Inde-
    pendence; civil religion
Bosniac, 7, 13, 76, 77, 83, 113, 146

Bosnian Croat, 13, 76, 77, 146
Bosnian Serb, 13, 76, 77, 146, 154
Bosnian war, 83, 114
Bürgergesellschaft, 130, 131

"chosen people," 20, 26, 46, 55, 117, 152
citizen nation, 93, 101
citizenship, 5, 24, 30, 31, 38, 45, 93, 95, 97,
    99, 103, 118n56, 120n71, 120n73,
    121n85
civil religion, 19, 20, 21, 61n32, 62n45, 153.
    See also Bellah, Robert N.
civil society, 65n69, 114n21, 114n25,
    115n32, 120n74, 129, 130, 131, 132,
    136, 155n6, 156n7, 156n8, 156n10,
    156n12, 156n13
"clash of civilizations," 66, 127
Clinton, Bill, 28, 31
"coalition of the willing," 75, 113n13, 135,
    136, 142
Cold War, 16, 17, 48, 67, 71, 82, 89, 90, 91,
    132, 143, 147, 154, 160n42
collective self-image, 16, 36
colonialism, 19, 61n33, 116n39, 148, 160n46
"compassionate conservatism," 131, 155n4,
    156n11
constitution, 21, 25, 34, 40, 58n16, 111
    Bosnian, 12, 76, 77, 110, 111, 112n11,
        113n16, 123n95
    US, 33, 34, 48, 53, 54, 57n7, 57n9,
        59n26, 59n27, 60n31, 62n40, 107,
        122n89, 154, 162n60

Council of Europe, 1, 52, 69, 111, 112, 121, 123, 157, 162, 164
culture nation, 93, 94, 95, 101

Dayton Agreement, 1, 2, 12, 15, 31, 53, 54, 56, 68, 69, 70, 71, 72, 73, 75, 76, 77, 78, 79, 110, 111, 154, 165
death penalty, 46. *See also* Supreme Court (US), 34
denationalization, 126, 127, 128, 140
"destatification," 126
displacement, 7, 12, 73, 95, 119, 127
division of labor, 133

Eastern Bloc, 55
Eisenstadt, Schmuel N., 19, 29, 56n5, 61n35, 62n38, 62n45, 63n45, 118n54. *See also* "American way of life"
Enlightenment, 44, 46, 47, 49, 91, 92, 93, 95, 96, 101, 102, 105, 107, 143, 145, 147, 148, 149, 153, 161
"ethnic cleansing," 5, 8, 12, 70, 76, 81, 95, 98, 101, 110, 112n4, 119n64
ethnicization, 8, 76, 78
Eurocentrism, 148, 149, 150
European Convention on Human Rights, 1, 2, 22, 51, 69, 111, 113, 139
European Court of Human Rights, 1, 51, 53, 69, 158n28
European Social Charter, 51
European Union, 6, 7, 31, 37, 49, 50, 52, 67, 68, 95, 96, 97, 98, 99, 106, 110, 119n65
exclusivity, 45, 90, 118n54

Federal Republic of Yugoslavia, 31, 32, 103, 141, 142, 159n37
foreignness, 37, 38, 87
French Revolution, 20, 23, 25, 33, 37, 44, 45, 49, 59n25, 62n40, 80, 85, 89, 91, 93, 101, 102, 103, 106, 107, 143, 147, 156n6
fundamentalism, 22, 23, 122n87, 142, 150, 159n35
  Islamic, 22
  Protestant, 23

gated communities, 39, 40, 108
Gellner, Ernest, 20, 58n15, 58n21, 82, 114n26, 129. *See also* "awakening"; "slumbering state"
Geneva Conventions, 42
Grande Nation, 101, 102, 105, 146
group rights, 102, 104, 105, 106, 123n81
Guantanamo Bay, 42, 50, 62n39, 76
Gulf War, 142

Hague, The, 50, 137
Holbrooke, Richard, 31, 32
horizontal social contract, 24, 26, 28, 46, 59n29, 60nn29–30, 78, 140

identity
  civic, 12, 13, 14, 79, 89, 96, 130, 131
  cultural, 95, 96, 97, 98, 99, 100, 101, 102, 103, 104, 106, 119n65, 143, 144, 146, 147, 149
  democratic, 34
  group, 148
  legal political, 109, 132
  monolithic ethnic, 7, 9, 10, 11, 12, 13, 15n6, 77, 78, 86, 87, 126, 131
  national, 20, 21, 55, 88, 89, 92, 94, 96, 97, 98, 99, 100, 102, 104, 105, 106, 111, 117n46, 117n47, 118n56, 119n65, 126, 128, 144, 147
  social, 128
imperialism, 92, 153
  Western, 2, 162n61
inclusivity, 89, 90
individualization, 18, 76, 78, 87, 104, 126, 139
intellectual history, 19, 49, 75, 85, 89, 90, 91, 93, 111, 129, 132, 133, 134, 140, 148, 152, 154, 165, 166
  intellectual offering, 150, 151
Inter-American Human Rights Convention, 51
International Court of Justice, 50, 139
International Criminal Court, 63n57, 65n71, 137, 139, 140, 142, 151, 152
Iraq, 129, 162n60

Kosovo, 32, 38, 159n34, 160n37

law
  Anglo-Saxon, 138
  criminal, 46, 137, 138, 139, 140, 158n26,
    164
  humanitarian international, 42, 129, 139
  international criminal, 75, 133, 134,
    136, 141, 142
  private, 157n21, 158n21
  public, 59n24, 114n25, 158n21
"law of the stronger," 132, 133, 136, 137, 148
legal order, 41, 43, 48, 49, 108, 109, 113n13,
  134, 135, 148, 159n33
  international, 75, 133, 134, 136, 141,
    142, 156n13

melting pot, 87, 88
Middle Ages, 18, 23, 87, 91, 128, 158n30
Milošević, Slobodan, 31, 38
minorities, 35, 78, 102, 104, 105, 121n79,
  121n81, 121n82
monolithic ethnic identity. *See* identity,
  monolithic ethnic
moral values, 148. *See also* universal morality

Napoleonic Wars, 93, 146
nationalism, 81, 82, 86, 87, 92, 93, 97, 98,
  100, 1115n37, 115n38, 119n64,
  120n65, 120n68, 123n94, 126, 128
nationality, 50, 93, 95
  culture nations, 93, 94, 95, 101
nation-state, 6, 20, 23, 24, 81, 90, 91, 93,
  94, 95, 96, 97, 99, 101, 102, 103, 105,
  106, 107, 110, 119n62, 121n76, 126,
  144, 160n44
NATO, 3, 7, 67, 69, 141, 142, 159n37
New World, 18, 19, 26, 40, 49, 123n90, 125, 134
NGO (non-governmental organization),
  26, 53
non- or "not yet" citizens, 64n64, 99,
  115n31, 120n74

Old Testament, 26, 46, 117n47
Old World, 19
Organization for Security and Co-operation in Europe (OSCE), 2, 3
"other," the, 124, 145, 149, 150

Parliamentary Assembly of the European
  Council, 25, 162n59, 164

Peace of Westphalia (1648), 18, 19, 57n6, 141,
  159n31. *See also* Thirty Years' War
  crossroads of, 20, 26, 35, 84, 108, 127,
    128, 142, 151
peace order, 50, 54, 93, 106, 109, 124, 127, 148
pledge of allegiance, 29, 39, 55
pragmatism, 28, 32, 41, 42, 50, 54, 63n55,
  71, 72, 142, 152, 162n58
privatization, 126, 136
public order structure, 26, 79, 81, 82, 83,
  84, 85, 86, 115n30, 27, 131

racism, 87, 88, 89, 126
Reformation, the, 18
republic, 25, 33, 53, 91, 92, 93, 95, 96, 97,
  100, 101, 143, 144, 147, 159n35
République, 26, 63n45, 146, 153
revolution, 40, 60n30, 60n40, 62n41,
  114n21, 114n22, 155n3
  American. *See* American Revolution
  French. *See* French Revolution
  Russian. *See* Russian Revolution of 1917
revolutions of 1989, 80, 93, 114n22, 132
Romanticism, 91, 92, 93, 94, 95, 96, 107,
  119n64, 128, 143, 145, 146, 147, 148,
  149
Russian Revolution of 1917, 90

Sarajevo, 1, 3, 4, 5, 7, 8, 9, 14, 15n3, 72, 76,
  83, 98, 114n29, 115n37, 116n43,
  119n60, 119n61, 121n83, 164, 165
  siege of, 7, 98
Šarčević, Edin, 8, 15n5, 110, 113n15,
  123n92
secularization, 21, 22, 23, 59n29, 84, 97,
  100, 115n35, 120n76, 121n85,
  122n87
September 11, 16, 17, 26, 28, 47, 54, 66n73,
  75, 79, 83, 87, 125, 133, 141, 151,
  152, 166
"slumbering state," 115n38, 120n69,
  121n78. *See also* "awakening"; Gellner, Ernest
social cohesion, 65n66, 120n65, 127, 128
social market economy, 85, 90, 125
sovereign people, 33, 34, 38, 40, 45, 4, 80,
  147
sovereignty
  absolute, 136

individual, 55, 107, 111, 134
international, 136
popular, 33, 34, 37, 45, 48, 62n40,
  62n44, 106, 108, 110, 111, 118n54
shared, 44, 55, 79, 106, 107, 108, 109,
  111, 125, 127, 128, 135
state, 6, 108, 136, 141
state nation, 23, 93, 94, 95, 101
"strength of the law," 132, 133, 136, 137,
  142, 143, 148, 149, 157n14
subsidiarity principle, 95, 96
Supreme Court (US), 34. *See also* death
  penalty, 46

Taliban, 32, 42, 50, 62
third factor (state as a), 24, 26, 28, 40, 45,
  78, 79, 128, 129, 140, 156n12
Thirty Years' War, 18, 155n3, 158n30. *See
  also* Peace of Westphalia
thought structure, 32, 33, 150
Tito, Josip Broz, 5, 6
transatlantic differences, 2, 3, 14, 16–66, 67,
  68, 71, 78, 79, 85, 88, 104, 105, 107,
  111, 123n90, 132, 134, 135, 149, 150

UN Human Rights Commission, 51
Universal Declaration of Human Rights,
  51, 120n76, 139, 141, 158n27

universal morality, 41. *See also* moral
  values
universal principle(s)/values, 140, 141, 145,
  146, 147, 160n42
universalism, 92, 121n77, 148

Vance-Owen Plan, 70, 112n4
Venice Commission (European Commission for Democracy through Law),
  69, 70, 113n15, 164
voluntarism, 27, 113n13, 134, 135, 136

welfare state, 2, 17, 25, 125
Western Europe/East Central Europe/
  United States triangle, 68, 78, 80–82,
  84, 90, 102, 104, 111, 143
World War I, 4, 5, 70, 93
World War II, 4, 5, 6, 50, 70, 82, 93, 97, 138,
  139, 151, 153

xenophobia, 87, 88, 89, 126

Yugoslav People's Army, 7
"Yugoslavism," 5